Courage to Connect

A Quality Schools Action Framework

María "Cuca" Robledo Montecel, Ph.D.
Christie L. Goodman, APR
editors

INTERCULTURAL DEVELOPMENT RESEARCH ASSOCIATION
MARÍA "CUCA" ROBLEDO MONTECEL, PH.D., PRESIDENT & CEO
5815 CALLAGHAN ROAD, SUITE 101
SAN ANTONIO, TEXAS 78228
210.444.1710 • FAX 210.444.1714
CONTACT@IDRA.ORG • WWW.IDRA.ORG

Questions and requests for permission will be most generously handled by: Intercultural Development Research Association; 5815 Callaghan Road, Suite 101; San Antonio, Texas 78228; Ph. 210-444-1710; Fax 210-444-1714; E-mail: contact@idra.org; www.idra.org

ISBN 978-1-935737-35-3

Distributed by the Intercultural Development Research Association. Manufactured in the United States.

"I believe it is time to dream together – to dream about education not for a lucky few but for all. And it is time to make the dream of education for all become fact."

– Dr. María Robledo Montecel,
IDRA President & CEO

Contents

Editors Note

The Quality Schools Action Framework (Robledo Montecel, 2005) provides a way for schools and communities to work together to examine a school's outcomes and identify leverage points for improvement so that all students are successful. This book discusses the indicators and elements in detail. Each chapter examines one aspect of the framework and includes recent selected articles from the *IDRA Newsletter*. Each chapter opens with a chapter preface along with a poem to harmonize with the prose. In the Appendix, we've provided two articles as a bridge from our earlier years through our day to day work with schools and communities to the present. Additional resources, including podcasts and videos regarding the book and the Quality Schools Action Framework, are available on the IDRA web site (www.idra.org/couragetoconnect). We would love to hear from you. Please share with us your questions and stories of your experience in creating schools that work for all children.

María "Cuca" Robledo Montecel, Ph.D.
Christie L. Goodman, APR

Foreword

A Word to Those Who Did Not Graduate, Class of 2010

As the days grow longer, as tree buds burst into bloom, and as swimming pools hear their first splashes, high schools gear up to hold splendid graduation ceremonies. Valedictorians draft their speeches, orchestras practice stanzas from Pomp and Circumstance, fancy programs are printed, and lavish decorations are pulled out. It's an important occasion. The final send-off of students schools cared for during their precious late teen years.

But so many of our young people won't have the chance to cross that stage. For them, there won't be invitations, parties or graduation gifts. They won't be throwing their caps in the air. They will never hear *te aventaste, mi'jo.*

They will not hear a commencement speech that celebrates their accomplishments and points them to their exciting future. For them, graduation day will be just another day.

So as we commit to changing education for all students and for our children's children, we would like to offer a few final thoughts, some words of commencement, to them.

To those who did not graduate, Class of 2010:

It is usual in a commencement address to congratulate you on your graduation, but we cannot do that. We can only say that we are sorry.

We want to speak volumes of your accomplishments, but we feel as if we hardly know you. We saw you falling, but somehow didn't catch you.

We want to talk about work with you, what interests you, what speaks to you. We want to listen to your dreams with you. But we know some doors will not be open.

Many will tell you that you have failed and weren't persistent enough. Only you know whether or not that is true.

What we know is that we are all held up by many people.

At our best we are like birds flying in a formation. You may have heard about how geese migrate in a "V" pattern. Birds use that formation because it conserves energy. Each one flies slightly above the bird in front of him, cutting into the wind and making it easier for those who follow. And flying in formation makes it easy to keep track of every bird in the group.

But there is something that you may not know about geese. When one bird weakens, is wounded and falls from the formation, two others will follow and tend to him, bringing him back to the group.

When you started slipping, the school might have followed you. Teachers or counselors might have reached out to you. If they had, you would have known, without doubt, that they valued you, that they were not going to leave you behind.

If you had slipped from the school, your parents or friends, might have reached for you. They would have held you up and mended your wings. They would have flown beside you.

If you felt yourself drop and start to free fall, you would have remembered that there was someone to hang on to. You would have reached out to get the support you needed from family, friends or faculty. You would find help and take the risk to accept it. You also might have reached back to help others from falling out of formation.

For you to have left school, all of this failed.

As a scientist, Albert Einstein, helped us see the universe and ourselves in completely new ways.

He once said: "The world is a dangerous place, not because of those who do evil, but because of those who look on and do nothing."

We all will miss your graduation. That unique stride, all yours, crossing the stage. But today we commit never again to look away, never again to look on and do nothing. Today and tomorrow and the day after tomorrow and for the long haul, we promise to transform our caring and our willingness to serve into action.

María Robledo Montecel

María "Cuca" Robledo Montecel, Ph.D.

Christie L. Goodman

Christie L. Goodman, APR

The Framework

Prologue

Aurelio M. Montemayor, M.Ed.

We are people of faith, I tell you,
But no religious sect predominates:
We share, beyond being primates,
Stubborn belief in children's value.

When teachers think the worst of kids,
Method's checked by point of view.
It's ancient bias, nothing new --
Yet children's learning hits the skids:

When we expect them geniuses to be
Expression, tone and looks do beam:
A teacher's glance emits a gleam,
As student's thoughts and words float free.

None is expendable, we vouch this true.
We advocate for all, not a select few.

Holding On to the Goal of Quality Education for Every Child

by María "Cuca" Robledo Montecel, Ph.D.

U.S. Secretary of Education Arnie Duncan calls education "the civil rights issue of our generation" and notes that "if we are to emerge from this global recession and ensure the future prosperity of our nation, every school must provide every child with a quality education that offers the path out of poverty and toward equal opportunity" (July 2, 2009).

We have a choice. Equal educational opportunity can remain a well-intended but unfulfilled promise or move to becoming the engine of shared prosperity for generations of Americans. Much depends on the clarity and the urgency with which we approach the challenge.

If the past decade is prologue to the next, it is difficult to know if we will have both the clarity and urgency that is needed to do the hard work of sustainable change. On the one hand, the last decade has seen a shift toward an expectation that schools "bring all students to high standards of academic proficiency" (Mosher & Smith, 2009). Also, more Americans now believe that education beyond high school is a necessity, with a large shift toward that belief occurring since the year 2000 (Lumina, 2009).

On the other hand, there is much evidence that the last decade has seen a widening of the economic and education gaps and that the "pressure for reform has increased but is not yet the reality" (Fullan, 2007).

Today and over the next several years, the grip of the economic crisis and the din of competing priorities may put education in a holding pattern that is interrupted only to wish for a return to the good ole days, that in reality weren't so good for much of the population; to bemoan the next school, district, state or national report card; or to pine for the next magic silver bullet.

Thankfully, there is another option. We can pursue shared prosperity by keeping our eyes on the goal of quality education for *every* child in *every* school, understanding that education matters, community voices matter in education and much is known about what to do.

Education Matters to Shared Prosperity

Robust research evidence indicates that the quality of education affects economic opportunity for individuals and outcomes for society across generations. Data from the Economic Mobility Project (The Pew Charitable Trusts, 2009) underscore the connection between education and economic opportunity and the key role that educational opportunity plays in getting a fair chance at the American Dream.

There is also strong evidence that education matters to individuals and to society in other critical areas, including health, longevity and the vitality of civic life. *Goals for the Common Good: Exploring the Impact of Education* identifies critical areas linked to educational attainment, synthesizes research findings, and provides links to an online Common Good Forecaster (American Human Development Project, 2009).

However, disparities and gaps in educational opportunity and outcomes continue to divide Americans based on class and color. The average low-income high school senior has the same reading level as the average middle-class eighth grader, and the percentage of high-poverty schools that are high-performing is 1.1 percent compared to 24.2 percent of low-poverty schools that are high-performing (Kahlenberg, 2008). If you are Black or Latino, you are more likely to attend a high-poverty, segregated, under-funded school that is unable to graduate students and is unable to prepare students for college or today's competitive job market (Alliance for Excellent Education, 2009; Alliance for Excellent Education and the College Board, 2009).

> We can pursue shared prosperity by keeping our eyes on the goal of quality education for *every* child in *every* school, understanding that education matters, community voices matter in education and much is known about what to do.

Community Voices Matter in Education

Education matters to the individual and to society. But the quality of education provided in a *local school system* affects the *local community* in important ways. To examine the impact of educational quality on the local community, RAND researchers focused on a substantial body of literature and found strong evidence of: (1) effects on housing values in the school attendance area with an increase of 1 percent in reading or math scores associated with a 0.5 percent to 1 percent increase in property values; (2) effects on crime rates with a one-year higher educational level in a community associated with a 13 percent to 27 percent lower incidence of murders, assaults, car thefts and arson; and (3) effects on tax revenues with increased earnings and sales, and higher property tax revenues from residences and businesses. There also was evidence that educational quality in the community is associated with greater civic participation in that community, including more voter participation, more tolerance and acceptance of free speech, more involvement in community arts and culture, and higher newspaper readership. (Carroll & Scherer, 2008)

Maintaining urgency and clarity in sustainable education reform depends in large measure on community will and informed engagement at the local community level. Schools, after all, belong to the community, and change is too important to be left to schools alone. Community engagement that is based on active participation by both the school and the community produces results for students (Petrovich, 2008; Mediratta, et al., 2008; Levin, 2008). IDRA work in building and informing school-community teams demonstrates success in these partnerships and coalitions (Rodríguez & Scott, 2007; Montemayor, 2008; IDRA, 2008).

The Harlem Children's Zone has established a cluster of community programs to serve neighborhood families and their children from birth to college graduation (Shulman, 2009). This "unique, holistic approach to rebuilding a community" is generating dramatically improved student achievement and parent engagement as well as positive financial impact to the neighborhood (HCZ web site).

Community buy-in and oversight stemming from shared understandings and data about the why, the how and the results of school change is a critical but largely untapped change strategy in school reform efforts. For example, community teams can use data about their local dropout and graduation rates, disaggregated by subgroups, and data on the related school factors of parent involvement, student engagement, curriculum access and teaching quality in order to develop comprehensive plans of action to graduate all students (Robledo Montecel, 2007).

Much Is Known About What to Do

There is a growing sense around the country that real, long-lasting change is urgent, indispensable and possible. The U.S. Department of Education is working with others to frame and fund an agenda that includes setting benchmarked standards, developing data systems to track growth and tailor instruction, boosting the quality of teachers and principals, and turning around the lowest-performing schools. Forty-six states have signed on to create benchmarked K-12 standards that prepare students for the 21st Century global knowledge-based economy.

Foundations also are focusing their strategies and leveraging their investments in education reform by setting goals and funding the detailed work that will achieve those goals. The Bill and Melinda Gates Foundation will invest $500 million over the next five years in learning how to improve and measure teacher quality. The Lumina Foundation is focused on assuring that, by 2025, the proportion of Americans with higher education credentials increases to 60 percent from the current 39 percent.

Unprecedented successes in unexpected places are defying the perception that achievement gaps are inevitable (Chenoweth, 2007). For example, IDRA led a group of middle school teachers, a principal, counselor and social worker to create a small professional learning community, in conjunction with IDRA's Coca-Cola Valued Youth Program, focused on the academic success of students who were considered at risk of dropping out of school. Both teaching quality and student engagement improved, transforming student results (Montemayor & Cortez, 2007).

High-poverty urban schools are improving demonstrably by using additional monies coming to them by court order to good effect. In New Jersey, poor schools that received an infusion of funds as a result of the *Abbott vs. Burke* case are demonstrating improved student achievement (Anrig, 2009). In Texas, student achievement on national tests improved in 2008 due in part to a decade of improved and equitable funding that had been provided to Texas schools (Cortez, 2009).

For the last four years, IDRA has utilized the Quality Schools Action Framework (Robledo Montecel, 2005) as a frame for our work in education reform (see graphic on next page). The Quality Schools Action Framework brings together what we know about educational change efforts. The framework:

1. is empirical, experiential and practical.

2. is results oriented and tracks expected outcomes both on (a) *student* metrics of success at many levels including college, and (b) *school* metrics of success focused on the school's ability to keep students in school and learning through to graduation.

3. focuses attention and action, singularly and in tandem, on the four system indicators that are key to success: parent and community engagement, student engagement, teaching quality, and curriculum quality and access.

4. points to governance efficacy and fair funding as crucial fundamentals that interact with indicators and outcomes.

5. highlights change strategies that build individual and collective capacity within and across school and community.

6. couples capacity-building with active coalitions that have an urgent agenda to produce results for students.

7. positions knowledge-building and utilization as a core feature of accountable leadership, enlightened policy and engaged citizens.

8. uses knowledge, information, evidence and outcome data not only as "rear mirror" assessments but also as integral to informing present and future strategy.

A number of our partner schools and coalition organizations have used the framework and the companion online portal to assess baselines, plan and implement strategies, and monitor progress in educating all students to high quality (Posner, 2009; Posner & Bojorquez, 2008).

Our experience with the framework so far is that it is a useful tool in many ways: to conceive, design and manage change at the school or district level; to encourage thoughtful and coherent selection of best practices that are grounded in the reality of the schools and their communities; to focus on particular strategies and/or instructional approaches (e.g., bilingual

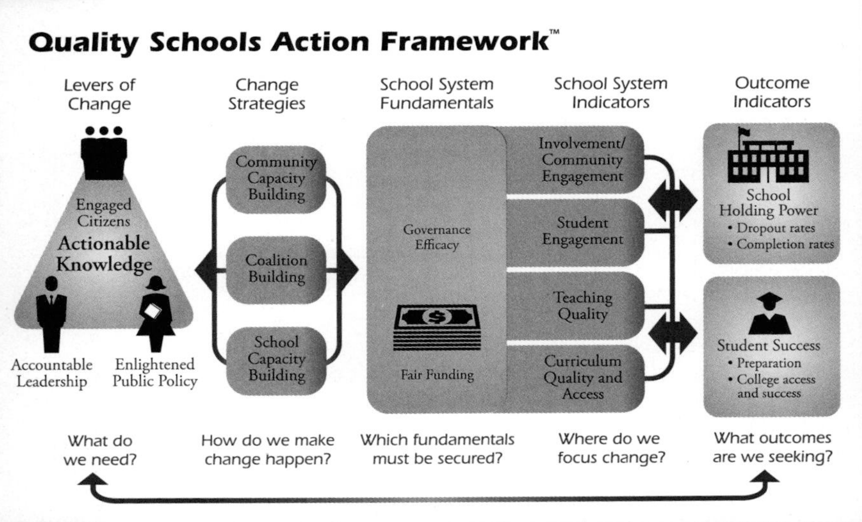

education) without losing track of the contexts that matter (e.g., teaching quality, school/district leadership, funding); to inform evidence-based community collaboration and oversight in productive ways; and to inform meaningful comparisons across campuses and districts.

As a "change model," the Quality Schools Action Framework also may prove useful in making the link between benchmarked standards and sustainable school reform that ties desired outcomes to indicators of quality at the local level.

Lisbeth Schorr (2009) has eloquently stated that the "search for silver bullets is giving way to an understanding that, to make inroads on big social problems, reformers must mobilize multiple, interacting strategies that take account not only individual needs but also the power of context." It is at the local level, with schools and communities working together, that the power of context can be a source of genuine and long-lasting change that benefits every student in every school with a quality education.

Resources

Alliance for Excellent Education and College Board. *Facts for Education Advocates: Demographics and the Racial Divide* (Washington, D.C.: Alliance for Excellent Education, copublished with College Board, 2009).

Alliance for Excellent Education. *Students of Color and the Achievement Gap* (Washington, D.C.: Alliance for Excellent Education and College Board, 2009).

American Human Development Project. *Goals for the Common Good: Exploring the Impact of Education* (American Human Development Project and United Way, 2009).

Anrig, G. *Educational Strategies That Work* (New York, N.Y.: The Century Foundation, March 2009).

Carroll, S.J., and E. Scherer. *The Impact of Educational Quality on the Community: A Literature Review* (Santa Monica, Calif: The RAND Corporation, 2008).

Chenoweth, K. *It's Being Done: Academic Success in Unexpected Schools* (Cambridge, Mass.:

Harvard Education Press, 2007).

Cortez, A. *The Status of School Finance Equity in Texas – A 2009 Update* (San Antonio, Texas: Intercultural Development Research Association, 2009).

Duncan, A. "Partners in Reform," remarks before the National Education Association recognizing the 45th anniversary of the enactment of Title VI of the Civil Rights Act of 1964, which prohibits discrimination in public schools (Washington, D.C. U.S. Department of Education, July 2, 2009).

Fullan, M. *The New Meaning of Educational Change*, fourth edition (New York, N.Y.: Teachers College Press, Columbia University, 2007) pg. 6.

Harlem Children's Zone. Web site (http://www.hcz.org).

Intercultural Development Research Association. Capacity Building Evaluation for the Rio Grande Valley Grantees, unpublished report memorandum to The Marguerite Casey Foundation (January 15, 2008).

Kahlenberg, R.D. Can Separate Be Equal? The Overlooked Flaw at the Center of No Child Left Behind (New York, N.Y.: The Century Foundation, 2008).

Levin, B. *How to Change 5000 Schools. A Practical and Positive Approach for Leading Change at Every Level* (Cambridge, Mass.: Harvard Education Press, 2008).

Lumina Foundation for Education. *Lumina Foundation's Strategic Plan: Goal 2025* (Indianapolis, Ind.: 2009).

Mediratta, K., and S. Shah, S. McAlister, D. Lockwood, C. Mokhtar, N. Fruchter. *Organized Communities, Stronger Schools: A Preview of Research Findings* (Providence, R.I.: Annenberg Institute for School Reform at Brown University, 2008).

Montemayor, A.M. "Authentic Consultation – NCLB Outreach Leadership and Dialogues for Parents, Students and Teachers," *IDRA Newsletter* (San Antonio, Texas: Intercultural Development Research Association, June-July 2008).

Montemayor, A.M., and J.D. Cortez. "Valuing Youth – Reflections from a Professional Learning Community," *IDRA Newsletter* (San Antonio, Texas: Intercultural Development Research Association, March 2007).

Mosher, F.A., and M.S. Smith. "The Role of Research in Education Reform from the Perspective of Federal Policymakers and Foundation Grantmakers," in *The Role of Research in Educational Improvement* (John D. Bransfor, Deborah J. Stipek, Nancy J. Vyie, Louis M. Gomez, and Diana Lam, eds.) (Cambridge, Mass.: Harvard Education Press, 2009) pg. 19.

Petrovich, J. A *Foundation Returns to School: Strategies for Improving Public Education* (New York: Ford Foundation, 2008).

Posner, L. "Actionable Knowledge: Putting Research to Work for School Community Action," *IDRA Newsletter* (San Antonio, Texas: Intercultural Development Research Association, August 2009).

Posner, L., and H. Bojorquez. "Knowledge for Action – Organizing School-Community Partnerships Around Quality Data," *IDRA Newsletter* (San Antonio, Texas: Intercultural Development Research Association, January 2008).

Robledo Montecel, M. "Graduation for All Students – Dropout Prevention and Student Engagement Strategies and the Reauthorization of the No Child Left Behind Act," testimony before the Committee on Education and Labor, U.S. House of Representatives, in a hearing on "NCLB: Preventing Dropouts and Enhancing School Safety" (April 23, 2007).

Robledo Montecel, M. "A Quality Schools Action Framework," *IDRA Newsletter* (San Antonio, Texas: Intercultural Development Research Association, November-December 2005).

Rodríguez, R.G., and B. Scott. "Expanding Blueprints for Action – Children's Outcomes, Access, Treatment, Learning, Resources, Accountability," *IDRA Newsletter* (San Antonio, Texas: Intercultural Development Research Association, May 2007).

Schorr, L. "Innovative Reforms Require Innovative Scorekeeping," *Education Week* (August 26, 2009).

Shulman, R. "Harlem Program Singled Out as Model: Obama Administration to Replicate Plan in Other Cities to Boost Poor Children," *Washington Post* (August 2, 2009).

The Pew Charitable Trusts. *The Economic Mobility Project* (Philadelphia, Pa.: The Pew Charitable Trusts, 2009).

Originally published in the *IDRA Newsletter*, September 2009

Chapter One – The Framework Explored

Frame that Works / Transforms

Aurelio M. Montemayor, M.Ed.

A framework for creating quality schools,
Comprehensive and grounded in practice,
From years of research and service
Brings rigorous and strategic tools.

With the end in mind: schools holding on to students,
Maintaining learning, for college prepared and bound:
This framework proposes levers and strategies sound,
Fundamental funding fair, governance with prudence.

To measure success clear indicators are needed,
From engaged families in manners authentic
To engaged students with 'real' teaching, not hallucigenic:
Accessible curriculum and proof students succeeded.

Deficit models don't bring positive school change:
Transformation, not student desks to re-arrange.

Chapter Preface

Before the early 1980s, the country largely ignored the fact that a significant percentage of students were dropping out of school. But changes in economic trends and employer needs for a skilled workforce led to increasing interest as the issue. It was during this period that IDRA was contracted by the Texas Department of Community Affairs to conduct the first-ever comprehensive study of the dropout problem in Texas. (An excerpt from the Texas School Dropout Survey Project summary document is in the Appendix.)

Texans were shocked to see high school attrition rates of 33 percent. The study outlined 10 areas that the state needed to address, such as a standardized dropout definition and procedures for calculating the dropout rate, tracking mechanisms that would result in more appropriate program interventions, early dropout intervention efforts given the large numbers of students who leave before the ninth grade, model dropout prevention and recovery programs for particular types of high risk groups, evaluation of dropout prevention and recovery efforts, linking public and private sector initiatives, and investing in dropout prevention and recovery efforts that is commensurate with the magnitude of the problem and its economic impact. (See cost study article in the Appendix.)

Yet, here we are today still losing one-third of our high school students. Since 1986, Texas schools have lost more than 2.5 million students. One is lost every four minutes. At current pace, the state will lose an additional 2.3 million to 6 million students before reaching an attrition rate of zero in 2042.

The picture is just as bleak across the country. Nationally, we are losing more than 1.2 million students every year.

It is time to do things differently.

- In "Framing Systems Change for Student Success," María "Cuca" Robledo Montecel, Ph.D., outlines promising strategies for improving achievement.
- And in "A Quality Schools Action Framework – Framing Systems Change for Student Success," Dr. Robledo Montecel presents an overview of the Quality Schools Action Framework.

The remaining chapters discuss each element of the framework and strategies for success.

Framing Systems Change for Student Success

by María "Cuca" Robledo Montecel, Ph.D.

> *Editor's note: The following are excerpts from a speech presented by Dr. Robledo Montecel, IDRA President and CEO, at a conference in Chapel Hill, North Carolina, entitled "High Poverty Schooling in America: Lessons in Second-Class Citizenship" in October 2006. The event was held by the North Carolina Law Review; the University of North Carolina Center on Poverty, Work and Opportunity; the UNC Center for Civil Rights; and the UNC School of Education.*

Landmark civil rights cases like *Brown vs. Board of Education* and *Mendez vs. Westminster* opened new paths toward integration and equity. More than 50 years later, the promise of educational opportunity for all remains largely unfulfilled. In fact, research suggests it may be slipping further out of reach. The nation is more and more at home with segregation. And segregation is not only on the rise, but our country seems to be more *at home* with a system of haves and have nots.

So education is absolutely at a crossroads in America. But how are we to achieve results? How do we guarantee that all of our children succeed?

If the past is any prophet of the future, we cannot layer new accountability measures on old educational inequities and expect to get different results. It isn't going to happen. Of course, there are exceptions. There are always highly successful high-poverty schools that belie the trends. But results for all children are not about exceptions, they are about creating a regularity of success.

What are the most promising strategies to improving achievement in high poverty schools?

A Framework for Action

The Quality Schools Action Framework that IDRA has developed in our collaboration with schools and communities in Texas and other parts of the country offers a model for assessing school outcomes, identifying leverage points for improvement, and focusing and effecting change.

The model is based on three premises. The first is that if the problem is systemic – and it seems to me that it is – the solutions must address schools as systems.

The second is that if we are up to student success, then we have to develop a vision, and that vision for children has to seek outcomes for every child, no matter where they come from, no matter the color of their skin, no matter the side of town they come from, no matter the language they speak.

And the third premise of this framework is that schools are not poor because children in them are poor or black or brown. Schools are poor because we have poor policies, poor practices and inadequate investments.

We might then ask three questions: What do we need? How do we effect change? and What fundamentals and features must be in place?

What do we need?

The first and most important thing that we need is to keep the *public* in public education. Americans support public schools. There has always been a vocal minority that has fought the integration and the diversity that comes with public schools.

As public education was first conceived and began to take shape in our country, various groups raised questions. See if these questions still sound current: Why does everyone need to go to school? Why do *they* need an education? Wouldn't ex-slaves and their children be more comfortable in their own schools? Why spend money on immigrants; they can't even speak English? Well… OK… maybe spend a little bit of money, but only enough to keep them out of the streets. But surely, those children are not going to attend school with *our* children. And so it went.

After the *Brown* decision, in the Jim Crow south, White institutions dragged their feet, and private White academies became commonplace. Separate but equal would, in this way, stay in place.

Today, private schools funded by public sources are a reality in some states. We seem to be moving from dual schools to dual systems, one public and one private – with our public money diverted to privatizing through vouchers, private charters, home schools, virtual schools and tax credits.

The *No Child Left Behind Act* requires unprecedented parent reporting and mandates parent involvement (tied to Title I funds for serving economically disadvantaged students) but implementation of the law has been overwhelmingly focused on testing. While school data are increasingly available to parents, databases are often designed to help them "shop" for schools, rather than, as citizens, to invest in their neighborhood public schools. And that is part of the problem.

The question of course becomes, if we are to keep the public in public education, who is the public? The demographics in this country are changing in a way that the public has to engage and has to assure that we include diverse communities that surround neighborhood public schools. Much of our rhetoric is about doing *unto* high poverty schools and *unto* high poverty neighborhoods. The *public* in keeping the public in public education must include people of color and the poor and must acknowledge the power, the privileges and the prejudices that come with racism.

To keep the public in public education we need engaged citizens, we need accountable leadership, and we need enlightened public policy.

Let me give you one example. We have been working on an effort called Graduation Guaranteed/*Graduación Garantizada* that would give a minimum of high school education to all children. We call it "school holding power" rather than dropouts to emphasize the accountability of the school in keeping kids in school and graduating. Our School Holding Power Portal includes dropout data that neighborhoods at the local level can use to know what is going on in their school and to call themselves into action around this, whether it be into action around policy, around investment or around the quality of their neighborhood public schools (http://www.idra.org/portal; also see article on Page 45). Local communities in Texas together with schools can look at the rate at which their students disappear, the actual numbers of students, whether or not they pass minimum competency tests, the differences by ethnic group, the ACT/SAT rates, and the state of teaching quality.

So the public in public education can know not only about outcomes but also about what leads to those outcomes. The public becomes armed with actionable data that can lead to good results.

How do we effect change?

For the second question, we must build capacity and collaboration for the common good. We clearly need to collaborate across traditional sectors. Economic injustice and poverty kept African Americans and Latinos apart or competing for measly slices of the same pie. In the 1940s, Hispanic workers (some of whom had been brought to this country as part of the Bracero Program) and African American workers competed for many of the same low paying jobs. Tensions have escalated whenever African Americans have determined not to defend the rights of immigrant workers or when Latinos have decided not to support desegregation efforts because it might antagonize Whites.

Recently, wrapped in the fear of national security, our nation's political leaders quickly returned to the march against the outsider, against the immigrant. Since September 11, 2001, we have seen the renewed push toward policy that would restrict the civil liberties of immigrants, a push to conflate immigration with terrorism.

Building common ground is a big task and an important one. IDRA's framework calls at the local level to develop capacity in the community, in the school and with coalitions to work together on this very serious divide.

The basis for this relationship cannot be a continued blaming of students because they are black or brown or poor, or of blaming of schools because they cannot meet accountability standards without the resources that are necessary.

What fundamentals must be in place to improve our public schools?

For the last question, we must invest in the changes that matter most. In Texas, with House Bill 1 that was passed in May of 2006, we estimate that the fiscal equity gap has grown by 30 percent. Texas' top 50 wealthiest schools are 72 percent White. Texas' poorest 50 schools are 94 percent Hispanic.

On the Quality Schools Action Framework then, while we look at the features that matter – and this is what research tells us matters – parent and community engagement, engagement of students, teaching quality, and curriculum quality, it is essential that the foundations be in place as well: governance efficacy and funding equity.

True sustainable action that fundamentally changes the experiences of children in the classroom must address the root causes and the trends that first gave rise to inequity. These causes have taken root in schools and systems and not in children or families. But addressing root causes can be carried out in a very local, very real practical way in terms of policy, practices and investment at the community-school-neighborhood level.

The Quality Schools Action Framework speaks to the need and possibility of engaging citizens, leaders and policymakers around high quality data that call all of us as members of the community to act, to establish common ground, to strengthen education, and finally and most importantly and fundamentally, to align our values with our investments in the school system: fundamentals and features that we know are needed – from teaching quality, to engaged students, engaged parents and families, and a high quality, authentic curriculum so that students in every neighborhood and of every background can in fact have equal educational opportunities.

Originally published in the *IDRA Newsletter*, January 2007

A Quality Schools Action Framework

by María "Cuca" Robledo Montecel, Ph.D.

The pipeline, or path, from pre-kindergarten to high school graduation and success in higher education, is marked by cracks and disjunctures. IDRA's InterAction forums in late 2004 and early 2005 reaffirmed that, in many cases, students experience no connection between early education and secondary school, much less between high school graduation and higher education (IDRA, 2005).

Without strong connections in the education pipeline, too few Texas students transition from secondary schools to four-year universities; fewer still are prepared to go on to earn bachelor's, master's or doctoral degrees. As an indispensable conduit to college, graduation with a diploma, backed by an excellent education, must be a focal point for systems change. It also must be central to any efforts for reform, as the problem of student attrition is not only longstanding, but growing.

IDRA released its 19th statewide attrition study for Texas this past October 2005, using the same methodology developed for its inaugural baseline study in 1986. The study reveals a grim picture. The latest attrition rate of 36 percent is higher than the original rate of 33 percent that alarmed so many community and education leaders almost two decades ago. IDRA's latest attrition study shows that Texas high schools lose one out of every three students before they graduate. Since 1986, schools in Texas have lost a total of more than 2.2 million students. In sum, one student in Texas is lost to attrition every four minutes (see October 2005 issue of the *IDRA Newsletter*; see IDRA's web site for the latest figures at http://www.idra.org).

Attrition rates among Hispanic students were higher in 1986 than they were for any other group and have increased over the last 19 years, from 45 percent to 49 percent – one student out of two. During this same period, the attrition rates for Black students have increased even more, from 34 percent to 44 percent.

This is not to suggest that for White students attrition should go unnoticed. While attrition rates of White students have declined from 27 percent to 22 percent, this rate still represents roughly one White student in five who does not graduate.

At these rates, Texas and other states are not only leaving children behind, but, as the Harvard Civil Rights Project has said in a recent report on dropouts, we are "losing our future" (Orfield, et al., 2004).

For those students who do graduate, only one out of five enrolls in a Texas public university the following fall. Thirteen out of 19 public universities in Texas graduate less than half of their students; six graduate less than a third. This picture is not very different across the country.

If Texas continues on this course, education cannot fulfill its promise as a path to opportunity for all; instead it represents a vanishing future (see figure below).

Texas Education – A Vanishing Future

"In Texas, the pre-kindergarten through 20 pipeline is not only clogged at various transition points, it is, in fact, nonexistent. There is no pipeline that moves students from quality early childhood education to college graduation and beyond."

– *Dr. María Robledo Montecel, IDRA President & CEO*

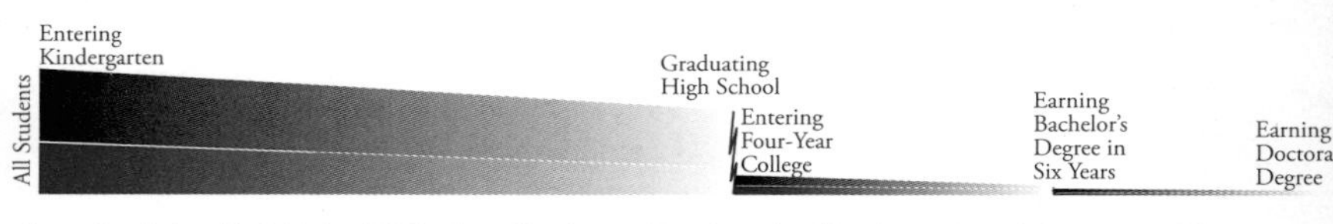

Source: InterAction – The Initiative: A Call to Action (San Antonio, Texas: Intercultural Development Research Association, 2005).

A Framework for Action

Clearly, to achieve different results, we must envision a dramatically different process and undertake a new strategy. IDRA has begun to outline one such process, a Quality Schools Action Framework, described here. We are examining its usefulness through IDRA's ongoing collaboration with communities and schools to assure that all children have access to quality neighborhood public schools.

The Quality Schools Action Framework is based on experience and empirical evidence that emerges from existing theories of change. These models suggest that because schools operate as complex, dynamic systems, lasting systems change depends on sustained action within and outside of those systems. Research on best practices of high performing schools, for example, has examined the links among a constellation of indicators (e.g., teaching quality and effective school governance; parent engagement and student success). Less examined, however, are the contextual and moderating factors that may impede or accelerate school system change. The Quality Schools Action Framework aims to bridge this gap.

The framework offers a model for assessing school conditions and outcomes, identifying leverage points for improvement, and informing action. In essence, the framework poses five key questions: (1) What do we need? (2) How do we make change happen? (3) Which fundamentals must be secured? (4) Where do we focus change? and (5) What outcomes will result?

The framework draws on both current research and knowledge of the field. It also seeks to be intuitive and reflect common sense. It is widely recognized, for example, that students are far more likely to succeed when they have the chance to work with highly qualified, committed teachers, using effective, accessible curricula; when their parents and communities are engaged in their education; and when they, themselves, are engaged in their learning. We also know that effective schools depend on good governance to guide their success and on fair funding to effectively serve all of their students each school day.

What is less well understood is which change strategies and school and community capacities will ensure that schools *as systems* can hold on to all students and secure their success. The Quality Schools Action Framework zeroes in on three key strategies: first, *building community capacity* to strengthen schools; second, *creating coalitions* and action networks that amplify parent and community voices, work and impact; and third and essentially, *building school capacity* to ensure that every child receives an excellent education. To have lasting impact, these kinds of strategic action are needed at local, state and federal levels. At every level, powerful levers are the key to initiating change.

In physics, levers apply mechanical force to move or lift heavy objects. Like crowbars, wheelbarrows and pliers, levers give people a "mechanical advantage" to accomplish work that might at first seem far beyond their capacity and strength. *Engaged citizens*, who actively express their concern for the quality of education and are engaged as partners in school improvement, play a critical role. *Accountable leadership* that recognizes that schools belong to the communities they serve and that fully and consistently reports and takes stock of school performance, is an essential lever. *Actionable knowledge* – clear, quality data – gives education and community leaders the information they need to make good decisions about school policy and practice. *Enlightened public policy*, which provides both the appropriate standards and resources schools need to serve all children, is also an indispensable lever for change.

Using the Framework for Increasing School Holding Power

In assessing student outcomes for secondary schools, the Quality Schools Action Framework suggests that we consider two key indicators: school holding power and student success. *School holding power* refers to the ability of schools to guarantee graduation for all students. *Student success* refers to the academic preparation both to graduate with a diploma and to graduate prepared for college access and success. Following this approach, any plan to increase school holding power must begin with a review of student outcomes and, if needed, have us redefine our goals.

It has never been the case in the history of this country that most minority students graduated from quality high schools or from any type of high school. It has never been the case that schools prepared every student to succeed in college or in a good job that sustains them, their families and their communities. Further, it has never been the case that all sectors – communities, business owners, public officials and the voters who elect them – demanded a quality education for all students.

To date, the goal of dropout prevention has been damage control. Trying to lower the dropout rate bit by bit is considered the best that can be done. This seems rather reasonable given the fact that Texas, for example, has never even been in the ballpark of the 95 percent graduation rate set by the State Board of Education back in the 1980s.

Not too long ago, however, it seemed unreasonable to think that this country would have universal education through elementary school. It was not until the mid-19th century that states began to enact compulsory attendance legislation, and even these laws only called for children to attend school for three months of the year. Many states did not require that children attend elementary school until the early 20th century.

And the gap between required attendance and available public schooling was great. Until the 1950s, education beyond the third grade was neither expected nor accessible for many children. In less than one hundred years, the nation has come to unquestioningly view elementary school as a universal prerequisite.

High school is the new educational minimum. Why is it unreasonable now to think that Texas and the nation can have universal education through high school? Former U.S. Department of Labor Secretary Alexis Herman has said: "This is a labor market that will be unforgiving to those persons without the necessary skills. To compete in a global marketplace, a high school diploma is *just* the beginning" (U.S. Department of Labor, 2003). Half of our nation's 20 fastest-growing occupations require not a high school diploma but an associate or bachelor's degree just to get in the door. In this economy, in this global market, graduation guaranteed – 100 percent graduation – is the only reasonable goal.

Strengthening Schools as Systems

It is obviously not enough just to set a new goal. In Texas, the official 95 percent graduation goal has produced no result. Across the country, despite laudable goals, many children are still left behind. Nationally, the highest poverty schools and schools with the highest concentrations of minority students have nearly double the proportion of inexperienced teachers as schools with the lowest poverty rate (20 percent vs. 11 percent) and the lowest concentration of minority students (21 percent vs. 11 percent) (NCES, 2000).

Segregated minority schools are far more likely to be low wealth schools, characterized by less qualified teachers (Orfield, et al., 2004).

To move from good *intentions* to good *results*, the Quality Schools Action Framework would have us examine schools as systems and to identify and address system factors, such as these, in need of change.

Dropout prevention programs, even the most effective ones, have never been able to address widespread attrition. While these programs can make a profound difference for the specific students they serve, they are simply not designed to transform school systems. Also ineffective have been approaches that tacitly or directly blame parents, students or their backgrounds for crisis-level attrition. These biases not only further disengage students who might already feel marginalized by educational systems, but discredit a schools' significant capacity to serve a diverse population of students.

Emphasizing school and community capacity building, student, parent and family engagement and a systems-based approach, the Quality Schools Action Framework avoids silver bullet solutions and moves toward a comprehensive approach.

To graduate students who are prepared for later life, schools need competent caring teachers who are well-paid and supported in their work. *Teaching quality* is defined by the preparation of teachers and the placement of teachers in their field of study. Teaching is informed by continual professional development. Teaching quality also refers to the practices that teachers use in the classroom to deliver comprehensible instruction that prepares all students to meet academic goals and ensures that no child is left behind or drops out of school.

To increase holding power, schools need consistent ways in which to partner with parents and engage the communities to which they belong. Effective *parent and community engagement* builds partnerships based on respect and a shared goal of academic success for every child. Engagement depends on the meaningful integration of parents and community members into the decision-making processes of schools.

Student engagement is also integral to any plan to reduce attrition. System-wide, schools need ways to get to know students and in turn, to have students know that they belong. Schools need the capacity to create environments and activities that value students of all backgrounds and to incorporate them into the learning process and other social activities within the school, with academic achievement as a result.

School systems that strengthen holding power depend on a high quality, enriched and accessible curriculum. *Curriculum quality and access* encompasses the educational programs of study, materials and other learning resources – such as technology – and their accessibility. It also relates to the fair and unbiased assessment of students and the degree to which schools take responsibility for the academic success of all students.

To have these basic features, school systems must secure two fundamentals: the resources to effectively serve all students and good governance that facilitates academic achievement and success. *Governance efficacy* strengthens school holding power when administrative and supervisory personnel have the capacity to deliver quality educational services to all students, along with the policymaking and pro-active support of a school board to hold on to every student. *Fair funding* is a lynchpin of school success, as it assures that school districts have equitable resources to support a quality educational program for all students.

Strengthening Community Capacity

But to make anything happen, citizens across diverse sectors must reconnect for reform. To address high school attrition, the Quality Schools Action Framework would have us examine how communities, leaders and policymakers can use *actionable knowledge* on attrition to inform and leverage change. The framework would have us examine how to reconnect communities and strengthen coalitions for reform.

Parents and communities have played vital roles in every school reform effort – from fighting for fair funding to making sure that students are not ignored or punished because of the language they speak. As partners in education and catalysts for education policy and funding reform, their role can be critical to helping local neighborhood schools turn the tide of student attrition.

If students are to reach the halls and classrooms of colleges and universities, stakeholders must consider schools as systems and reforms must span the education pipeline. Looking back one length in this line, if students are to enter and succeed in institutions of higher learning, they must be well-prepared and graduating with a diploma from high school. The Quality Schools Action Framework can be used to make sure that schools are places where all children can and do succeed.

Resources

Johnson, R.L. "Little Improvement in Texas School Holding Power – Texas Public School Attrition Study, 2004-05," *IDRA Newsletter* (San Antonio, Texas: Intercultural Development Research Association, October 2005).

Intercultural Development Research Association. *InterAction – The Initiative: A Call to Action* (San Antonio, Texas: Intercultural Development Research Association, 2005).

National Center for Education Statistics. (Washington, D.C.: NCES, Dec. 2000) pg. 14.

National Center for Public Policy and Higher Education. *Measuring Up – The State Report Card on Higher Education* (San Jose, California: NCPPHE, 2004).

Orfield, G., and D. Losen, J. Wald, C. Swanson. *Losing Our Future: How Minority Youth are Being Left Behind by the Graduation Rate Crisis* (The Harvard Civil Rights Project & The Urban Institute, 2004).

U.S. Department of Labor. *Tomorrow's Jobs* (Washington, D.C.: Bureau of Labor Statistics, 2003).

Originally published in the *IDRA Newsletter*, November-December 2005

Chapter Two – Levers of Change

Just Lift!

Aurelio M. Montemayor, M.Ed.

Lifting school buildings is an easier task
Than changing the people inside:
Knowledge for action, persistently applied
Can transform: citizens, ask, ask, ask!

Informing data can enlighten policy
If the facts are current, not stone-age.
The present school picture is the page
Leaders must hold up for all to see.

As families engaged excellence demand,
Responsible leaders give honest accounts.
With voice in unison the pressure mounts:
Enlightened policy, strike up the band.

Enlightened, Accountable and Engaged:
Look at student data: all should be enraged!

Chapter Preface

"Keep Your Eyes on the Prize" / "Hand on the Plow," the gospel hymn that became an American civil rights anthem, showed that real and lasting change comes first from vision, then from holding on to see that vision through to fruition. Where transformation seemed out of reach and problems intractable, the song called for individual and collective action – a concerted movement for fundamental change.

Transforming U.S. public schools into places of excellence and equity in every community – as we must – also calls upon each of us to work for change. This is true as long as low-income and minority students are more likely to attend under-resourced schools and be assigned less qualified teachers. It is true as long as a school's surrounding property wealth prescribes the quality of its books, buildings and academic programs. And it is true as long as high schools graduate only one in two African American, Latino and Native American youth on time with a diploma. Inequity affects us all. If the nation does not address its dropout problem, it stands to lose $3 trillion over the next decade (Rouse, 2005). The loss in human capital is immeasurable.

Schools, as public institutions at the nexus of policy and practice, need our collective energy, engagement and leadership if they are to serve all students well. As starting points, IDRA's empirically-based Quality Schools Action Framework outlines three indispensable levers of change – *engaged citizens, accountable leadership* and *enlightened public policy* – that, in turn, depend on the production and use of *actionable knowledge.*

- First and foremost, engaged citizens, people who actively express their concern about the quality of education and act as partners in school improvement, are essential to transforming schools. "Our Power is Now – Joint African American and Latino Leadership in Education," by Rosana G. Rodríguez, Ph.D., and Bradley Scott, Ph.D., tells the story of how communities across the south are partnering with educators to improve their own schools. With a process developed by IDRA for community-based issues roundtables to catalyze local action, these cross-sector dialogues between African American and Latino communities are using education as common ground for collaboration.
- A second critical lever is accountable leadership, which continuously takes stock of school performance and takes action to improve it. In "Strengthening School's 'Immune Systems' to Fight Mediocrity and Failure," Abelardo Villarreal, Ph.D., shows how healthy schools draw strength and resiliency from diverse, accountable leadership.

- To leverage change, education policy cannot simply extend the status quo or promote incremental reform. It must be enlightened by rejecting two-tier (have/have not) solutions and by securing systems that work for all children. In "Assessing Policies for Success of Minority Children," Albert Cortez, Ph.D., and Abelardo Villarreal, Ph.D., provide a set of tools to assess the implication of policies on minority students and those with special needs at the local level, with examples of how a rubric can be used to assess state policy reforms. This article provides a way of assuring the equity context suggested by Dr. Scott.
- At every level, from policy to practice, people need clear, accurate, and timely information to assess what is needed to strengthen schooling, take action and make sure it is on the right track. "Actionable Knowledge – Putting Research to Work for School-Community Action," by Laurie Posner, M.P.A., considers how educators and grassroots community leaders are putting research to work and how to make knowledge more actionable.

In physics, levers apply mechanical force to move or lift heavy objects. Like crowbars, wheelbarrows and pliers, levers give people a mechanical advantage to accomplish work that might at first seem far beyond their capacity and strength. When it comes to transforming education so that it works for all students, a history of experience and research shows that we must leverage reserves beyond school walls. Real, lasting change comes when people are engaged at all levels, from state capitols to board rooms, from classrooms to community centers and kitchen tables, and where people have the knowledge they need to take the right steps on behalf of all children.

Resources

Rouse, C.E. "Labor Market Consequences of an Inadequate Education," Paper prepared for the symposium on the Social Costs of Inadequate Education, Teachers College Columbia University (New York, N.Y.: Teachers College Columbia University, October 2005).

Engaged Citizens

Our Power is Now

Joint African American and Latino Leadership in Education

by Rosana G. Rodríguez, Ph.D., and Bradley Scott, Ph.D.

Inspiration calls us to be who we are. IDRA's cross-sector and cross-race leadership development work has spanned several years of issuing a call and offering inspiration and support for leaders within communities to take up the charge of strengthening their public schools.

In 1999, inspired by the national One America initiative to engage the nation in moving toward a stronger, more just and united country, offering opportunity and fairness for all people, a collaborative was created between IDRA and several organizations in the San Antonio community. In an effort to engage individuals and organizations in dialogue about issues related to race and ethnicity, the goals of the One America initiative were to promote a vision of a unified community, engage in constructive dialogue to work through the issues of race and identity, and develop solutions in critical areas, such as education, economic opportunity and health care.

More recently, with funding from the Annie E. Casey Foundation and with support from the U.S. Department of Education-funded South Central Collaborative for Equity, IDRA launched its Blueprints for Action initiative, a series of community dialogues aimed at fostering cross-race, joint African American and Latino leadership in education. In 2006, IDRA hosted three "Blueprints for Action" community dialogues in Dallas, Houston and Tyler, Texas. In 2007, with encouragement and support from a national consultative group of civil rights leaders, IDRA expanded the dialogues to Albuquerque and Little Rock. This year and next, with continued Annie E. Casey Foundation funding and additional support from the Charles Stewart Mott Foundation, IDRA is hosting dialogues in four more states: Alabama, Louisiana, Mississippi and Oklahoma.

A Cross-Sector Multi-Racial Approach

The dialogues use a cross-sector multi-racial approach for gathering educators, parents, business and community representatives, and state educational leaders to engage in the tough work of joint planning and action in tackling their communities' persistent problems in education: equitable funding, quality schooling, high school graduation and access to higher education. Building on past dialogues and incorporating the voices of participants, IDRA uses a three-part process to support joint leadership at the pre-event, event and post-event levels.

Student voices are a critical component to the process. For example, in Albuquerque, students presented a photo gallery of their perspectives within their school district about the fulfillment of the promise of equity made by the court rulings in *Brown vs. Board of Education* and *Mendez vs. Westminster*. These powerful images and stories became the center of discussions on what remains to be done (see Page 58).

In Little Rock, students gave oral presentations and wrote articles about equity and access to quality education within the historic Central High School. Working in teams, students identified eight concerns and issued a call to action. An article by student, Brandon Love (printed in the April 2007 issue of the *IDRA Newsletter*) riveted the community in discussions that are continuing today.

The dialogue process is building momentum and having lasting impact. Beyond just talk, communities are taking up the charge through action after these events take place. For example, in Dallas, participants created the South Dallas Consortium involving five communities, including school districts, chambers of commerce and institutions of higher education. Their goal is to ensure that minority students graduate from high school and go on to college. This group has created a five-year strategic plan to accomplish this with assistance from the IDRA South Central Collaborative for Equity.

In Little Rock, participants have become part of two key taskforces for their school district, one of which works on increasing student achievement for all learners based on a new legislative initiative. They are using the dialogue documents as part of their foundation for the taskforce work and are creating recommendations to address the state-level mandate for educational improvement. The other taskforce is investigating school environmental and policy issues.

The action planning process is an effective prototype for inspiring local leaders from all walks of life to tackle hard issues, set aside differences that have kept them apart and build a strong common vision for success for their children. Together, local leaders…

- Build cross-sector and cross-race alliances as advocates in education to catalyze local action;
- Create a common discourse on the proper ends of education, based on what forms a good and just society that supports and prepares all children for graduation, college and civic engagement;
- Begin to build policy agendas and action blueprints on dropout prevention for improved graduation rates;
- Create a legacy of shared leadership, accountability and joint action around education issues for minority children; and
- Leverage and complement work underway to address the education needs of all youth.

IDRA is leveraging its work through technology enhancements that are underway to help prepare and orient participants prior to and after their dialogues and to encourage the exchange of information. Web site enhancements are being designed to facilitate a sustained engagement process beyond the dialogues that will help connect communities across states and regions (http://www.idra.org/mendezbrown/).

Through these enhancements, information is available about the two historic *Brown* and *Mendez* cases that undergird this work. Both cases concluded that the obligation of public schools to provide access to non-segregated and quality educational experiences is a matter of equal protection of rights under the U.S. Constitution.

The Challenge of Brown and Mendez

Every year, more than 1.2 million children are "lost" or drop out prior to their high school graduation. One student is lost from public school enrollment every two minutes. This tragic loss is felt in families, communities and at the national level. We must maintain uncompromising efforts in our expectation for graduating all students. As such, IDRA's president and CEO, Dr. María "Cuca" Robledo Montecel has issued a call to immediate action to address these issues. The key principle in her call to action is that all students should be expected and supported to graduate from high school.

More than ever, what is needed is broad and deep engagement of diverse racial communities acting together in building strong and responsive public schools that value and support Latino, African American and other minority children.

We are at a critical juncture in our nation's history with the upcoming reauthorization of the *No Child Left Behind Act*. Most of us would agree that our children deserve to be nurtured and supported to become the powerful creators of their future they are born to be. Each generation merits our support throughout their schooling, from pre-K through college, to be, do and have all they can dream in this lifetime.

But how can our society build confident young leaders for the future when divisions among our groups continue to persist and erode the very social capital our diversity represents? More than ever, what is needed is broad and deep engagement of diverse racial communities acting together in building strong and responsive public schools that value and support Latino, African American and other minority children.

The challenge that lies before us is to create new networks of collective action built on trust and a shared vision of success for all youth. In cultivating a just and civil society, we must mitigate our differences and forge new alliances to create a blueprint for access, equity and excellence in education that will ensure the fulfillment of the *Brown* and *Mendez* rulings for every child.

This is our national imperative: increase support for public schools and the communities they serve to ensure that diverse learners are not denied access to an excellent education that will facilitate college success and lead to a full and productive life. The blueprints for change – while critical for the success of minority students, whose achievement lags well below their Anglo counterparts in all indices of well-being, including education, health and college attendance – are vitally important for all children.

Will our diverse communities and sectors pull together and concentrate on building a better educational future? IDRA believes that communities and public schools, given equitable and appropriate support, are the hope for the future for all children. Unleashing the potential of joint leadership in action has power to transcend differences and build upon the cultural, linguistic and racial strength of this nation that is reflected in our diversity.

In his dissenting opinion in the *Parents Involved in Community Schools vs. Seattle School District No.1* case, Justice Breyer wrote: "For much of this nation's history, the races remained divided. It was not long ago that people of different races drank from separate fountains, rode on separate busses and studied in separate schools. In this court's finest hour, *Brown vs. Board of Education* challenged this history and helped to change it. For *Brown* held out a promise… It was the promise of true racial equality – not as a matter of fine words on paper, but as a matter of everyday life in the nation's cities and schools. It was about the nature of a democracy that must work for all Americans." (2007)

The challenge lies before us in the decisions we make and the actions we take, together. Let us not turn our backs on so many minority children who continue to be trapped in a mire of tragic inequity, with under resourced schools and less than excellent teaching. This nation was built on the premise that our public schools are the bedrock of democracy, the great equalizing factor in preparing citizens for the future.

Julian Bond said: "We must persevere… only with renewed commitment can our country become the nation it should be. Only with renewed commitment will we fulfill the promise of *Brown*." (2007)

Together, we can create that reality. The moment for joint leadership is long overdue. Our power is in our now.

Resources

Bond, J. "We Must Persevere," *Teaching Tolerance* (Fall, 2007) pg. 19.

Breyer, S. *Parents Involved in Community Schools vs. Seattle School District No. 1*, dissenting opinion (Supreme Court of the United States, June 28, 2007).

Love, B. "A Tale of Two Centrals," *IDRA Newsletter* (San Antonio, Texas: Intercultural Development Research Association, April 2007).

Rodríguez, R.G., and B. Scott. "Expanding Blueprints for Action – Children's Outcomes, Access, Treatment, Learning, Resources, Accountability," *IDRA Newsletter* (San Antonio, Texas: Intercultural Development Research Association, May 2007).

Robledo Montecel, M. "Fulfilling the Promise of Brown vs. Board of Education," *IDRA Newsletter* (San Antonio, Texas: Intercultural Development Research Association, November-December 2003).

Originally published in the *IDRA Newsletter*, June-July 2008

Accountable Leadership

Strengthening Schools' "Immune Systems" to Fight Mediocrity and Failure

by Abelardo Villarreal, Ph.D.

In the November-December 2005 issue of the *IDRA Newsletter,* Dr. María "Cuca" Robledo Montecel, IDRA executive director, presented a model for assessing school conditions and outcomes, identifying leverage points for improvement, and informing action (2005). This Quality Schools Action Framework is based on experience and empirical evidence that emerges from existing theories of change. The framework and related definitions are available on the IDRA web site (http://www.idra.org). This article examines ways leaders can strengthen school capacity.

The human body is equipped with an immune system that protects it from outside biological influences. A school is like a human body. It has an "immune system" that equips it with the capacity to fend off internal and external influences that hinder its ability to successfully educate all children. For purposes of this article, *capacity* refers to a school's *immune system* that, when activated, has an extraordinary ability to fight hurtful influences. Just like the biological immune system, schools have a first line of defense to continuously ward off damaging influences and a capacity to strengthen this line of defense through external intervention and assistance.

Understanding and banking on this capacity for self-renewal is basic to finding effective remedies to many education problems. This article demonstrates how this immune system can ensure that all of a school's interacting parts can be aligned to create a healthy school by: (1) describing what constitutes a healthy school, (2) briefly discussing two major woes that threaten a healthy school's existence and functionality, and (3) outlining ways to build up a school's immune system.

What is a Healthy School?

A healthy school may be described in two interdependent ways: (1) consistency and quality of outcomes as defined through success of all students regardless of ethnicity, race or socioeconomic status, and (2) access to strong and decisive governance and leadership, teaching quality, and a world class curriculum.

A healthy school has great accomplishments in student academic performance, a strong student holding power ability, no achievement gaps among student subgroups, high graduation rates, high college preparation rates as demonstrated through high college entrance examination scores, high college enrollment and graduation rates, and strong community and parent support for the school.

Also, a healthy school is filled with student excitement, engagement and inquiring minds that thirst for knowledge by questioning, hypothesizing and discovering. A healthy school draws strength from its leaders, teachers, community and parents. Its leaders are committed to excellence and equity for all students, its teachers are qualified and ensure that all students have access to knowledge, its community fully supports the school's efforts, and its parents are the unquestionable and best partners in education. With today's demands for excellence, healthy schools must be in a constant state of improvement.

Mediocrity and a dismal failure to teach students from diverse backgrounds and of low socioeconomic status are the two major illnesses that threaten the viability of our schools.

Threats to School Health

Unfortunately, a healthy school is a much-sought after luxury in many communities. *Mediocrity* and a dismal failure to teach students from diverse backgrounds and of low socioeconomic status are the two major illnesses that threaten the viability of our schools.

Mediocrity is defined as a paralysis of an educational institution that maintains the status quo regardless of its effectiveness, is content with its limited capacity to produce excellence, believes that improvement is out of its reach, and masquerades mediocrity as excellence. A school should look for signs of mediocrity and take immediate action. Some signs of mediocrity in schools are the following.

Misplaced and discouraged innovation. Mediocre schools make changes that fail to target critical areas of need. They fake change, are overly cautious, and do not promote innovativeness. Their leaders fail to share and promote leadership among staff. No risks are taken.

Blame the students and community. It is not uncommon for a mediocre school to exonerate itself of all blame for ineffectiveness. Mediocre administrators and teachers firmly believe that student performance in their school can never reach the level of excellence that other schools reach supposedly because their students are not capable and because parents and community are uncooperative.

The "now" is the limit. Mediocre schools grow sour in their student performance because they feel that the limit has been met given the students they have and the community that those students come from. Because of that circumstance, their school cannot expect and should not expect more than what it is accomplishing.

Systemic deception is the rule rather than the exception. Mediocre administrators and teachers circumvent policies and best practices because they have little hope and low expectations of their students and have no faith in the community served by the school. Pretexts abound for unfinished or unacceptable teaching. Dishonesty and keeping quiet about fraudulent behavior are common systemic regularities.

Unqualified staff. In mediocre schools, teachers are non-degreed, and many are teaching out of field. Administrators lack the leadership and management skills to guide a school through tough times. Teachers lack the desire and commitment to grow professionally and make a difference in the lives of students. For many, teaching is just a job, and these teachers have few accomplishments to show for their time. They lack self-efficacy and hold low expectations for themselves. They institutionalize low expectations across the school, having a negative impact on students, parents and community as a whole.

Under-funded schools and classrooms. Appropriate funding to provide the necessary opportunities to learn in a safe environment usually is missing in mediocre schools. Administrators and teachers use this lack of funding as grounds for their lack of accomplishment or their inefficiency in teaching students from diverse backgrounds.

Biased governance and leadership. The absence of leadership in the school board and the mismanagement of a school also are symptoms that contribute to mediocrity. A school board where infighting is common and micromanagement runs rampant is fertile soil to breed discontent, promote mediocrity and endorse inefficiency.

Lack of partnership with communities and parents. Schools where teachers and administrators feel foreign and have little in common with the community in which they teach become vulnerable to heartless, insensible, indifferent and mediocre teaching.

The second problem that beleaguers a school is its inability to increase the academic performance of all of its students. Many factors contribute to this. These factors are: (1) prevalent mediocrity; (2) inability to teach students from diverse cultural and linguistic backgrounds; (3) uncaring and mediocre staff; (4) no access to a world-class curriculum; (5) low academic expectations, particularly for low-income and minority students; and (6) a community that fails to require educational excellence from its schools. These factors also have a demoralizing and weakening effect on the school's immune system to protect its viability as a great equalizer.

Building a School's Immune System

How does one build up a school's immune system to deal with the two major woes that afflict schools? The first step is to assess the effectiveness of the school's critical interacting components and determine the health of each component. The box on Pages 27-29 provides a description of those interacting components of a healthy school.

The second step is to base the priority to act on each component in relationship to academic success and intensity of need as demonstrated through the assessment phase. Address each component starting with the ones that most directly affect student outcomes. Research has yet to establish the degree of interrelationship of the components and those outcomes.

The third step is to recognize that renewal is internal, and solutions and remedies to mediocrity and school failure must emerge from the school's immune system with strong support from external resources. Autoimmune forces (internal forces such as sabotage, disruption and incapacitation) must not stall the school's immune system. School leaders must create an environment of support and determination to guarantee the success of its remedies.

Excellence is prized; mediocrity and student failure must be out of favor. Schools must recognize that they have an immune system that must be activated and exploited. Solutions to education problems must emerge from within and have support from external agencies to be successful.

All students need to have access to a high-quality education that prepares them not only to go on to college but that also lays the groundwork for a life that includes the potential for economic success, full participation as a citizen of a vibrant democracy, and the ability to enrich themselves with ongoing learning experiences.

Resources

Advocates for Children of New York and the New York Immigration Coalition. *Creating a Formula for Success: Why English Language Learner Students are Dropping Out of School, and How to Increase Graduation Rates* (New York: Advocates for Children of New York and the New York Immigration Coalition, 2002).

Bell, J.A. "High-Performing, High-Poverty Schools," *Leadership* (September-October 2001).

Bilby, S. "Community-Driven School Reform: Parents Making a Difference in Education," *Mott Mosaic* (2002) 1, (2), 1-8.

Council of Chief State School Officers and The Charles A. Dana Center at the University of Texas at Austin. *Expecting Success: A Study of Five High-Performing Elementary Schools* (Washington, D.C.: Council of Chief State School Officers, 2002).

Cortez, A., and J.D. Cortez, M. Robledo Montecel. "Dropping Out of School in Arizona: IDRA Conducts New Study," *IDRA Newsletter* (San Antonio, Texas: Intercultural Development Research Association, September 2002).

Foley, R.M. "Professional Development Needs of Secondary School Principals of Collaborative-Based Service Delivery Models," *High School Journal* (2001) 85 (1), 10-23.

Kroll, J., and R.F. Sexton, B.N. Raimondo, H.D. Corbett, B. Wilson. *Setting the Stage for Success: Bringing Parents into Education Reform as Advocates for Higher Student Achievement* (Lexington, Ken.: Prichard Committee for Academic Excellence, 2001).

National Dropout Prevention Center/Network [Online]. *Effective Strategies Having the Most Positive Effect on Dropout Rates.* http://www.dropoutprevention.org/effstrat/effstrat.htm.

Robledo Montecel, M. "A Quality Schools Action Framework – Framing Systems Change for Student Success," *IDRA Newsletter* (San Antonio: Intercultural Development Research Association, November-December 2005).

Robledo Montecel, M., and J.D. Cortez. "Successful Bilingual Education Programs: Development and the Dissemination of Criteria to Identify Promising and Exemplary Practices in Bilingual Education at The National Level," *Bilingual Research Journal* (2002) 26 (1).

Spencer, S.S., and K.R. Logan. "Bridging the Gap: A School-Based Staff Development Model that Bridges the Gap from Research to Practice," *Teacher Education and Special Education* (2003) 26 (1), 51-62.

Originally published in the *IDRA Newsletter*, January 2006

School's Interactive Components and Description

Components	Description
Fair Funding is the availability of funds in a school district to support a quality educational program for all students.	• The district provides enough to fund a quality school program. • The district provides enough additional funds for a quality school program for students with special needs. • The district provides enough to fund educational programs to help students who are not having success in school. • Funding is fairly distributed among the various schools in the school district. • Funding is fairly distributed among the schools in the state.
Governance is the policy making and pro-active support of a school board to support a quality educational program for all students in a school district.	• School board actively supports a quality educational program for all students. • School board sets policies that support programs for students who are successful academically. • School board sets policies that do not affect negatively the quality of education that some students receive. • School board provides for funding and other resources to implement policies that support programs for students who are not successful academically. • School board supports efforts by school administration to ensure high achievement and no achievement gaps among different student groups. • School board tracks and acts on inequalities within the various schools' academic achievement performance. • School board tracks and acts on inequalities within the various schools' access to resources and quality curriculum.
Leadership is the ability and inclination of administrative and supervisory personnel to deliver quality educational services to all students and pride itself for its ability to hold on to students in a school setting.	• School leaders know the needs and educational programs for the various student populations. • School leaders know the needs of a diverse student population. • School leaders actively promote and ensure that the needs of a diverse student population are met. • School leaders represent the ethnicity of the student population in the school. • School leaders involve parents in the decisions affecting the quality of education that their children receive.

Components	Description
School culture is an educational environment that promotes safety and high expectations for all students, reflects high energy and commitment across the board to do what is needed to ensure that students stay in school, and guarantees academic success for all students.	• School personnel at all levels reflect attitudes and beliefs that all students can and will learn in that school. • School personnel at all levels respect and value all students regardless of ethnicity, religion and lifestyle. • All students feel safe and are able to express themselves without fear of ridicule or embarrassment. • Students from various ethnic groups respect each other and learn in a cooperative setting.
Community involvement is the creation of a partnership based on respect and the shared goals of academic success and integration of the community into the decision-making processes of the school.	• The community has an interest in becoming an integral part of the education community of the school. • The community takes a pro-active role in ensuring that all students receive a quality education. • The school actively promotes the involvement of the community in school activities and decisions. • The school perceives community involvement as an essential partner in its campaign to teach all students.
Teaching quality is the preparation of teachers, the placement of teachers in their fields of study, and the opportunities provided teachers to grow professionally.	• Teachers have the highest preparation available to teach students from different cultures and languages. • Qualified teachers (bilingual or English as a second language teachers for English language learners) are placed in appropriate classrooms. • Teachers teach in their discipline. • Teachers have ample opportunities for professional growth.
Assessment and accountability are the school practices related to fair and unbiased assessment of students and the degree to which schools take responsibility for the academic success of all students.	• The school uses fair and unbiased tests that are reliable for students from diverse cultures and languages. • The school uses assessment data in planning and delivering instruction. • The school communicates assessment data in a comprehensible way to parents and the community. • The school feels responsible for serving a diverse student population.
Curriculum is the educational programs of study, materials and other learning resources, such as technology, and their accessibility to all students.	• Academic goals for the school are congruent with district and state goals. • Curriculum meets federal, state and local requirements. • The school offers quality bilingual or ESL programs of study for English language learners.

COMPONENTS	DESCRIPTION
	• The school offers quality educational programs for students with disabilities. • The school capitalizes on the power of technology to enhance the delivery of instruction. • The school offers the most challenging state graduation plans available. • The school has agreements with colleges and universities to offer courses that carry college credit. • Students, regardless of ethnicity or home language, have access to the most challenging graduation plans and courses.
Instruction is the practices that teachers use in the classroom to deliver comprehensible instruction that prepares all students to meet academic goals and ensures that no child drops out of school.	• Teachers use appropriate teaching techniques that are aligned with student characteristics and learning styles. • Teachers feel responsible for teaching all students. • Teachers capitalize on cultural resources in the community to enhance their teaching. • Teachers articulate high expectations through their actions and beliefs. • Teachers communicate with other school personnel to coordinate the best instruction for all students.
Student engagement is the school activities designed to incorporate students into the learning process and other social activities within the school that ensure academic achievement.	• Teachers know and practice the value of connecting students socially and academically. • All students believe that school personnel want them engaged in the academic and socialization processes of the school. • There is evidence that all students have access to and are supported in the academic and socialization processes of the school. • All students feel valued and respected and engage themselves in the academic and socialization challenges provided by the school.
Support systems are programs and activities designed to support students academically, psychologically and socially to ensure that students reach the goals set by the school.	• Counseling programs are sensitive to cultural and linguistic characteristics of the student population. • Counselors are trained and committed to work with students from different cultural and linguistic backgrounds. • Counselors and teachers encourage and prepare all students to enroll in college. • The school provides academic programs to address students who have fallen through the cracks. • The school has been successful in addressing students who are falling through the cracks.

Enlightened Public Policy

Assessing Policies for Success of Minority Children

by Albert Cortez, Ph.D., and Abelardo Villarreal, Ph.D.

At one time, only a small subset of schools were asking what changes needed to be made in public education to improve outcomes for minority children. But now, as the nation's schools grow increasingly diverse, the challenges of answering this question have expanded to reach the majority of school systems in all parts of this country.

This article defines and describes the role of policy in shaping the quality of educational services to minority children and to those with special needs. In addition, it describes a set of criteria to assess the adequacy and appropriateness of policies that ensure students' full participation, engagement and success in the educational process. Further, it assesses two major policies using the criteria outlined.

The Role of Policy in Shaping Education Services

Policy as defined in Webster refers to a "governing principle" or "written contract." As a *governing principle*, a policy reflects a basic stance or position. Thus, it is intended to result in certain changes in practice associated with related issues.

An example of a policy is a state requirement for schools to report numbers of students by certain characteristics. The information is then used to inform an understanding of a school's enrollment profile. Additionally, the policy may provide information deemed necessary to guide specific services for students.

The state of Texas, for example, already has an array of policies that are designed to identify minority students and impact the education programs that are provided to them. State policies often require collection of data on students' racial and ethnic status and the income status of their families. These data are used to develop state and district profile summaries to allow for targeted funding resources based on academic achievement and for disaggregating information to enable state leaders to compare the relative achievement performance levels of different minority groups.

Prior to desegregation, no data were used to track the educational status of minority and non-minority students, as any policy review could focus on simply looking at school-level information. After school integration, district information was collected at an aggregate level, with no sub-group breakouts – providing an average of performance for the school or district as a whole.

The shortcomings of using such averages to inform education policy were best summarized by Dr. José A. Cárdenas, IDRA founder and director emeritus. He explained that the problem with averages is that a person could have one foot in a bucket of ice and the other in a bucket of scalding water, and the resulting average temperature of 72 degrees would disguise the reality that neither foot was in very good straits. Thus, policies that are designed to specifically identify minority student status can be useful in guiding policy efforts.

It is no doubt that policy impacts the nature and quality of educational services provided to minority students. National policy that evolved from the *Brown vs. Board of Education* Supreme Court decision led to efforts to dismantle segregated school systems. And this eventually influenced state-level policies that mirrored the national requirements.

At the state policy level in Texas as in other states, school districts are required to identify students who have limited English proficiency and to provide specialized services to address those needs. The data also are used to provide supplemental funding to schools to help them provide the specialized services needed.

As the nation as a whole continues to experience growing diversity, there is a need for tools to assess the implications of polices on minority students and communities. Following is a framework developed by IDRA's Dr. Rosana Rodríguez and Dr. Abelardo Villarreal for assessing education reform policies.

Criteria for Assessing Policies that Impact Access and Success

Policies that have positive impact on access and success for all students are characterized by the following attributes.

Inclusivity – The policy includes communication and participatory processes that embrace diverse perspectives from the community being served. Key questions to ask are:

- Does the policy address the diversity of the community in its focus and purpose?
- Does the policy address the diverse nature of the state's student population by pro-actively ensuring that low-income and minority students receive maximum benefit?
- Do the decision-making bodies and leadership who will implement the policy reflect diversity?

Funding Equity – The policy provides for adequate funding for varied responses that serve a diverse student population. Key questions to ask are:

- Are appropriate resources committed to ensure that problems are addressed?
- Does the policy promote equity and excellence through equitable and appropriate funding for all students?
- Is there a mechanism to acquire or disperse funding, and is it fairly and equitably designed?
- Is there recourse to correct disparities that might occur?
- How will the recourse be clearly articulated and disseminated?

Priority – The policy assigns high priority to graduation and academic success of minority students. Key questions to ask are:

- Does the policy pro-actively articulate the highest level of commitment to the academic success of every student?
- Does the policy promote the highest level of commitment and requirement for action from the institution?

Quality of Action – The policy provides an action framework that ensures programmatic activity is consistent with the highest quality instruction for a diverse student population. Key questions to ask are:

- Does the policy propose viable solutions that are of the highest quality and aimed at minority student access and success?
- Does the policy reflect an approach that is appropriate to the setting with viable goals, stated objectives and means to measure the outcomes for students?
- Will the targets selected for the policy yield the greatest positive impact in supporting access, student persistence, academic success and graduation for minority students at key junctures in the educational pipeline?
- Are the barriers that prevent inclusivity, access and success addressed?

Flexibility – The policy is flexible and adoptable to address various contexts within an action framework. Key questions to ask are:

- Does the policy provide for an intentional process that allows for adjustments or changes as needed to better serve students?
- Is there a method for evaluating the impact and effectiveness of the policy at regular intervals in order to provide feedback for assessment and planning?
- Is there a means of adapting the policy to meet local needs and contexts to better serve students?

Goal Appropriateness – The policy focuses appropriately on the goal of access and success of every minority student. Key questions to ask are:

- Does the goal correctly acknowledge the various problems associated with the lack of access and success for every student?
- Does the policy derive from a focused analysis that identifies and processes institutional responses that present access and success?
- Is the policy on target in addressing the systemic changes needed to support student access and academic success at key junctures in learning?

Agency Accountability – The policy includes structures that provide for enforcement and agency accountability. Key questions to ask are:

- Does the policy foster shared accountability to support access and success for every student?
- Does the policy have a method of enforcement for accountability?
- Have means been identified to share broadly and receive feedback regarding the enforcement of the policy at regular intervals?
- Have benchmarks been identified?

Institutional Accountability – The policy requires institutional accountability. Key questions to ask are:

- Is there a provision to regularly conduct assessments of progress in serving students and report results through disaggregated means?
- Is there a means of accountability for the policy that appropriately places responsibility on the system to support student success?
- Does the institution open itself to a shared, formal examination of progress in supporting student access and success?
- Is there a commitment to use the data collected as part of continued planning?
- Is there a means of shared accountability to see students successfully transition from high school to college and college graduation?
- Is engagement built into the systems of evaluation and reporting?

Educational Impact – The policy holds promise for making positive and lasting impact on access and success for all students. Key questions to ask are:

- Does the policy provide a viable means for closing the achievement gap?
- Does the policy support positive and effective solutions to increase student achievement?
- Does the policy create a vehicle to increase enrollment, institutional persistence and graduation rates for minority students?

Inter-connectedness – Acknowledge the inter-connectedness of systems from pre-kindergarten through higher education. Key questions to ask are:

- Does the policy foster connections at key junctures in the pipeline from pre-kindergarten through higher education?
- Does the policy promote interaction and shared accountability across traditional boundaries within the educational pipeline?
- Does the policy foster greater articulation between systems in support of student success?

Assessing Recent Policy Reforms via the Policy Assessment Framework

In its recently-completed special session on school finance, the Texas Legislature adopted numerous new education reform policies. One such reform provided a new high school allotment of $275 for students in grades nine through 12 to help schools reduce dropouts, improve preparation for college and support expanded college enrollment. An assessment of the provisions of this new policy initiative however shows it has mixed implications.

As the nation as a whole continues to experience growing diversity, there is a need for tools to assess the implications of polices on minority students and communities.

On the one hand, the program partially meets the *inclusivity* criteria, but because it is provided to all schools without regard to relative needs of school districts, it is not effectively inclusive. On the *funding equity* issue, the new plan calls for an allocation that is not run through any equalization mechanisms found in most state aid formulae, so it fails this assessment. Because it targets the funds on graduation, enrollment and academic success, it gets an A+ in that area. *Quality of action* requirements are minimally addressed with local systems given great latitude in deciding how monies provided will be utilized at the local level. *Flexibility* is worked into the new reform, but it may provide so much flexibility that it may actually hamper targeting of new funding. On the *goal appropriateness* indicator, the new reform acknowledges critical issues that need expanded state action. *Agency accountability* is worked into the plan in the form of required progress reports, but requirements to evaluate program effectiveness are non-existent. The new high school allotment recognizes *connections* at key junctures, focusing primarily between high schools and colleges.

Another new reform policy calls for awards for teachers and schools that show notable improvement in achievement. On the surface this pay for performance sounds good in that there is an emphasis on overall improvement in achievement for all students. Judged against the framework however, the new policy promises to create more concerns than solutions for minority students.

Some positive features of one such proposal include initial targeting of schools needing improvement, some flexibility to allow local decision-making, appropriate emphasis on improvement, some accountability in use of funding, etc. Its major shortcomings, however, include lack of sufficient provisions to ensure that minority, low-achieving students do not become victims of efforts to exclude them from selected classes or schools so that those educators and schools are better positioned to receive rewards for improvement. Competition for rewards may also result in less collaboration among colleagues and actually decrease the level of peer support, as educators compete with each other for available rewards.

These sample applications of the policy reform assessment framework provide an insight of how one can use these criteria to assess whether policies have the potential for improving access and success of minority students enrolled in schools.

We would encourage policymakers, educators and community members to review major education reforms using these factors as markers for potential improvement. Though not intended as the ultimate assessment, its application may help provide some structured process for assessments for people concerned with the array of education reforms that have emerged in recent years. At best, it may help inform refinement of proposed policies before their eventual adoption. At least, it may help review whether existing policies support or actually hinder commonly shared goals of improving achievement for all students, and particularly those students who have been historically ill-served or under-served in our educational institutions.

Originally published in the *IDRA Newsletter*, June-July 2006

Actionable Knowledge

Actionable Knowledge –

Putting Research to Work for School-Community Action

by Laurie Posner, M.P.A.

Since as long ago as 1845, when the Boston School Board gave a uniform test to its elementary students, schools in the United States have been gathering data to gauge how well they are educating students (Coe & Brunet, 2006). These early report cards planted seeds for what would later become a plethora of reports on the performance of American organizations and systems.

Standardized report cards emerged relatively quickly in the field of health care. In the early 1860s, Florence Nightingale pressed for mortality statistics to be published by London hospitals to raise standards of hospital sanitation. By 1917, the American College of Surgeons was using a cross-system report to publicize the performance of almost 700 hospitals (Coe & Brunet, 2006).

In the field of education the "report card" became the centerpiece of individual student assessment and, by the end of the 20th Century, the central trope for state and national assessment of school effectiveness. In its *Round-up of National Education Report Cards*, the Center for Public Education (2007) identified more than a dozen such reports, spanning a spectrum from pre-kindergarten to post-secondary education, from K-12 school funding to college scholarships, and from measures of international standing to state, school district and individual student performance.

Such report cards include the National Center for Education Statistics' well-known "National Assessment of Educational Progress" (or NAEP) reports, the U.S. Chamber of Commerce's *Leaders and Laggards: A State-by-State Report Card on Educational Effectiveness*, Education Week's *Quality Counts* series, and the National Center for Public Policy and Education's "Measuring Up" study. As the field has become increasingly meta-analytic, even assessment of assessment, such as *The State of State Standards* produced by the Thomas B. Fordham Foundation, has become commonplace.

Rankings of our nation's performance in public education in these last few decades have tracked business objectives, advocacy aims and policy preoccupations. In 1983, *US News and World Report* published its first edition of *America's Best Colleges*. At that time, blue-collar workers were being hit hardest by the recession, and low-income students had increasingly limited access to public higher education (Fligstein & Shin, 2004). But college-going rates and college revenues rose dramatically in the 1980s, with tuition increasing during the period by 106 percent (Levine, 1994).

Such increases justified the marriage between ranking and advertising. A report card, in this context, was as much about packaging schools for consumer choice as assessing quality.

The link between outcomes-based assessment (accountability) and consumer choice also was famously inscribed in the *No Child Left Behind Act* of 2001, which envisioned accountability ratings and parent choice as twin levers for raising performance locally and across school systems.

As a result of widespread rankings and ratings, more data are available to Americans than ever before about how our schools are doing. At a mouse click, we can locate public schools nationwide by name, find demographics and dropout rates, and compare student outcomes on state-mandated tests, national standards, and college entrance exams.

But raising national awareness of school performance has not necessarily coincided with better national outcomes. Graduation rates have hovered at about 75 percent since the 1960s (Heckman & LaFontaine, 2007), and disparities in, for example, fourth grade reading and mathematics outcomes over the last decade have persisted (NCES, 2009).

You might say that this is to be expected. Research, report cards and the presentation of data cannot be counted on to change school systems. After all, the correlations between research, policy and practice are inherently messy. School systems are complex organic organizations.

Information must be available to people who need it most at the district- and school-level and it must be crafted around organizing and action.

And policymaking for public education is similarly complex. As Vivien Tseng points out in a review of the role of research in policymaking and practice, research is "rarely used in… a clear-cut linear way [and] rarely offers a definitive answer to any policy or practice question… requiring instead that practitioners discern if research evidence is relevant to their particular needs and judge whether they can use it given political, budgetary and other constraints" (2008).

Still, reports and indicator systems contribute far less then they could to school improvement. In IDRA's experience, they fall short for several reasons. First, their purposes and intended audiences are often diffuse or ill-defined. Second, they tend to focus too much on ranking and not enough on exemplary practices and models for action. Third, many data sets are overly tied to consumer choice and not enough to citizen engagement. Finally, despite vast improvements, research remains inaccessible to many people, bringing knowledge online but not infusing it into capitols, classrooms and kitchen-table problem-solving (Robledo Montecel, 2006).

Just as a father who finds out that his son has earned a "D" in algebra can do little with this data without information on how to make a difference, school, community and family leaders need more than annual yearly progress (AYP) scores and discrete outcome data to make a difference in schools that are struggling. Information must be available to people who need it most at the district- and school-level and it must be crafted around organizing and action.

"Actionable knowledge," as researcher Chris Argyris has written, "is not only *relevant* to the world of practice, it is *the knowledge that people use to create that world*" (1993, emphasis added).

The good news is that with good information, school, community and family leaders can and are making a difference. In *Organized Communities, Stronger Schools*, for example, Kavitha Mediratta and her colleagues at the Annenberg Institute for School Reform (2008) chronicle seven community organizing efforts that use actionable knowledge in school reform. In Oakland and Philadelphia, community and school action led to new small schools that resulted in higher attendance and improved graduation rates. In Miami, a combination of improvements in literacy programming for elementary students with community engagement raised student outcomes on the Florida Comprehensive Assessment Test (FCAT).

According to Mediratta and her colleagues, the most effective organizing combines "community members' knowledge… and insights… with analyses of administrative data and best practices identified by education research. The combination of data and local knowledge enabled groups to develop reform initiatives uniquely suited to local school conditions and needs." (2008)

The Annenberg findings echo those of Janice Petrovich at the Ford Foundation, who, in a reflection on the foundation's investments in community involvement in education from 1950 to 1990 (2008) points out that "no matter how well crafted or well intentioned [school] reforms may be, they will not endure without community support – and that community support is won not through public relations campaigns, but through active participation." Promoting such participation requires the capacity "to clearly identify research questions and data needs, to find ways of obtaining these data and to use research evidence to bolster their arguments."

Such findings also have been central to IDRA's experience. IDRA's partnership with the nonprofit organization, ARISE, is one example. ARISE is a faith-based organization, founded in the late 1980s, dedicated to supporting children for educational success and strengthening families from within. For the Latina leaders at ARISE working to improve Texas border communities, a guiding tenet is to "look around you, assess what's going on, make a response, evaluate and celebrate."

In keeping with this principle, IDRA designed a series of training sessions on family leadership in education with ARISE centers through IDRA's Parent Information and Resource Center. Through these forums, parents have shared concerns about how their children were doing in school and looked together at data on dropout rates, college-going rates and student test scores. In deepening their knowledge, a group of families in the Rio Grande Valley has been moved to action: This summer, ARISE families formed a PTA *Comunitario* to formalize their role as advocates to improve the quality of education. Through the PTA *Comunitario*, family leaders will consider why school outcomes are not matching up with their hopes and goals for their children and will form partnerships with their local neighborhood public schools for action.

Research and experience show that knowledge must be made actionable in order to have impact. Actionable knowledge:

- Is framed around the right questions – for example, asking how schools as systems can go beyond dropout prevention and recovery to strengthen "holding power" across grades.
- Tracks not just school outcomes but the conditions that give rise to them and effective practices – providing teachers, administrators, family and community members the data they can use to make a difference.
- Presents data in context – including meaningful comparisons among peer schools and districts and information on school funding, resources and data that are disaggregated by student groups to help people assess and improve both educational quality and equity.
- Bridges data divides – presenting data online and in-person, in families' first languages; answering burning questions; and embedding salient knowledge into community forums, school-community partnerships, and professional development for educators and school leaders.

Incorporating these features in partnerships, like the ones profiled above, researchers, educators, and family members are building on the data-gathering strengths of the accountability era in their efforts to improve schools. To realize our aspirations for children more broadly, we need to make sure that these examples become the rule rather than the exception.

Resources

Argyris, C. *Knowledge for Action: A Guide to Overcoming Barriers to Organizational Change* (San Francisco, Calif.: Josssey-Bass Inc., 1993).

Coe, C.K., and J.R. Brunet. "Organizational Report Cards: Significant Impact or Much Ado about Nothing?" P*ublic Administration Review* (January 2006) Vol. 66, No. 1, pp. 90-100(11).

Center for Public Education. "Round-up of National Education Report Cards," web site (2007).

Fligstein, N., and Shin, T. "The Stakeholder Value Society: A Review of the Changes in Working Conditions and Inequality in the United States, 1976-2000," in *Social Inequality* (Kathryn M. Neckerman, ed.) (New York, N.Y.: Russell Sage Foundation, 2004) pg. 407.

Heckman, J., and P.A. LaFontaine. *The American High School Graduation Rate: Trends and Levels* (Bonn, Germany: The Institute for the Study of Labor. December, 2007).

Levine, A. *Higher Learning in America, 1980-2000* (Baltimore, Md.: Johns Hopkins University Press, 1994).

Chapter Two – Levers of Change

Mediratta, K., and S. Shah, S. McAlister, D. Lockwood, C. Mokhtar, N. Fruchter. *Organized Communities, Stronger Schools: A Preview of Research Findings* (Providence, R.I.: Annenberg Institute for School Reform at Brown University, 2008).

National Center for Education Statistics. *The Condition of Education: Learner Outcomes* (Washington, D.C.: May 2009).

Petrovich, J. *A Foundation Returns to School: Strategies for Improving Public Education* (New York: Ford Foundation, 2008).

Robledo Montecel, M. "Knowledge and Action – From Dropping Out to Holding On," *IDRA Newsletter* (San Antonio, Texas: Intercultural Development Research Association, November-December 2006).

Tseng, V. "Studying the Use of Research Evidence in Policy and Practice," *William T. Grant Foundation 2007 Annual Report* (New York, N.Y.: William T. Grant Foundation, 2008).

Originally published in the *IDRA Newsletter*, August 2009

Chapter Three – Change Strategies

Tools Changing Schools

Aurelio M. Montemayor, M.Ed.

Our dreams must go beyond fond wish
We must proceed awake and smart.
Wisdom and clarity must surpass the heart.
Absent strategies strong, hopes are foolish.

Clear eyed strategies change will cause,
Through community, schools and coalitions,
The arenas for strategic change missions.
Communities, for one, knowing the laws.

No arena an island, all interconnect.
Coalitions are examples in fact
Of the connections and the contact
Based on common goals and respect.

Strengthening families and schools,
Forming unions: those are the tools.

Chapter Preface

Within the Quality Schools Action Framework, we have major categories that are connected and interdependent. Change strategies are preceded by the levers of change that are in turn centered on actionable knowledge. Each of the three levers is a static, unmoving tool unless directly connected with a change strategy. For example, engaged citizens with actionable knowledge are energized and set in motion through community capacity building. Enlightened public policy becomes a reality through dynamic and strategic coalition building. Each lever, parallel and also integrated, does its heavy lifting when connected to each of the three strategies for change: *community capacity building, coalition building and school capacity building*. The articles in this chapter illustrate the change strategies.

- Community capacity building involves building, strengthening and giving content to the community in the process of transforming schools. Information must be presented in a user-friendly and comprehensible manner. In "Knowledge for Action – Organizing School-Community Partnerships Around Quality Data," Laurie Posner, M.P.A., and Hector Bojorquez posit that "without accessible data on school success, parents and communities often remain disengaged or rely on solutions driven by supposition and anecdote." This article introduces a dynamic web-based tool – IDRA's School Holding Power Portal (http://www.idra.org/portal) – to support understanding and use.
- In "This We Know – All of Our Children Are Learning," by Aurelio M. Montemayor, M.Ed., we see how parents, regardless of educational background and class, can investigate the quality of instruction and give valid feedback. The article documents an actual case of parents who, upon being informed of the lack of student achievement in math at a large high school, participated in a dialogue that brought up questions about the data and resulted in a community survey initiated and carried out by parents, with the data analyzed and interpreted by students themselves.
- With a focus on coalition building, the article "Expanding Blueprints for Action – Children's Outcomes, Access, Treatment, Learning, Resources, Accountability" by Rosana G. Rodríguez, Ph.D., and Bradley Scott, Ph.D., discusses how it is critical and timely that African American and Latino communities come together in fostering lasting and meaningful coalitions that can help fulfill the promise of the two historical cases, *Mendez vs. Westminster* and *Brown vs. Board of Education*. Blueprints for Action, dialogues using a cross-sector multi-racial

approach, are described and recommended for further action.

- The article, "Valuing Youth – Reflections from a Professional Learning Community," by Aurelio M. Montemayor, M.Ed., and Josie Danini Cortez, M.A., demonstrates the third change strategy of school capacity building. The 26-year-old Coca-Cola Valued Youth Program was enhanced with a planned variation that introduced two approaches to the tutors' teachers: mentoring and a small professional learning community. The processes and impact described here reflect the IDRA valuing principles, carefully documented and evaluated.
- In reality, the change strategies must build on each other. As an example, in "Community Conversations about Math Learning and Teaching," Kristin Grayson, M.Ed., and Aurelio M. Montemayor, M.Ed., illustrate how, in working with school personnel and with parents, change strategies can be even more strategic and effective. Schools and teachers are under immense pressure to improve student math achievement scores from state and federal regulations. More importantly, most students of color are not achieving satisfactorily. The article describes several specific activities that schools and parents have done together to address this challenge through school data math conversations, parent conversations about everyday math, and parent-initiated math surveys. In each case, IDRA worked with teachers and administrators together with parents to collect and present data in a manner that facilitated dialogue between school and families.

It is clear that in transforming schools we must connect the dots from actionable knowledge to families, the broader community and schools through strategic actions that give new life, mobilize and give all involved the evidence that change and transformation for the better is possible. Connections, collaborations and coalitions established and nurtured provide a dynamic and strong enough effort to affect the inertia of public educational institutions. The articles here both illustrate the particular strategies and give evidence that none is really effective in isolation and that there is a positive and accelerating impact when these are seen as parallel, co-existing and mutually energizing.

Community Capacity Building

Knowledge for Action

Organizing School-Community Partnerships Around Quality Data

by Laurie Posner, M.P.A., and Hector Bojorquez

Without accessible data on school success, parents and communities often remain disengaged or rely on solutions driven by supposition and anecdote. Schools are mandated to send accountability report cards to parents. Yet there are few mechanisms for helping parents interpret data on school performance. There are even fewer resources to guide authentic parent-school collaboration and engagement resulting from analysis of the data. This article encourages these joint efforts and introduces a dynamic web-based tool – IDRA's School Holding Power Portal (http://www.idra.org/portal) – to support them.

A Gateway to Action

IDRA's School Holding Power Portal is structured around IDRA's Quality Schools Action Framework. Grounded in research and years of experience in the field, the framework proposes that because schools (like other public organizations) are complex, multi-faceted entities, they rarely benefit from patchwork, silver bullet or short-term solutions.

Instead, what is needed to strengthen schools is a systems-level approach that engages the commitment and leadership of school, family and community partners around high quality actionable data. Quality schools emerge, the framework suggests, through enlightened policymaking, accountable leadership, equitable funding and an engaged public. Quality schools reflect teaching quality, student engagement, parent and community engagement, and quality curricula. (Robledo Montecel, 2005; also on Page 29)

By providing data on these key indicators of quality schooling, IDRA's School Holding Power Portal helps schools and communities gather information as a backdrop to partnerships that can leverage their distinct roles and shared strengths. In this way, this online portal has been developed around three premises: (1) that public schools can provide an excellent education for every student; (2) that school-community-family partnerships are fundamental to this success; and (3) that quality data about schools is indispensable in identifying areas of strength and need, leading change in the right direction and assessing whether or not changes are making a difference.

Although the portal is intended to help school community partners work together on complex challenges, it invites partners to begin this work around a shared vision that can be – though profound – quite straightforward and simple. One school district in South Texas described its shared vision this way: that each and every student, bar none, achieves academic success.

Value of Partnerships

It is clear from research, direct experience and common sense that parent and community engagement in public education matters. In their meta-analysis of 51 studies, Henderson and Mapp found a "positive and convincing relationship between family involvement and benefits for students, including improved academic achievement" (2002).

> Families and communities can offer extraordinary human capital to school reform. But good information is key to meaningful engagement.

Payne and Kaba also found that recognizing parents and community members as assets to the process of raising student achievement can predict the quality of a school (2001).

IDRA's Texas Parent Information and Resource Center, recently featured in the U.S. Department of Education's *Engaging Parents in Education* guide, affirms through years of partnerships with parents that "parents are powerful advocates of excellent schools as peer teachers, spokespersons, catalysts, problem solvers and resource linkers" (IDRA, 2008).

Parent Involvement Often Stymied

While community and parent involvement is pivotal to school success, significant barriers prevent meaningful engagement. These obstacles often have included language, cultural and logistical barriers, as well as deficit-based interactions that suggest to parents that they are either irrelevant to school reform or the principal cause of student failure.

Parents naturally are not compelled to engage an institution that does not value their contributions or that simply sees them as part of the problem. Where logistical and language barriers are addressed, many schools still struggle to create meaningful relationships among schools, families and communities or to provide access to the kind of information that spurs joint action to strengthen schools.

Dearth of Data for Engagement

Newer, user-friendly education databases, produced by the independent sector, have substantially improved public information about school performance. However, these databases typically resemble a consumer's guide ("buyer beware") approach to education as opposed to facilitating collaboration among parents and schools. Much of the school accountability data available tends to rely solely on *No Child Left Behind Act* testing measures to rate schools.

For many parents and communities, this is simply not enough to gauge success beyond school halls. College access and success rates are rarely part of any state agency databases. By design, NCLB does not hold schools accountable for how well they prepare students for higher education. Yet, parents and communities hold college-going rates at a higher premium than just scoring well on a state-mandated test that does not guarantee success beyond high school.

Families and communities can offer extraordinary human capital to school reform. But good information is key to meaningful engagement.

A Place for Collaboration and Transparency

IDRA's School Holding Power Portal is a web-based resource designed to provide school, community, family, student and business leaders in Texas with key information to assess school holding power and student preparation and, where needed, to develop a school-community action plan to improve outcomes.

In conjunction with a school district's internal use of the School Holding Power Portal and other research tools and products for professional development, school leaders can use the portal as part of an effort to engage families and communities in:

- Analyzing school data, conducting needs assessments and targeting the most effective approaches to reducing dropout rates and increasing college readiness.
- Convening solution-oriented community-school forums that bring various stakeholders together around a shared vision of student success and quality data.
- Designing a plan that is informed by research-based best practices, builds on school-community strengths, is aligned with the current school improvement plan and engages stakeholders in ownership, accountability and success.
- Identifying and implementing models with proven success and providing tailored professional development and training.

The portal provides easy-to-access data and helps school-community partners explore questions like:

- *How well does the school keep and graduate students?* The portal provides data on how many students are lost from school enrollment before they graduate (student disappearance rates) and how this compares to Texas as a whole and to other schools.
- *How well does the school prepare students to achieve academically?* The portal provides data on how students are doing on Texas Assessment of Knowledge and Skills tests and if they are college-ready.
- *How well does the school prepare students for college?* The portal provides data on how well a school prepares students for SAT and ACT tests.

- *How well does the school perform in getting students into college?* The portal provides data on how many high school seniors are attending college and how many are attending two- vs. four-year institutions.

Getting Started

When embarking on community-school partnerships, schools and educators can use the IDRA School Holding Power Portal to guide them through a three-step process.

1. Disseminate comprehensible data – *Create opportunities for parents to use the portal in groups to galvanize discussions about strengths and weaknesses.* This portal can be used by anyone at any time. It is an easy-to-use tool that is available at no cost. The power of the tool, however, can best be harnessed by groups. Educational institutions can create opportunities for using the portal with parents and community members.

A lone parent viewing a school's AYP status, or ACT/SAT scores, or college-going rates may feel discouraged. A group of parents viewing the same scores in a school lab, surrounded by the instructors or administrators are more likely to feel empowered. Why? A by-product of transparency is trust. When a school opens its doors and welcomes parents regardless of poor or mediocre test results or less-than-stellar college preparation rates, the message is clear: "This is our responsibility, and we welcome your help."

Having schools create opportunities for data dissemination and discussion does not have to be difficult. School leaders can plan a schedule of gatherings throughout the year with parent-teacher organizations, local community-based organizations and faith-based communities. They can use Title I funds designated for parent education and leverage all resources, such as parent volunteers and parent liaisons.

2. Facilitate community and parent networks – *The portal facilitates information dissemination to informal networks through simple tools.* The IDRA portal gives users the ability to navigate to any high school and receive simple graphs about a school's general performance and capacity to produce satisfactory results for children. Users can go a step further and take notes online about their own ideas, observations and recommendations about the school. These notes can be saved for later use, printed out and shared with other parents or e-mailed directly to other community members.

Parents are empowered by this simple ability to receive information and disseminate it to all parties concerned with educational institutions. This simple, easy-to-use feature can help bring more parents and community members into a school. The results lead to schools and communities working in partnership.

3. Set shared goals – *As groups gather and grow, weaknesses and strengths can be identified with input by the community stakeholders that a school serves.* Educational data generally have been used in two ways: (1) as diagnostic tools to help institutions inform their decisions, and (2) as a means to increase accountability through public dissemination to communities. Unfortunately, either through inadequate standards or narrow focus, school achievement remains stagnant regardless of data-driven decision making or public awareness.

The IDRA School Holding Power Portal can serve both of those ends but through purposeful community-school use. The data can help institutions and parents identify problems and seek solutions not previously seen through the narrow lens of single measure standards.

Simply, when schools and communities look at the data together and have frank discussions, they can set shared goals that address a range of issues from inadequate funding and classroom size to pedagogy and school-home ties.

Resources

Henderson, A.T., and K.L. Mapp. *A New Wave of Evidence: The Impact of School, Family, and Community Connections on Student Achievement* (Austin, Texas: Southwest Educational Development Laboratory, 2002).

Intercultural Development Research Association. "Texas IDRA PIRC Valuing Assumptions," IDRA web site (current 2008).

Payne, C.M., and M. Kaba. "So Much Reform, So Little Change: Building-level Obstacles to Urban School Reform," *Journal of Negro Education* (2001) 2(1), 1-16.

Robledo Montecel, M. "A Quality Schools Action Framework – Framing Systems Change for Student Success," *IDRA Newsletter* (San Antonio, Texas: Intercultural Development Research Association, November-December 2005).

Originally published in the *IDRA Newsletter*, January 2008

This We Know – All of Our Children Are Learning

Brief Rumination on Parent's Qualifications for Judging the Quality of the Teaching Their Children are Receiving, Using Math as an Example and Considering the NCLB/Title I Section 1118 Parent Engagement Rules

by Aurelio M. Montemayor, M.Ed.

Prologue: Which Students Can Learn – Algebra

A parent in a south Texas community brought a letter received from her son's high school announcing that the school was not meeting adequate yearly progress (AYP) because of math. In a problem-solving conversation, a group of parents wondered if the problem was that the teachers were unprepared or uncertified to teach algebra. But further probing revealed that most of the teachers were in fact certified and seasoned practitioners of mathematics. Instead, they learned of an algebra teacher who stated that most students in the school "do not have the capacity to learn higher math." (See article on Page 66 for more.)

In another example, while conducting a training of trainers session for Eisenhower Grant Scholarship elementary teachers, IDRA was preparing these selected teachers to develop workshops and presentations to extend their knowledge in the teaching of math and science to their campus peers. Upon reviewing some very exciting, participatory and creative plans for presentations in science teaching, the facilitator asked where the parallel workshop plans were for pre-algebra instruction. The response was: "Oh no, we cannot do that for these teachers and students. Algebra is just too abstract!"

Seeing students through these cloudy lenses ensures that few students will ever master algebra. The status quo was proof of prejudice.

All Children Ahead in Math

Math prejudice directly contradicts the premise of "leaving no child behind." It also presents a critical locus to meet the parent involvement requirements in the law: engaging parents in judging the teaching quality when a school is not meeting AYP.

Math is *not* too abstract for the so-called masses.

- See the work lead by Kathryn Brown in IDRA's Math Smart! institutes for creative answers to that myth (Brown, 2006).
- Check with Bob Moses' Algebra Project (Moses & Cobb, 2001; Moses, et al., 1989).
- View the movie Stand and Deliver (1988), with the caveat that calculus is really for a broader audience than a select number of bypassed and ignored Latino geniuses.
- Math is a great litmus test of teaching quality. The parent-useful and friendly assessment is: How well are children learning to use and apply math, algebra and so-called "higher mathematics"?

Parent's Math Teaching Skills? Not in This Approach

Before we explore some questions parents can ask, let us be clear about the domain we are working in. Parenting training is a broad aspect of working with parents, targeted to improving parent's skills in bringing up and educating their children. Within this domain, the math-teaching-quality conversation would shift to the parent as math teacher. There is a large body of literature that focuses on the literacy of the parent, especially the mother, and points to children's literacy skills directly flowing from the caretaker's skills.

> A parent does not need to know the content, the language of instruction or effective teaching pedagogy to judge whether children are learning and succeeding.

Likewise there is a comparable emerging body connecting parents and families and math. In contrast, we are concentrating on those aspects of parent involvement that highlight the parent as resource to the school, as decision makers about the quality of the education of their children, and as leaders in creating schools that work for all children.

Parents as Resources for Quality Math Education

Parents, families and others in the community can inquire without any further preparation than their faith in their children and their desire to have high quality schools. One first thing to check is if the secondary math teachers are prepared and certified to teach their classes. Second, find out whether any of these teachers consider algebra and beyond as appropriate only for a select few students. If a major block is the lack of resources to hire sufficient, highly qualified teachers, parents are a powerful ally to administrators whose pleas for added resources are not being heard.

At the elementary level, first find out if any teacher is mouthing some version of " I was never good in math." Then ask the principal how that lack is being made up for. Are the best and brightest teachers in math accessing the children whose classroom teachers admit to limitations in that area?

A parent does not need to know the content, the language of instruction or effective teaching pedagogy to judge whether children are learning and succeeding.

What is the Question?

Ask students: "What helps you learn math?" and "What blocks you from learning math?"

Ask teachers: "Do you think all children can learn math?," "What do you do if students don't learn math with the way you are currently teaching?," and "How do you change your teaching to engage the students that are not mastering the required skills?"

Ask principals, "What are you doing to encourage the modification of the curriculum and the teaching approaches so that all children are learning?" and "How are tutoring and other supplementary educational services helping to engage students and support their academic success?"

See the following suggestions from "10 Tips for Parents Who Choose to Stay Put" (KSA-Plus Communications, nd).

- "Get extra help for your child. If the school fails to meet its learning goals for three straight years, your child is eligible for additional academic help, such as afterschool tutoring, paid for by the federal government. Some schools offer extra help after the second year to keep parents in the school. You can press your school to do this. Check to see what extra help your school is providing. Often this support is provided by community organizations, such as a local YMCA, library, or Boys and Girls Club."
- "Make sure the school's improvement plan focuses on areas where the school is not doing well. All schools now have to publish annual report cards, showing how all students are doing in reading and math. If the data show that math scores are low, for instance, you'll want to make sure that the school's improvement plan has steps for strengthening the math program. Maybe the school will spend more time on math during the school day, create an after-school program to help struggling students, improve staff training for teachers and so on. These annual report cards also need to describe how different groups of students are performing. For instance, if low-income students are lagging, the school improvement plan should describe what will be done to help those students. Start by asking if all classes offer high quality teaching and a challenging curriculum so that all children will meet the standards."

Also see the following pages for sample surveys one community is using.

Epilogue: Parents as Advocates and Catalysts for Quality Teaching

There are many more questions that laypersons can ask of educators (*As A Parent, Here are 12 Things You Should Know about and Expect From Your Schools… and Yourself*, KSA-Plus Communications, nd). None of these require that the inquirer be an expert in mathematics or teaching. The answers will cause the educator to rethink and come up with better ways to support academic success for all children: truly high quality teaching for all students.

Resources

Brown, K. "Making Math Real for Students," *IDRA Newsletter* (San Antonio, Texas: Intercultural Development Research Association, March 2006).

Brown, K. "Re-Invigorating Math Curricula," *IDRA Newsletter* (San Antonio, Texas: Intercultural Development Research Association, April 2006).

Internet Movie Database, Inc. "Plot Summary for Stand and Deliver (1988)" http://www.imdb.com/title/tt0094027/plotsummary.

KSA-Plus Communications. *10 Tips for Parents Who Choose to Stay Put* (Lexington, Ken.: Center for Parent Leadership at the Pritchard Committee, no date).

KSA-Plus Communications. *As A Parent, Here are 12 Things You Should Know about and Expect From Your Schools… and Yourself* (Lexington, Ken.: Center for Parent Leadership at the Pritchard Committee, no date).

Moses, R., and C. Cobb. *Radical Equations: Math Literacy and Civil Rights* (Boston: Beacon Press, 2001).

Moses, R., and M. Kamii, S. Swap, J. Howard. (1989). The Algebra Project: Organizing in the Spirit of Ella (Waltham, Mass.: Civic Practices Network).

Originally published in the *IDRA Newsletter*, May 2007

Parents and Students Examine Math Curriculum and Instruction at their High School

A group of parents participating in a parent leadership series led by IDRA at a high school in Texas decided that their leadership project would be to survey parents and students. These parents are very concerned about the math curriculum and instruction, because this year their children's high school was put on the list of not achieving adequate yearly progress (AYP) for the first time. They had collected anecdotal evidence of what the problem might be but wanted to have more data in terms of family and student opinions about the situation. At first, they decided to just ask two questions of other parents and caretakers: What helps your children learn math? and What blocks them from learning math? After further conversation, they decided to conduct a more extensive survey and to include students.

Following are their surveys. The first is for parents who will survey other parents, and the second is for students who will survey other students.

Adult/Adulto Name/*Nombre*____

Mathematics Survey / Encuesta sobre la Matemática

Please mark (fill the circle) that best indicates your opinion. *Por favor marque (rellene el circulo) que mejor indica su opinión.*

1 My children have high grades in math.
Mis hijos tienen altas calificaciones en matemáticas.

Never *Nunca*	Rarely *Raramente*	Sometimes *A Veces*	Often *Seguido*	Always *Siempre*
☐	☐	☐	☐	☐

2. Students are encouraged to ask questions.
Se les anima a los estudiantes que hagan preguntas.

Never *Nunca*	Rarely *Raramente*	Sometimes *A Veces*	Often *Seguido*	Always *Siempre*
☐	☐	☐	☐	☐

3. When students don't understand a concept, different ways are used to teach it.
Cuando los estudiantes no entienden un concepto, se usan distintas maneras para enseñarlo.

Never *Nunca*	Rarely *Raramente*	Sometimes *A Veces*	Often *Seguido*	Always *Siempre*
☐	☐	☐	☐	☐

4. The supplementary educational services, such as tutoring, help the students to succeed in their classes.
Los servicios educativos suplementarios como profesor particular les ayudan a los estudiantes para tener éxito en sus clases.

Never *Nunca*	Rarely *Raramente*	Sometimes *A Veces*	Often Seguido	Always *Siempre*
☐	☐	☐	☐	☐

The next two questions require a brief answer. Please give your honest opinion. *Las siguientes dos preguntas requieren una respuesta breve. Por favor de su opinión franca.*

5. The most important thing that school can do to help a student learn math is:
La cosa mas importante que la escuela puede hacer para ayudarle a un alumno para que aprenda matemáticas es:

6. The biggest block in school for a student to learn math is:
La barrera más grande que existe en la escuela para que un alumno aprenda matemáticas es:

Student/*estudiante* Name/*Nombre* ______________________________

Mathematics Survey / Encuesta sobre la Matemática

Please mark (fill the circle) that best indicates your opinion.
Por favor marque (rellene el circulo) que mejor indica su opinión.

1. I have high grades in math.
Yo tengo altas calificaciones en matemáticas.

Never *Nunca*	Rarely *Raramente*	Sometimes *A Veces*	Often *Seguido*	Always *Siempre*
☐	☐	☐	☐	☐

2. I am encouraged to ask questions in math class.
Se me anima a que yo haga preguntas en la clase de matematicas.

Never *Nunca*	Rarely *Raramente*	Sometimes *A Veces*	Often *Seguido*	Always *Siempre*
☐	☐	☐	☐	☐

3. When I don't understand a concept, different ways are used to teach it.
Cuando no entiendo un concepto, se usan distintas maneras para enseñarlo.

Never *Nunca*	Rarely *Raramente*	Sometimes *A Veces*	Often *Seguido*	Always *Siempre*
☐	☐	☐	☐	☐

4. The supplementary educational services, such as tutoring, help me to succeed in my classes.
Los servicios educativos suplementarios como profesor particular (tutoría) me ayuda a tener éxito en mis clases.

Never *Nunca*	Rarely *Raramente*	Sometimes *A Veces*	Often *Seguido*	Always *Siempre*
☐	☐	☐	☐	☐

The next two questions require a brief answer. Please give your honest opinion.
Las siguientes dos preguntas requieren una respuesta breve. Por favor de su opinión franca.

5. The most important thing that school can do to help me learn math is:
La cosa mas importante que la escuela puede hacer para ayudarme a aprender matemáticas es:

6. The biggest block in school for me to learn math is:
La barrera más grande que existe en la escuela para que yo aprenda matemáticas es:

Coalition Building

Expanding Blueprints for Action

Children's Outcomes, Access, Treatment, Learning, Resources, Accountability

by Rosana G. Rodríguez, Ph.D., and Bradley Scott, Ph.D.

Previous *IDRA Newsletter* articles have described IDRA's work in Texas creating cross-sector and cross-race leadership to improve access, excellence and equity in education. As background, the U.S. Supreme Court unanimously ruled in *Brown vs. Board of Education* more than 50 years ago that sending children to separate schools purely on the basis of race was unconstitutional. Seven years prior, the U.S. Circuit Court of Appeals, Ninth Circuit ruled in *Mendez vs. Westminster and the California Board of Education* that Mexican American children could not be denied access to public school or a quality education because they were Mexican American.

While these two decisions, among others, transformed the nature of U.S. public education, the objectives of these rulings have not been fully met. According to the Harvard Civil Rights Project, 40 percent of Black students attend schools that are 90 percent Black. This is up from 3 percent in 1988. In nine out of 10 of these schools, the majority of children are poor.

Latino children are the most segregated and attend the poorest schools. They receive the poorest preparation by the least trained teachers and have little access to rigorous curriculum that would prepare them for college.

In addition, "75 percent of the 4.5 million students who speak a language other than English have a seat in the classroom but are left out of the class because of English-only policies that are concerned with politics instead of learning" (Robledo Montecel, 2003).

Clearly, the promise of *Brown* and *Mendez* is not yet met. And the current anti-immigrant environment certainly threatens the promise even further.

It is critical and timely that African American and Latino communities come together in fostering lasting and meaningful coalitions that can help fulfill the promise of these two cases for all children in this nation and particularly for African American and Latino learners.

Rev. Dr. Martin Luther King Jr. reminds us that we are "inextricably linked" in a web of mutuality. And Cesar Chavez emphasized that the end result of education must surely be service to community, not only for their sake but for our collective good.

Blueprint Dialogues in Communities

To this end, with funding from the Annie E. Casey Foundation, IDRA has implemented three "Blueprints for Action" dialogues in Texas, and recently two more in Albuquerque, New Mexico, and Little Rock, Arkansas, with plans to expand to other states. The dialogues use a cross-sector multi-racial approach for gathering participants, educators, parents, business and community representatives engaged in a roundtable discussions focusing on actions to address key education issues in their communities, including equitable funding, ensuring graduation for all, quality schooling and access to higher education.

The groups create "blueprints" for action, based on these questions:

- What are the challenges to access and success for *all* students?
- What resources, strengths and assets can be tapped to create local blueprints for action that will result in access and success?
- What opportunities can be seized upon to accomplish this goal?
- What local actions are needed to fulfill the promise of *Mendez* and *Brown*?

Hearing Student Voices

The dialogues held in Albuquerque, New Mexico, brought in a critical component that is often overlooked in education: the importance of student voices. Prior to the dialogues and with assistance from IDRA and Critical Exposure, local students learned about the landmark cases and began to take pictures of their realities within schools, capturing in their words and through their eyes whether or not the promises of *Brown* and *Mendez* were being fulfilled in their school districts.

These powerful images became part of a gallery to be appreciated by the entire community before the dialogues began. Participants had an opportunity to meet and hear from the students and consider these pictures as a powerful reminder of what remains to be done. The images and stories became a critical component in setting the stage throughout the next day's dialogue planning.

In Little Rock, Arkansas, IDRA staff met with African American, Latino and Asian students representing three public school districts. Students participated in an assessment of strengths, weaknesses, opportunities and threats (SWOT) relative to the fulfillment of the promises of *Mendez* and *Brown* in their communities. Working in teams, students identified eight key issues. Students presented these to roundtable participations at an evening reception of community members and school leaders, and issued a call to action. (The article by student Brandon Love in the April 2007 issue of the *IDRA Newsletter* was a product of this interaction.)

IDRA continues to foster new and strengthened alliances among groups with local leaders committed to continuing this work through sustained dialogues and action. Toolkits for taking local action are provided as follow-up to the dialogues, and the IDRA web site is poised to leverage the meetings at state and national levels (http://www.idra.org/mendezbrown).

Student Voices

High school students in Albuquerque, New Mexico, participated in the Blueprints for Action dialogues by sharing through photographs and their words whether or not the promises of *Brown* and *Mendez* were being fulfilled in their schools. Here is a sample of their insights.

Separate Tables
"These pictures were taken of a photography class. It shows how students are separate – there are tables for White students and other ones for African American students. They don't interact together in class!"

– Randa Hussein, Grade 11

Moldy Ceiling
"This picture is of my government class that has a moldy roof. The mess was caused by a leaky roof, which is a problem in many other rooms and in the hallways. This is a way that the *Brown* and *Mendez* cases aren't being fulfilled, in that our schools aren't receiving [the support] they desperately need. I took this picture to show people that, even though we set high standards, that high standards may not always be fulfilled."

– Jazmine Ralph, Grade 12

Broken Fence
"This picture is of a broken fence in the back of my school. I took this picture for a couple of reasons. Because the fence looks and appears to be broken, I felt that the fence represented and symbolized the promises desired from the *Brown* and *Mendez* cases. While they appeared to be fixed on the surface, if you look deeper or beyond the surface, there is still much to be changed and fixed. We cannot continue to just attempt to mend those problems of which the cases fought for. We have come a long way, but we have still have further to go."

– Fatimah Martin, Grade 11

Insights

Important insights are emerging of national significance from the Blueprints for Action dialogues.

- **In terms of process**, communities of color must have opportunities and support at the local level to voice concerns regarding access to education. People in communities yearn to communicate with one another across groups but often lack opportunities or a process to do so in ways that result in collective and focused action. Facilitated interaction can yield greater interconnectedness, build on assets, strengthen will for effective action and focus on results.
- **In terms of context**, valuing and engaging students and communities are essential elements for school success. Students and community are where great reservoirs of strength and insight can be found. Each community needs information about its local schools in order to hold schools accountable for fulfilling the promises of *Mendez* and *Brown*. While complexity and diversity within and among groups pose challenges, these serve as launch points for building trust and taking collective action on behalf of all children.
- **In terms of issues**, the dialogues underscore that accountability in education is good and must be shared and accomplished through multiple measures that do not hurt kids. Coalition building of diverse sectors working toward a shared vision of excellence, access and success for all children must span across disciplines and sectors.

Partnering with the Annie E. Casey Foundation, IDRA is drawing upon prior work of a National Consultative Group of key leaders from educational and civil rights organizations that was convened in 2005. To bring the work to national scale, IDRA is exploring possibilities to foster a national shared vision and a common discourse for building cross-sector and multicultural alliances as advocates in education.

Presentations at the National Conference of Public Education Network in Washington, D.C., in December of 2006 gave yet another opportunity to meet with national leaders and explore the following key questions:

1. What are the most strategic ways to advance a national scale-up of the *Brown* and *Mendez* community action dialogues?
2. What are the next steps and the supports needed for a national scale-up effort?
3. How can we seize the potential to work collaboratively for the greatest national impact?

As a resource for communities, IDRA has developed *A Community Action Guide – Seven Actions to Fulfill the Promise of Brown and Mendez* (which is available free online at http://www.idra.org/mendezbrown) that supports local leaders in taking specific steps to fulfill the promise of *Brown* and *Mendez*. This resource outlines key areas emerging from local dialogues, such as equitable funding, accountable schools, quality schooling, ensuring access and inclusion, and strengthening school holding power. This resource is intended to spark cross-sector cross-race action for joint leadership aimed at what must be done and what can be done together across all racial groups to create schools that are equitable and excellent for all children.

All children have equal rights to quality education, regardless of where they live and who they are. Educational equity is not just morally right, it is right for kids, right for learning and right for democracy. IDRA's stand on this issue is not just for some, not just for most, but for every single child.

Resources

Robledo Montecel, M. "Fulfilling the Promise of Brown vs. Board of Education," *IDRA Newsletter* (San Antonio, Texas: Intercultural Development Research Association, November-December 2003).

Rodríguez, R.G., and B. Scott, A. Villarreal. *A Community Action Guide-Seven Actions to Fulfill the Promise of Brown vs. Board of Education and Mendez vs. Westminster* (San Antonio, Texas: Intercultural Development Research Association, 2005).

Originally published in the *IDRA Newsletter,* May 2007

School Capacity Building

Valuing Youth

Reflections from a Professional Learning Community

by Aurelio M. Montemayor, M.Ed., and Josie Danini Cortez, M.A.

Almost 30 years ago, as Dr. José A. Cárdenas, IDRA's founder and director emeritus, addressed a migrant education management training workshop in San Diego, California, on how to make power work for children. His statement is as timely today as it was then: "I have found that the most effective parents and professionals… are effective not because of what they do but because of the philosophical understandings they bring to the task. It is not so much a matter of strategy as it is a matter of approach… I have seen in such individuals, regardless of their economic or educational achievement, an intelligence and a dignity that pervades all that they do in the name of children, and it is neither transitory nor occasional" (1995).

Dr. Cárdenas went on to say that there are three elements to making power work for children: purposefulness, perspective and leadership. Individuals must be clear and united in their purpose as advocates for children. Their purpose must be aligned with their perspective of what needs to change. Finally, their leadership must be: "dedicated to the development, nurturance and maintenance of the group's strength: sharing information, visibility and rewards generously and diligently… [They] must operate from a secure level of self-knowledge and knowledge of each other that will enable them to deal with the unfamiliar, ambiguous and rapidly changing situations with success" (1995).

This purposefulness, perspective and leadership permeates IDRA's work this past year with administrators, teachers and staff at a middle school in south Texas. IDRA launched the pilot test of its Professional Learning Community and Mentoring Model (PLCM) to create a successful school experience for children. Five content area teachers, one counselor and one social worker at the school formed the professional learning community and mentoring group. They, in turn, became mentors for 16 migrant students, most of whom were also Coca-Cola Valued Youth Program tutors.

IDRA's Coca-Cola Valued Youth Program, when implemented as designed, reduces the dropout rate for students deemed at risk of dropping out and concurrently lowers absenteeism and disciplinary referrals, improves student self-concept and attitudes toward school, and increases academic achievement.

The Professional Learning Community and Mentoring Model was designed and researched as a planned variation of the Coca-Cola Valued Youth Program and centers on the program's valuing concepts and effective mentoring characteristics. With this planned variation, participating teachers are expected to develop greater competencies in instruction, self-knowledge and teamwork.

IDRA provided extensive research-based resources to the participants throughout the year in order to develop a collective grounding for the implementation of this learning community. One of those resources included the *SEDL Outcomes of Professional Learning Communities for Students and Staff* reports (Hord, 1997).

> "The most important aspect of this program is that it focuses on the students… on what they are doing, how they are doing it; it deals with both academic and home issues."

These reports have indicated that professional learning communities have improved outcomes for staff and for students. For staff, those improvements include:

- Reduction of teacher isolation,
- Increased commitment to and increased vigor to strengthen the mission and goals of the school,
- Shared responsibility for the total development of students and collective responsibility for students' success,
- Powerful learning that defines and creates new knowledge and beliefs about good teaching, learning and classroom practice,
- Increased understanding of the content that teachers teach and the roles that they play in all students' achievement,
- Teachers more likely to be well-informed, professionally renewed and inspired to inspire students,
- More satisfaction, higher morale and lower rates of absenteeism,
- Making teaching adaptations more quickly for students,
- Commitment to making significant and lasting changes, and
- Higher likelihood of undertaking fundamental, systemic change.

For students, the results include:

- Decreased dropout rate and fewer classes "cut,"
- Lower rates of absenteeism,
- Increased learning that is distributed more equitably in smaller high schools,
- Larger academic gains in math, science, history and reading than in traditional schools, and

- Smaller achievement gaps between students from different backgrounds.

Model Key Components

The key components of the model are as follows.

- **Students Assigned to Participating Teachers** – Student tutors are scheduled in linked courses to the same content area teachers.
- **Team Planning** – Teachers in team planning focus on tutors' success; during team planning, teachers, counselor and social worker (PLCM team) have collective discussions and bring in-depth understanding of students' problems and "check for understanding."
- **Mentoring** – Each teacher mentors, counsels and advocates for two to three tutors. Teachers and mentees meet weekly.
- **Professional Development** – Four retreats guided by IDRA also serve as teacher renewal.
- **Guided Reflection and Case Studies** – Teachers reflect on their mentees' issues and success.
- **Administrator Support** – The middle school principal supports the learning community variation by allowing PLCM teachers to have the same planning period and allowing program tutors to be assigned to the PLCM teachers.
- **Teacher Compensation** – PLCM teachers are paid a stipend for participation in professional development retreats.
- **Content Area Focus** – PLCM teachers focus on any teaching issues, such as competencies in English as a second language and sheltered instruction as well as connecting heuristics (natural knowledge) to content area.

Findings and Reflections

The participants mapped out assisting and restraining forces in the establishment of a learning community. The *assisting* forces included community leaders and role models, extracurricular activities, teachers nurturing respect and politeness, communication and the Coca-Cola Valued Youth Program. The *restraining* forces included limited or negative expectations, student peer pressure, adult prejudice, and a stereotyping of English language learners and migrant families.

Case studies and guided reflection became an integral part of learning community process. Each focused conversation would key-in on four questions:

- How do you measure your students' progress?
- How is their English language development and fluency?
- How is their behavior and attendance in your class?
- How well are they learning the concepts in your class?

Sharing of Content Knowledge and Peer Support

The Professional Learning Community and Mentoring Model allows for a sharing of content knowledge and peer support for students needing help in particular subjects. Following are comments from participants.

- "I think a prime example is… the math scores were kind of low… And so, we realized that it was an issue, and we said okay, we need to fix this… Okay, you're going to do math here… you're going to do math there… and everybody said okay. We're going to do it. And we're doing it! Ms. L. is helping me teach math."
- "It's not whether you taught three years or 33 years, because you can teach one year 33 times."
- "It is not about me succeeding; it is about all of us succeeding."
- "The most important aspect of this program is that it focuses on the students… on what they are doing, how they are doing it; it deals with both academic and home issues."
- "You actually have time for reflection. You have discussions about the end of the day, and not only about the individuals but also as an educator, what am I doing to help these kids."

Student Feedback

Participating teachers are affirmed by their students' success and their students' feedback:

- "I had the kids write an essay about what they like and don't like to do in science. It was going to be fun reading them, but I never expected to see several essays saying that they like the way I teach, the way I explain things, and that if they don't understand it, I go back and make sure they understand."
- "You feel that you are touching their lives; you are making a difference. And that is what teaching is, you want to make a difference."

Checking for Understanding

Participating teachers now take the time to "check for understanding" with their students and help build their students' confidence:

- "Another student… He's one of our special students… I knew he had a question but he didn't ask me… I told him, 'Why didn't you ask me how to do it?' I have a sign in my room … 'If you never ask a question, you will never know the answer.' So I told him, 'Look, read that sign'… Yesterday he came up to ask me a question, and I'm like, 'Oh, awesome.' I guess he feels confident to come and ask me… And I felt really good; it's just like one of those awesome moments."

Seeing Student Gifts

Teachers have learned to see the gifts and talents their students bring with them and to tap those for academic success:

- "How can we look at them [students] in such a way that we start helping them see the array of their gifts and talents and how those connect very specifically to decisions I make in the classroom? Because we all know that no matter how we plan it, things will change or something will just not work with some kids and will work with others."

IDRA is expanding its Professional Learning Community and Mentoring Model this year with all of the middle school content area teachers participating. Initial findings are even more promising with teachers, staff and administrators realizing their individual and collective power to make schools work for children.

Resources

Cárdenas, J.A. *Multicultural Education: A Generation of Advocacy* (Needham Heights, Mass.: Simon and Schuster Custom Publishing, 1995).

Center on English Learning and Achievement. "Teachers Share Their Views About Effective Professional Development," *English Update* (Albany, N.Y.: CELA, Winter 2002).

Crawford, B.A., and J.S. Krajcik, R.W. Marx. "Elements of a Community of Learners in a Middle School Science Classroom," *Science Education* (1999).

Fulton, K.P., and M. Riel. "Professional Development Through Learning Communities," *Edutopia Online* (San Rafael, Calif.: George Lucas Educational Foundation, 1999).

Hord, S.M. *Professional Learning Communities: Communities of Continuos Inquiry and Improvement* (Austin, Texas: Southwest Educational Development Laboratory, 1997).

Loucks-Horsley, S., and K. Stiles, P. Hewson. "Principles of Effective Professional Development for Mathematics and Science Education: A Synthesis of Standards," *NISE Brief* (Madison, Wis.: National Institute for Science Education, University of Wisconsin-Madison, May 1996).

Pearce, K.L., and K. Gusso, L. Schroeder, R. Speirs, J. Zwaschka. "The Impact of a Teacher Learning Community on School Climate," *Journal of School Improvement* (2002).

Roffman, J.G., and J.E. Rhodes, J.B. Grossman. *An Overview of School-Based Mentoring* (2002).

Russo, A. "School-Based Coaching: A revolution in professional development – or just the latest fad?" *Harvard Education Letter* (Cambridge, Mass.: Harvard Graduate School of Education, July/August 2004).

Sweeny, B. *Defining the Distinctions Between Mentoring & Coaching* (Wheaton, Il.: Best Practices Resources, 2001).

Thompson, S.C., and L. Gregg, J.M. Niska. "Professional Learning Communities, Leadership, and Student Learning," *Research in Middle Level Education Online* (Springfield, Mo.: Missouri State University, 2004).

Tinto, V. "Learning Better Together: The Impact of Learning Communities on Student Success," *Promoting Student Success in College* (nd).

Originally published in the *IDRA Newsletter*, March 2007

Change Strategy Combinations

Community Conversations about Math Learning and Teaching

by Kristin Grayson, M.Ed., and Aurelio M. Montemayor, M.Ed.

We all continue to hear critiques about the state of mathematics learning and teaching:

- "Math Crisis? Students Don't Get It. If improving science and math education is a national priority, someone apparently forgot to tell the parents and the students" (Associated Press, 2006).
- "U.S. 15-year olds [are] outperformed by other nations in mathematics, problem-solving" (U.S. Department of Education, 2004).
- "In our K-12 we were doing okay at the fourth-grade level, we were doing middle-of-the-road in the eighth grade, and by 12th grade we were hovering near the bottom in international tests related to math," states Tracy Koon, Intel's Director of Corporate Affairs (Friedman, 2005).

Schools are under immense pressure to improve student math achievement scores. Many schools and teachers are under the added pressure of district, state and federal scrutiny because of their adequate yearly progress (AYP) status for math under the *No Child Left Behind Act.*

So, how can parents and students be brought into this conversation?

There are ways that schools can use the support of their parents to make a difference in student math achievement. Parents are a critical piece to the solution. This article describes several specific activities that schools and parents have done together to address this challenge.

School Data Math Conversations

Alan H. Schoenfeld, of the University of California, Berkeley states, "To fail children in mathematics, or to let mathematics fail them, is to close off an important means of access to society's resources" (2002).

One of the essential features of parent involvement is to *have meaningful conversations about the knowledge that schools and parents possess.* Schools have data from many sources that they can share with parents, such as past and current math achievement scores on district benchmark tests, mandated state test results, percentage of students enrolled in higher level

On Shortchanging Children

"Mathematics education is a civil rights issue," says civil rights leader Robert Moses, who argues that children who are not quantitatively literate may be doomed to second-class economic status in our increasingly technological society. The data have been clear for decades: poor children and children of color are consistently shortchanged when it comes to mathematics. More broadly, the type of mathematical sophistication championed in recent reform documents, such as the National Council of Teachers of Mathematics' (2000) Principles and Standards for School Mathematics, can be seen as a core component of intelligent decision making in everyday life, in the workplace and in our democratic society. To fail children in mathematics, or to let mathematics fail them, is to close off an important means of access to society's resources.

– Excepted from Alan H. Schoenfeld, University of California, Berkeley in "Making Mathematics Work for All Children: Issues of Standards, Testing, and Equity"

math, percentage of students taking advanced placement and college entrance tests, percentage of students repeating required algebra (known as the gate-keeper course for graduation), and how the district or school compares with others.

IDRA has just launched an interactive School Holding Power Portal that the public can access that puts these types of data and other data together in a coherent way for the state of Texas (http://www.idra.org/portal).

This sharing of information can be the springboard to the posing of the question: "What does the data mean?" This can generate lots of fruitful conversation.

In several school districts, IDRA trainers have done just this. And parents critically examined the data, pointed out where the numbers of an ethnic group were not adequate to make generalizations, and asked for clarification about the many types of data that were reported ("What test was this?" "What was this test compared to in order to get that ranking?" etc.).

Parent Conversations About Everyday Math

Brainstorming a list of ways that parents use math in everyday life is another way that deep conversations about math can be initiated. In sessions with IDRA, parents listed keeping a budget, calculating needs for food and gas and tracking cell phone minutes. Talking about these specific examples acknowledges that we all use math every day and are capable of doing advanced calculations even without formal education or the language of the school.

This also models how parents can encourage their children to think about mathematical concepts just by having conversations about daily activities.

As the conversations about math scores and daily math activities continue, parents can be encouraged to engage their children in discussions about mathematical concepts. Even if they have never taken a particular math course, parents can ask their children to explain a concept or relate it to something in real life.

Math Survey – Parent Initiated

At a school district in West Texas, a group of parents decided to create a student math survey. They distributed it through the schools' math departments to all math students (see Pages 54-55). The survey was short, bilingual and included several items that students were to rate on a Likert Scale from 1 to 5.

Statements included: "I usually get good grades in mathematics" and "When I don't understand a concept, I am encouraged to ask questions in class."

Open-ended statements also were included on the survey, such as "The most important thing that school can do to help a student learn math is…" and "The biggest block in school for a student to learn math is…"

At an urban school district, after collecting the student feedback from the same survey, parents first predicted how they thought their teenagers had

Math Survey – Facilitator Questions

As parents review responses to their survey, facilitators guided the conversation with the questions below in brown.

1. My children have high grades in math.
How do you know this? With whom, other than your children, have you had a conversation about your children's academic achievement in mathematics?

2. Students are encouraged to ask questions.
Why is this important information? What are other students' responses beyond what your own children say?

3. When students don't understand a concept, different ways are used to teach it.
Why is it important that math be taught in a variety of ways? What happens when only one way of teaching is used?

4. The supplementary educational services, such as tutoring, help the students to succeed in their classes.
How should tutoring differ from regular class instruction? What is most helpful to students in afterschool tutoring? What are some things about tutoring that are not helpful or motivating to students?

5. The most important thing that school can do to help a student learn math is…
Why is it important to ask this question of students? What should we do about the answers students give?

6. The biggest block in school for a student to learn math is…
Why is it important to ask this question of students? What should we do about the answers students give?

responded to the questions. Then they compared their predictions to the actual survey results.

This generated deep conversation about the comments. (See sample facilitator questions below.) From the discussion, it was apparent that there were things teachers, families and communities could do to improve math achievement.

There is an equivalent survey that parents can complete about their children's math education that can then be used for meaningful conversation.

Using What is Learned

The final step of the parent conversations involved creating a graphic organizer that illustrated the ideas parents had shared about the specific suggestions for improving math achievement. Some of the ideas generated by one school district in Texas included finding ways for more men to serve as role models in the community, placing a suggestion box in each math classroom, and having more conversations related to math in families. A sample of this parent-generated organizer is available online at http://www.idra.org/newsletterplus/january_2008/.

The parent organizer was shared with the math teaching staff at a school departmental meeting, which generated another fruitful conversation.

Having meaningful communication among the three critical groups of parents, students and teachers is one of the beneficial outcomes of parent involvement in math discussions. Other benefits include increasing parent awareness of campus data and accountability issues and awareness of specific things parents can do on a daily basis.

These are all critical components for supporting students and their proficiency and achievement in mathematics.

Resources

Associated Press. "Math Crisis? Students Don't Get It Improving Science, Math is a U.S. Priority, But Many See No Problem," *CBS News* (February 14, 2006).

Brown, K. "Making Math Real for Students," *IDRA Newsletter* (San Antonio, Texas: Intercultural Development Research Association, March 2006).

Dieckmann, J., and A.M. Montemayor. "Can Everyone Master Mathematics?," *IDRA Newsletter* (San Antonio, Texas: Intercultural Development Research Association, September 2004).

Friedman, T. *The World Is Flat* (New York, N.Y.: Farrar, Straus and Giroux, 2005).

Schoenfeld, A.H. "Making Mathematics Work for All Children: Issues of Standards, Testing, and Equity," *Educational Researcher* (January-February 2002).

U.S. Department of Education. "Pisa Results Show Need for High School Reform," *Extra Credit* (December 7, 2004).

Originally published in the *IDRA Newsletter*, January 2008

Chapter Four – School System Fundamentals

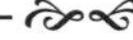

Back to Basics

Aurelio M. Montemayor, M.Ed.

Funding and governance are as fundamental
As concrete foundations public schools require.
Inadequate resources bring crises as dire
As inefficacious governing is detrimental.

Instead of demanding fair funding for schools
Of breadth and quality, what all children deserve,
Manic school critics with unmitigated nerve
Foment despairing messages, the fools.

Money is not the only need, agreed!
Our children merit schools well run;
But school resources under the gun?
Discriminatory, short-sighted greed.

Our children don't need punitive rules and tests:
Run schools well, and funded fairly: case rests.

Chapter Preface

Galvanizing the levers of change and change strategies requires support from strong leadership and resources for change to happen. Effective governance at both state and local levels while essential, however, cannot occur if school funding is inadequate or inequitable.

IDRA President and CEO, María "Cuca" Robledo Montecel, Ph.D., has stated: "Strong governance efficacy means that school leaders – at all levels – have the commitment and the capacity to deliver quality educational services to all students. And it means that school boards, school policies, and school procedures support graduation and success for every student."

At the state level, state boards of education must be driven to promulgate policy to support structures, procedures and practices that create school success, graduation, and college opportunities for all students. State legislatures must create structures that produce fair funding for local schools so that every student receives an appropriate, equitable, high quality educational experience that leads to high success and graduation no matter the levels of community wealth of the school district in which they reside.

At the local level, boards of education also must create policy that will support student success at every campus, at all levels, wherever students reside within a given school district. School boards must ensure that distribution of the funding needed to implement those policies – be it federal, state or local – in ways that are equitable and appropriate to lead all diverse learners to school success, graduation, college attendance and completion prepared for work and for life.

The articles in this chapter address issues that support these two key fundamentals in the Quality Schools Action Framework that must be secured to create schools that lead to student success and graduation.

- Abelardo Villarreal, Ph.D., begins the chapter by challenging school boards to assume their leadership role and responsibility to be guardians of educational excellence and equity in "School Board Accountability for School Reform that Supports Educational Equity." He offers five strategies to help school boards to assume this important role.

- In the next article, "The Role of School Governance Efficacy in Building an Equity Context for School Reform," Bradley Scott, Ph.D., challenges education stakeholders, including boards of education, to employ an equity lens to create a high equity context through which to conduct the work they do in support of quality, successful schools. He asserts that school boards have a responsibility to create and sustain this equity context through the policies they create and fund, and he offers strategies from research to assist them to do this.

- In "Fair Funding of Schools – Why and With What Results," Albert Cortez, Ph.D., focuses on the second critical role that states and school boards must address, the issue of fair funding and school finance equity. His examination of the history of this issue, its impact, and its promise is at once compelling, thought provoking, and challenging.

- Finally, we share an excerpt from the acclaimed *Texas School Finance Reform – An IDRA Perspective* by IDRA founder and director emeritus, José A. Cárdenas, Ed.D. In "Myths in School Finance," he discuses nine claims that are still made today in debates about school finance equity.

Whether at the level of school board, school administrator or teacher, effective governance requires developing the shared habit of vision that eschews the tired excuses of the past and creates schools that work for all students.

School Board Accountability for School Reform that Supports Educational Equity

by Abelardo Villarreal, Ph.D.

Thirty or more years of school reform efforts have yielded some positive educational outcomes. But these results have been slow in coming. And they have been accompanied by the same depressing statistics that have consistently described the academic landscape of this country, particularly with respect to American Indians, Hispanics and African Americans. Perhaps attempts to reform and make schools more responsive have been isolated. They have failed to engage, enlighten and develop ownership by those stakeholders most entrusted with the responsibility to provide leadership and support for quality education: the school board.

When was the last time you thought about initiating school reform by influencing school boards to develop an understanding of issues, solutions and policies to prod administrators to make school reform a reality? How many times have you seen school boards – as supreme bodies with responsibility to govern schools – take leadership in setting school reform goals, setting parameters for school reform, providing flexibility for school administrators to execute school board policies, assigning authority to ensure that school administrators operate research-based implementation and management practices, or establishing self-imposed and mandatory accountability measures that guide expectations and consequences at all levels of the school hierarchy?

It is time for school boards to demonstrate leadership in what happens in the schools that we entrust them with and to become accountable for exerting the leadership necessary to achieve educational success of each and every student entrusted to their custody.

In the research literature, knowledge about school reform efforts is concentrated on research-based practices for school administrators. Focusing on systemic changes by addressing solely school administrators and other personnel ignores the fact that school boards, as representatives of the public who elected them, have "unlimited" power to change the face of education in their communities.

It is time to hold school board members accountable for what they have not done to hold on to a greater number of students until they graduate, to provide them with a quality education that prepares them for college, and to close all achievement gaps.

School boards must be careful not to cross the line of administration, but they cannot rely solely on firing and hiring superintendents before they can take any other pro-active action to fend off mediocrity.

Walking a fine line not to cross into school administration entails strategic planning with the superintendent and other community stakeholders for targeted school transformation efforts that lead to strong student holding power and high student achievement. The use of external experts to advise this strategic planning group is essential. In such cases, the school board initiates strategy through its superintendent to plan and become fully engaged in creating a window of opportunity for greater support in the school reform effort.

Educational mediocrity reveals itself through a lack of academic accomplishments that is unacceptable and a threat to our democracy as a model of human dignity and equality. The fact that our academic accomplishments place us below many other nations in the world is reason for concern.

The loss in brainpower, human dignity and economic supremacy is immeasurable, with serious consequences to our social order and world leadership and security. School boards must wake up and assume their leadership roles more assertively and with greater dedication as guardians of educational excellence and equity.

How School Boards Can Become More Involved in School Reform Efforts

The role of school board members in creating systemic changes in our schools cannot be underestimated. For example in Texas, a school board "constitute[s] a body corporate and [has] the exclusive power and duty to govern and oversee the management of the district" (TEA Guidelines).

Its power to govern is enforced through policies that have the force of law. These policies shape the quality of education that a community offers its students. In other words, the quality of education is a reflection of the understanding, commitment and dedication of school boards to excellence and equity.

> By disengaging, board members abdicate the power and responsibility entrusted to them through the democratic process.

Five key strategies that can help school boards become more involved in issues that matter to students and schools are discussed below.

1. Become better informed of community assets and needs, student characteristics, and implications for a quality educational program. Although most states require that their school board members receive training during their tenure, the training rarely targets knowing their communities (assets, needs, student characteristics) or basic knowledge about a quality education program. How can we entrust the education of our children to persons who are responsible for school policy but who have a limited knowledge of quality education and quality teaching?

Unfortunately, it is not uncommon for school board members to become totally disconnected from their role and the duty that they are elected or appointed to carry out. The community that elected them should demand greater interest, action and leadership from them.

2. Engage in constant dialogue with community leaders and parents to ensure that schools work in partnership with community members and parents to enrich the quality of education to be provided. Successful school boards meaningfully engage their communities in periodic forums, meetings and reflection sessions to check the pulse of schools in graduating students who are ready for college, in ensuring that schools are holding on to students, and in creating school environments that are safe and responsive to the needs of all students.

School boards must wake up and assume their leadership roles more assertively and with greater dedication as guardians of educational excellence and equity.

Building community consensus and support for school transformations based on research and compassion are powerful methods. This also can neutralize the effects of political rivalry and enmity that cause school board paralysis, deadlock and inappropriate action. Too often school boards engage community only during election times.

3. Promote and facilitate partnerships with community members and parents as a powerful way of creating and sustaining educational change. Recently, a leading school superintendent lamented the lack of knowledge and commitment of school administrators to value and partner with their communities and parents to create a learning community that works and supports a quality educational program.

Effective school boards are strong advocates of meaningful engagement. They promote and facilitate partnerships with community and parents as a powerful way of creating and sustaining change that leads to student engagement and success. School administrators must realize that total student success will not be achieved until the school partners with all sectors of the community and parents and has the full confidence of students.

4. Become an integral part of a leadership team responsible for designing school reform efforts. Many times, school boards underestimate their contributions as citizens and elected representatives of the general public in school reform efforts. They bring different, essential perspectives into the planning and design phase of school reform. They are in a position to change policies to enable schools to make the necessary changes.

The total disengagement of school board members from school reform efforts can have a detrimental impact on schools' success. By disengaging, board members abdicate the power and responsibility entrusted to them through the democratic process.

5. Be accountable to the community for excellence and equity in the provision of services and the resultant academic accomplishments. If systemic changes were well-defined, understood and supported by an informed school board, they would be less vulnerable to disruption of educational services to students created by school leadership changes like a new superintendent or new principals. Many times, leadership vacuums left by superintendents' or administrators' sudden departure lead to complete school disarray and dysfunction.

When a school board is informed and engaged in the educational design process, continuity is sustained, transition can be less troublesome, and the implementation of effective policies and practices will not be disrupted.

In conclusion, the benefits of a more involved school board cannot be underestimated. School boards are at the root of an educational system founded upon democratic principles and promote the tenets of democracy and self government.

There is no doubt that ownership of school reform efforts by a school board can result in greater community support and acceptance, stronger collaboration among schools in a school district, and increased participation of community stakeholders. Our children cannot be the victims of an indifferent and unconscionable system that can be manipulated by self-serving and insensible politics. Our children deserve better.

Originally published in the *IDRA Newsletter*, June-July 2007

The Role of School Governance Efficacy in Building an Equity Context for School Reform

by Bradley Scott, Ph.D.

Much has been written on the need for school governance efficacy for school reform to result in high student achievement. But the research has been thin concerning the effect of school boards on student achievement. We must consider the importance of governance efficacy as one of the essential drivers for creating an equity context through which school reform occurs.

This article examines ways in which school governance can guide the creation and maintenance of an equity context within which reform can occur to create quality schools that appropriately educate, graduate and prepare all students for college and life.

In his confirmation hearing before the Committee on Health, Education, Labor and Pensions, the then designee for Secretary of Education, Arne Duncan, testified: "Quality education… is the civil rights issue of our generation. It is the only path out of poverty, the only road to a more equal, just and fair society. In fact, I believe the fight for quality education is about much more than education. It's a fight for social justice. I come to this work with three deeply held beliefs. First, that every child from every background absolutely can be successful. Rural, suburban, urban, gifted, special education, English language learner, poor, minority – it simply doesn't matter… When we as adults do our job and give them opportunities to succeed, all of our children can be extraordinarily successful. Second, when we fail to properly educate children we, as educators, perpetuate poverty and perpetuate social failure… And third, our children have one chance – one chance at a quality education, so we must work with an extraordinary sense of urgency. Simply put, we cannot wait because they cannot wait." (The Washington Post, 2009)

Secretary Duncan also noted in a presentation to the House budget committee: "There's a lot I don't like about *No Child Left Behind*, but I will always give it credit for exposing our nation's dreadful achievement gaps. It changed American education forever and forced us to take responsibility for every single child regardless of race, background or ability." (Nagel, 2009)

The notion of "taking responsibility for every child" has to become something more than a slogan or a phrase. It must become a rallying call for every school district to galvanize action across sector, race and circumstance to lead to transformation so that all students are successful.

Dr. María Robledo Montecel, IDRA president, has presented a way communities can take responsibility by examining "contextual and moderating factors that may impede or accelerate school system change" (2005). She presented the Quality Schools Action Framework as "a model for assessing school conditions and outcomes, identifying leverage points for improvement, and informing action." The framework poses five key questions: (1) What do we need? (2) How do we make change happen? (3) Which fundamentals must be secured? (4) Where do we focus change? and (5) What outcomes will result?"

Dr. Robledo Montecel named two fundamentals as critical to creating student success – fair funding and governance efficacy – "the resources to effectively serve all students and good governance that facilitates academic achievement and success."

> Quality schools that support high student achievement, school graduation, college attendance, and life success for all diverse learners can only occur in a context of educational equity.

She said, "Governance efficacy strengthens school holding power when administrative and supervisory personnel have the capacity to deliver quality educational services to all students, along with the policymaking and pro-active support of a school board to hold on to every student." (2005)

Governance Efficacy Defined

It is important then to define governance efficacy in detail. For the sake of this article, ***governance efficacy*** **is defined as the power of school boards, among others, to change the face of education in their communities through positive and appropriate policymaking, equitable resource allocation and transparent accountability for all stakeholders.** This definition is an expansion of a discussion of school board accountability offered by Villarreal (2007). Cortez and Villarreal also described policy attributes that positively impact access and success for students using a framework originally developed by Rodríguez and Villarreal (Cortez & Villarreal, 2006).

Authors Griffin and Ward identified five characteristics of an effective school board that also help define governance efficacy. According to them, effective school boards: focus on student achievement as the number one job; allocate resources to support students based upon their differing characteristics and needs; watch return on investment and report to the communities they serve with transparency and accountability; use good data to inform policymaking to support student success; and engage the communities they serve in providing real opportunities to give input into policymaking process (2006).

In a similar manner, the National School Boards Association defined the "Key Work of School Boards" by identifying a framework of eight interrelated actions that school boards should undertake to engage their communities and improve student achievement through effective governance. The actions involve work in the areas of: vision, standards, assessment, accountability, alignment, climate, collaboration and community engagement, and continuous improvement. (See a detailed discussion of each of these actions at the NSBA web site at http://www.nsba.org/MainMenu/Governance/KeyWork.aspx.)

There is one critical piece that is missing that seems to be strongly suggested by Secretary Duncan's comments above. Quality schools that support high student achievement, school graduation, college attendance, and life success for all diverse learners can only occur in a context of *educational equity*, such as where the Six Goals of Educational Equity and School Reform (Scott, 1999; Scott, 2000) create a high equity context for action, transformation and school reform. While it appears to be implied in the research and work of the authors cited, it is clear to this writer that the goal of equity must be specifically stated – not merely implied – and it must be fore-front in any work that seriously embraces "quality education as the civil rights issue of our generation."

I have previously described *systemic equity* as, "the transformed ways in which systems and individuals habitually operate to ensure that every student has the greatest opportunity to learn, enhanced by the resources and supports necessary to achieve competence, excellence, independence, personal and social responsibility, and self sufficiency for school and for life" (2000).

Strategic and focused implementation of the Six Goals of Educational Equity and School Reform is critical to the creation of systemic equity.

The Equity Context

The systems and structures a school district puts into place to ensure that no learner is denied the fair and equitable benefit of a quality, sound educational experience afforded to all other students regardless of race, gender, national origin, economic level and handicap is the lens through which all of the business of the organization is filtered. This is the work of school boards. It is the challenge of governance efficacy to create a culture that is a high equity context where systemic equity and the Six Goals of Educational Equity and School Reform become the regular practice of a district's operation (Scott, 2001).

The following questions must be posed and answered before an organization can say that it has employed an equity lens to serve all students regardless of their differing characteristics:

- How does this practice impact all learners?
- What policies, resources and/or other supports are needed to create equitability across different populations?

IDRA Six Goals of Education Equity and School Reform

Public schools can do what they choose to educate their students within certain limits and parameters, but they are accountable for educating all learners to high academic standards and outcomes regardless of differing characteristics of those learners. Bradley Scott, Ph.D., (director of the equity assistance center at IDRA) developed the following six goals of education equity, which have been embraced by the nine other equity assistance centers across the country.

Goal 1: Comparably high academic achievement and other student outcomes

Goal 2: Equitable access and inclusion

Goal 3: Equitable treatment

Goal 4: Equitable opportunity to learn

Goal 5: Equitable resources

Goal 6: Accountability

More information is available at:
http://www.idra.org/South_Central_Collaborative_for_Equity

- What might create a negative or adverse impact on any identifiable population?
- How might that adverse impact be avoided?
- What precautions should we take as we move forward?
- How do we monitor our work to ensure comparable high outcomes for all students?

The Iowa Lighthouse Project supports this notion of a culture of equity. The project is a 10-year study of the relationship between school board leadership and student learning. The original study was commissioned by the Iowa Association of School Boards in 1998. Over the 10 years since the original study, various phases of the implementation of the findings reveal that school boards make a difference in the creation of high student achievement (IASB, 2001). The study shows that boards in high achieving school districts are significantly different in their knowledge and beliefs about students and education from low-achieving districts.

The actions of school districts with high achieving students operated in five critically different ways. The school boards:

- Consistently expressed the belief that all students can learn and that schools can teach all students. This "no excuses" belief system resulted in high standards for students and an ongoing dedication to improvement.

- Were far more knowledgeable about teaching and learning issues, including school improvement goals, curriculum, instruction, assessment and staff development. They were able to clearly describe the purposes and processes of school and identify the board's role in supporting those efforts.

- Used data and other information on student needs and results to make policy decisions.

- Created a supportive workplace for the staff, including regular professional development, support for more effective, shared leadership and decision making, and regularly expressed appreciation to the staff.

- Identified how they connected with and listened to their communities and focused on involving parents in education.

Boards in high achieving school districts focused on policies supporting changes in the conditions and the environment, i.e., the context of practice. In other words, these boards used their authority, power and decision making capacity to promulgate policy that led to a transformation of the culture of schooling that ultimately improved achievement for all students.

This research describes an example of high equity context. The lens for increased student achievement reflects a push for the sustained implementation of systemic equity where the Six Goals of Educational Equity and School Reform are used to impact policy, administrative action, instructional practice, professional and human development, community and parent engagement and involvement, accountability by all stakeholders, and continual monitoring toward improvement to support high achievement for all diverse students.

Each element of the Quality Schools Action Framework developed by Dr. Robledo Montecel requires equity to be effective. With this framework as the starting point, boards would have to determine how high or low their equity context is. They would have to use their power to create and implement policy and provide the necessary leadership to raise the equity context if reform is to occur and be sustained to lead to increased achievement for all.

The Final Challenge

Secretary Duncan presented a challenge when he stated: "The biggest barrier, the only remaining barrier in my mind is: do we have the courage? It takes courage to expose our weaknesses with a truly transparent data system. It takes courage to admit our flaws and take steps to address them. It takes courage to always do the right thing by our children, but ultimately we all answer to the truth. Reforming public education is not just a moral obligation. It absolutely is an economic imperative. It is the foundation for a strong future and a strong society. Education is the civil rights issue of our generation. The fight for quality education is about so much more than education, It's a fight for social justice. It is the only way to achieve the equality that inspired our democracy, that inspired women to stand up for theirs, and then inspired minorities to demand their fair share of the American promise, and it inspires every child to dream." (The Washington Post, 2009)

Finally, it is important to close by noting that every educational institution has an obligation and is challenged to filter its business in support of student success through a lens of educational equity. This lens helps to protect the civil rights of every learner under the law, to guarantee equitable educational opportunity for every learner regardless of his or her differing characteristics, and to provide the appropriate educational supports for school success, post secondary school attendance and completion and life success supported by the necessary resources to make that success possible.

Governance efficacy is critical for creating and sustaining the high equity context for the reform that is needed, and education stakeholders must hold themselves and all others responsible for these outcomes.

Resources

Cortez, A., and A. Villarreal. "Assessing Policies for Success of Minority Students," *IDRA Newsletter* (San Antonio, Texas: Intercultural Development Research Association, June-July 2006).

Griffin, A., and C. Ward. "Five Characteristics of an Effective School Board: A Multifaceted Role, Defined – How does your school district measure up?" *Edutopia* (San Rafael, Calif.: George Lucas Educational Foundation, March 21, 2006).

Iowa Association of School Boards. *The Lighthouse Study* (Des Moines, Iowa: The Iowa School Boards Foundation, 2001).

Nagel, D. "Ed Secretary Duncan Wants to 'Flip' NCLB, Vows to Scale Up What Works," *The Journal* (March 13, 2009).

National School Boards Association. Key Works of School Boards, web site: http://www.nsba.org/MainMenu/Governance/KeyWork.aspx

Robledo Montecel, M. "A Quality Schools Action Framework – Framing Systems Change for Student Success," *IDRA Newsletter* (San Antonio, Texas: Intercultural Development Research Association, November-December 2005).

Scott, B. "A Comparative Study of Teacher Perception of Race and Race Relations in Two Selected Districts," unpublished dissertation (University of Texas at Austin, May 2001).

Scott, B. "We Should Not Kid Ourselves: Excellence Requires Equity," *IDRA Newsletter* (San Antonio, Texas: Intercultural Development Research Association, February 2000).

Scott, B. "From 'DAC? to 'EAC? – The Expanding Role of the Equity Assistance Center," *IDRA Newsletter* (San Antonio, Texas: Intercultural Development Research Association, February 1999).

Villarreal, A. "School Board Accountability for School Boards that Support Educational Equity," *IDRA Newsletter* (San Antonio, Texas: Intercultural Development Research Association, June-July 2007).

The Washington Post. "Arne Duncan Confirmation Hearing," CQ Transcript Wire (January 19, 2009).

Originally published in the *IDRA Newsletter*, June-July 2009

Fair Funding of Schools – Why and With What Results

by Albert Cortez, Ph.D.

School finance reform has been pivotal to IDRA's work to improve educational opportunities for all students. It was initially our primary focus, and the organization has since expanded its reform efforts to include extensive work in the areas of professional development for teachers and administrators, supporting expanded parent involvement, and encouraging improved student engagement and graduation in schools. Promoting and sustaining school finance equity however has remained a constant area of focus in IDRA's 36-year history.

This article examines the following critical questions about school finance equity and offers lessons learned during the course of our long involvement in this area: Why is funding considered so crucial for providing excellent and equitable education for all children? Does money really make all that much of a difference in the educational opportunities provided to students, and does it convert to improved outcomes? If it does, then how does one best achieve equitable funding and how do states best pay for such reforms? What options are available in states and communities that refuse to modify state funding plans that would ensure all students in all schools have equitable opportunities?

Recognizing the Need for an Educated Citizenry

It seems a no-brainer to understand that providing excellent and equitable education requires some level of investment. It is a given that operating schools requires expenditures for school buildings, for textbooks and instructional materials, for teachers and administrators, and for the staff needed to provide a wide array of support as well as to keep records, provide counseling, and maintain school property.

While there is no disagreement about the need to provide funding to support public education in the United States, there has always been dissension about how much funding to provide, for what purposes, and out of what pockets. Concerns about the need to have an educated citizenry in a political system that allocated much of its power to the electorate led to an early agreement to support public education.

The lack of consensus on the role that the federal government should play in that critical area was reflected in its exclusion from the U.S. Constitution. No doubt an article committing the federal government to support public education in all states would have resulted in a very different educational landscape than the patchwork of state-supported systems that exists today.

The exclusion of an education clause in the U.S. Constitution has resulted in the subsequent creation of state-based and state-controlled systems of public education and, with them, state-specific school funding plans. Research on these systems reveals that no two systems are the same (Augenblick, et al., 2001) with each reflecting the unique evolution of these plans within the contexts of each state's unique history.

Attendance Requirements and Inequity

In many states, public education was not an option available to all students. As states began to adopt compulsory attendance requirements, they also adopted processes for sorting students, such as designating separate school systems for White children and Black children in the South. In the Southwest, a variant created separate school environments for Latino students.

Finding ways to pay for schools that required student attendance, whether segregated or integrated, quickly led to a hodge-podge of state funding plans that varied extensively, ranging from schools funded by the state or primarily by local property taxes.

Texas is one example of that evolutionary process. Describing the early funding plans in the 1970s, legislative researchers note that Texas did not enter the modern era of school funding until 1949 (Texas House Research Organization, 1990; Walker & Kirby, 1986). Spurred by a strong education governor, a commission recommended major revisions to the heretofore locally-controlled enterprise and recommended the establishment of a "minimum foundation program of state and local financial support" (Cárdenas, 1997).

Known as the *Gilmer-Aiken Act*, this basic funding plan served as the primary vehicle for the support of Texas public schools for a few years until legal challenges to inequalities in public school funding caused the state to review its funding system.

Like many of its counterparts, Texas was plagued by very large differences in education spending per student. Many of the disparities were attributable to vast differences in the amount and value of taxable property within school systems, which ranged from a few hundred dollars to millions of dollars in taxable revenue per pupil.

The state's failure to recognize – let alone to equalize – these funding disparities would eventually be challenged in federal court. The historic case of *Rodríguez vs. San Antonio ISD* resulted in a 5-4 ruling that, despite the observation that the Texas system was "chaotic and unjust," it did not violate federal equal protection requirements.

The state's successful defense was short lived: in 1987 a state court found that the unequal school finance plan did in fact violate the Texas constitution. In the historic *Edgewood vs. Kirby* case (which came to be known as *Edgewood I*), the state's supreme court required Texas to modify its school funding plan in a way that provided every school district equal return for equal tax effort, instituting a process for equalizing school funding throughout the state (Cárdenas, 1997).

Other Considerations for Funding

Forcing states to recognize differences in local school districts' ability to support education, however, proved to be but one piece of a complicated puzzle. Advocates of equal opportunity for children had noted since the 1970s that students with differing needs would not be well served by providing the same amount of funding for educating them as students with no special needs.

> With fair funding, everyone benefits by having schools that are excellent and equitable.

In response to these issues, states developed funding mechanisms that recognized varying program costs. They used different strategies ranging from simple add-on funding to tying special program costs to funding for regular programs via weighting systems (where programs such as compensatory education were provided an allocation based on percentage of regular program costs) (Augenblick, 2001; Verstegen, 1988). Though an improvement, a major flaw in many of those state adjustments was the failure to collect and use actual add-on cost data to guide funding levels.

In addition to issues related to student counts and special needs, funding plans grew increasingly complex by incorporating adjustments for such issues as school district size, which impacted both operating expenses and efficiency.

Another funding issue that has confronted state leaders is how to deal with costs of constructing and renovating school facilities. Some states play little or no role in supporting local school construction, while others cover substantial portions of building costs. Some states incorporate equalization features that consider local district wealth factors, while others fund facilities outside an equalized system (ESC, 2009).

Impact on Student Achievement

The impact of school funding on student achievement has long accompanied debates about the amount and the type of funding provided to local schools. Research by Hanushek (1997; 1996) has argued that funding variations have no impact on student achievement, while Ferguson (1991) and Nechbya (2004) found that the amount of funding notably impacts the quality of schooling available to students in different school districts.

An interesting observation in Texas is that some of the state's wealthy districts had originally proposed that money did not make much difference but later complained that limited funding did not enable them to provide an adequate level of education for their students, especially their special needs students.

An outgrowth of decades-long debates on equitable funding of public schools is an effort to ensure that schools provide "adequate levels of funding" for all students in a state (Augenblick, et al., 1997). The emergence of adequacy studies led to the filing of a new round of court challenges based on the level of funding adequacy produced by a state funding plan. These were particularly effective in increasing funding in states (mostly in the South) that had previously provided minimal state funding for their public schools (Rebell, 2008).

Recent federal attention fueled by requirements in the *No Child Left Behind Act* have led to increasing federal funding for the nation's public schools. What began as supplemental support targeted for students with special needs has grown to increasing federal allocations that help cover costs of facilities, energy, technology and other issues of interest to federal officials.

While making a notably larger investment in public education, the federal percentage of total school allocations still accounts for less than 10 percent of most state public school budgets, though that amount may vary from state to state.

Funding for public education also has been challenged with the emergence of vouchers, which provide direct allocation of monies to private institutions. A radical departure from the goals of public education, these approaches have been vigorously opposed by public school advocates and the majority of the general public. Public school advocates affirm that the way to fix public schools is to focus attention on fixing public schools, rather than diverting resources to private enterprises.

Emerging research indicates that despite big promises, voucher programs have not resulted in dramatic improvements in achievement (Rouk, 2000), and at best, after years of implementation, have proven to be inconclusive (Gill, et al., 2001). At a symposium convened by the Institute for Education Sciences in Washington in 2005, a panel of experts continued to show that the evidence of voucher effectiveness at improving achievement was inconclusive.

Conclusion

As long as states, communities and federal agencies provide funding for public schools, we can expect continuing debates on what to fund, how much to fund and who will be responsible for covering those costs. As long as funding remains a state responsibility, IDRA believes that equity and excellence also is primarily a state responsibility.

On the other hand, while we understand the evolution of state education funding plans, we believe it is perhaps an appropriate time to consider adoption of a new federal constitutional amendment stating that equal educational opportunity is a birthright of every child living in the United States.

In an age when a student educated in one locale may grow up, work and raise a family anywhere in the country, it is not unreasonable to assure that an excellent and equitable education is accessible to all.

IDRA's president, Dr. María "Cuca" Robledo Montecel, has proposed imagining "a future in which the color of a child's skin, the language a child speaks and the side of town a child comes from are no longer considered barriers to a great education and a great life" (2009).

In the closing paragraphs of *Savage Inequalities*, Jonathon Kozol exposes the effect of unequal public school funding systems, noting: "From the top of the hill… the horizon is so wide and open… one wonders what might happen to the spirits of these children if they had a chance to breathe this air and stretch their arms and see so far… Standing there by the [river]… one is struck by the sheer beauty of this country, of its goodness and unrealized goodness, of the limitless potential that it holds to render life rewarding and the spirit clean. Surely there is enough for everyone within this country. It is a tragedy that these good things are not more widely shared" (1992).

When we establish a system of fair funding for schools, it will send the message that indeed every child is capable and is worthy of receiving the best quality education possible. Excellent schools will no longer be just for the families with the greatest financial advantages. With fair funding, everyone benefits by having schools that are excellent and equitable.

Resources

Augenblick, J.A. *The Status of School Finance Today – Education Finance in the States: Its Past, Present and Future*, ECS Issue Paper (Denver, Colorado: Education Commission of the States, 2001).

Augenblick J.A, and J.L. Meyers, M. Burk Anderson. *Equity and Adequacy in Education* (Princeton, N.J.: Princeton University Press, 1997).

Augenblick, J.A., and J.S. Hansen, J.W. Guthrie. *Education Finance in the States: Its Past, Present and Future* (Denver, Colorado: Education Commission of the States, 2001).

Cárdenas, J.A. *Texas School Finance Reform: An IDRA Perspective* (San Antonio, Texas: Intercultural Development Research Association, 1997).

Education Commission of the States. Finance, Facilities: What States are Doing, web site (Denver, Colorado: Education Commission of the States, 2009).

Farr, J.S., and M. Trachtenberg. "The Edgewood Drama: An Epic Quest for Education Equity," *Yale Law and Policy Review* (1999). Vol. 17, No. 2.

Ferguson, R.F. "Paying for Public Education – New Evidence on How and Why Money Matters," *Harvard Journal of Legislation* (1991). Vol. 28.

Fernández, R., and R. Rogerson. "Equity in Resources: An Analysis of Education Finance Systems," *Journal of Political Economy* (University of Chicago Press, 2002).

Gill, B.P., and P.M. Timpane, K.E. Ross, D.J. Brewer. *Rhetoric Versus Reality: What We Know and What We Need to Know About Vouchers and Charter Schools* (Santa Monica, Calif.: RAND Corporation, 2001).

Hanushek E.A. "Assessing the Effects of School Resources on Student Performance," *Education Evaluation and Policy Analysis* (Summer 1997). Vol. 19, No. 2, pp. 141-164.

Hanushek, E.A. "School Resources and School Performance," *Does Money Matter: The Effects of School Resources on Student Achievement and Adult Success*, Gary Burtless ed. (Washington, D.C.: Brookings Institution, 1996).

Imazecki, J., and A. Reschovsky. "School Finance Reform in Texas – A Never Ending Story," *State Aid and the Pursuit of Educational Excellence*, John Yinger (Cambridge, Mass.: MIT Press, 2003).

Kozol, J.A. *Savage Inequalities – Children in America's Public Schools* (New York: Harpers Perennial, 1992).

Maryland Department of Legislative Services. *Review of Selected State Responses to Facilities Survey*, presentation to the Task Force to Study Public School Facilities (Anapolis, Md.: December 2003).

McQuire K.C. *State and Federal Programs for Special Student Populations* (Denver, Colo.: Education Commission of the States, April 1982).

Nechbya, T.J. "Prospects for Achieving Equity and Adequacy in Education," *State Aid and the Pursuit of Educational Excellence*, John Yinger (Cambridge, Mass.: MIT Press, 2004).

Oden, A., and J.A. Augenblick, V.E. Philip. *School Finance Reform in the States, 1976-1977: An Overview of Legislative Actions, Judicial Decisions and Public Policy Research* (Denver, Colo.: Education Commission of the States, 1976).

Rebell, M.A. "Educational Opportunity and the Courts," *Phi Delta Kappan* (February 2008) Vol. 89, No. 06, 432-439.

Robledo Montecel, M. IDRA web site (San Antonio, Texas: Intercultural Development Research Association, 2009) http://www.idra.org.

Rouk, U. "Vouchers: Yea or Nay," *Insights on Education Policy, Practice, and Research* (Austin, Texas: Southwestern Educational Development Laboratory, September 2000).

Texas Association of School Boards. *A Guide to Texas School Finance* (Austin, Texas: Texas Association of School Boards, August 2008).

Texas House Research Organization. *An Introduction to School Finance* (Austin, Texas: Texas House of Representatives, February 1990).

Texas Legislative Budget Board. *Foundation School Program Fiscal and Policy Studies* (Austin, Texas: Texas Legislative Budget Board, March 2009).

Texas Legislative Budget Board. *Financing Public Education in Texas Kindergarten through Grade 12 Legislative Primer*, third edition (Austin, Texas: Texas Legislative Budget Board, October 2001).

Verstegen, D.A. *School Finance at a Glance* (Denver, Colorado: Education Commission of the States, 1988).

Walker, B.D., and W. Kirby. *The Basics of Texas Public School Finance* (Austin, Texas: Texas Association of School Boards, 1986).

Originally published in the *IDRA Newsletter*, May 2009

"Myths in School Finance"
Texas School Finance Reform – An IDRA Perspective

by José A. Cárdenas, Ed.D.

The following is a random listing of some of the myths of school finance which surfaced repeatedly during the past 22 years and are still widely perceived as reality by the general population.

Myth #1. Only the privileged care for their children

This misconception is not exclusive to school finance or education. Our entire society and its dysfunctional responses to societal problems is based on the myth that the rich and privileged have an interest and concern for their well-being and their children's well-being that is not shared by the general population. The rich are able to do a great deal for their children because they have the time, the money and the power to do so. The disadvantaged seldom have the resources or the skills for the manipulation of social institutions.

It is erroneous to conclude that educational benefits accrue to the children of one economic level and not to the children of other economic levels because of concern and care. On the contrary, it has been my experience that bonding in low socio-economic families is stronger than in the high sector, but unfortunately, too much of the result of their intense family ties is dissipated in trying to make ends meet, in avoiding exploitation of their economic plight, and in fighting the impact of their poverty.

In many cases, social institutions, including the schools, tend to create more problems for the child and his or her family than they attempt to solve.

Along with the concept that the privileged have better schools because they care more for their children, I have found a strong sentiment that the children of the rich are entitled to a better public educational opportunity. I find this attitude, which is so contrary to our democratic principles, very pervasive at all social and economic levels, and it may be one of the fundamental reasons for a general lack of support for school finance reform over the years.

Myth #2. The privileged have better schools because they pay higher taxes

For more than two decades, we have heard a justification for the disparities in available educational resources based on the argument that schools for children of privileged families are better because their parents are willing to make the necessary financial sacrifices to provide better schooling through higher taxes. This myth persists in spite of 20 years of school finance data that show that residents of low wealth districts make a much higher tax effort than residents of high wealth districts. The analysis of these data indicated early on that tax rates in the poorest school districts were commonly 50 times higher than the tax rates in the wealthiest districts.

Even after several years of court-ordered equalization, there remains a negative correlation between wealth and tax rates. The higher the wealth, the lower the tax rate; the lower the wealth, the higher the tax rate.

During the years of the school finance reform effort, there were three "military" school districts in metropolitan San Antonio. These school districts are located on military reservations, serve the children of servicemen and women, have the same status as other local districts, but have no taxable property since federal installations are tax exempt. The school districts received state funds but did not have access to local enrichment tax funds, although this constraint was more than compensated for by federal funds available under the impact aid program and from the Department of Defense. The amount of federal aid available was sufficient to rank the military school districts as the richest in the county, and the superintendent of one of these school districts was the highest paid of the 12 district superintendents in spite of the district being by far the smallest one in the county. In a budget-cutting move, the Department of Defense eliminated its subsidy for the operations of military school districts leading to a severe loss of funds available to them. In spite of the loss of federal funds, the military school districts still had revenues higher than those available to the poorest school districts in the county.

Immediately following the federal loss of funds, the Texas Legislature made the necessary amendments to its system of school finance in order to partially compensate the military districts for the loss. There was no discussion about a lack of state funds, the need for consolidation, or any of the dozens of arguments we had been hearing for two decades about the difficulty in implementing an equitable system. Additional funding was immediately provided to bring up the state share to the level of the average state and local share in the county. This immediate and emergency legislation provided for the military school districts to maintain a level of spending considerably higher than the levels for the low wealth school districts in San Antonio. Not only did low-tax-paying citizens in rich school districts have more funds for their children's education, children in some school districts without any property taxes still received more revenues than children in high taxing, low wealth school districts.

I applaud the efforts of the state education agency and the legislature in responding so effectively to the needs of the children in the military school districts. I regret that it took more than 40 years and extensive litigation for them to respond to the needs of children in the Edgewood school district.

Myth #3. Expenditures in high wealth school districts have little effect on low wealth districts

Immediately after the creation of TEE/IDRA and its commitment to reform the Texas system of school finance, I had an opportunity to meet with a group of superintendents from nearby low wealth school districts. I expected to find a very supportive audience eager to bring about drastic reform in the system, but I was disappointed in receiving only a lukewarm reception. After presenting a number of visuals depicting wealth, tax and revenue disparities, one of the superintendents in attendance responded with the statement that he was already aware of these disparities, and that he could live with them. He added that he was interested in what our organizations could do to raise the minimum level of funding for students in his school district, and he had no concern over high wealth school districts expending much more. The applause given his remarks indicated a strong consensus of agreement among the school officials present.

At one point in the state court trial, a spokesperson for the intervening school districts described existing inequities as desirable in that it forced the state to pump in new money each year. He compared the poor school districts to rabbits in a dog race serving an important purpose in giving the dogs something to chase.

This concern over amounts and quality of minimum programs and a lack of concern over disparities was a consistent attitude toward school finance reform during the two decades of our activity. Of the more than 1,000 school districts in Texas, with more than 500 being below the state median in district wealth, only 13 of the poorest districts signed on as plaintiffs in the state court case. Although many others intervened in behalf of the plaintiff districts, many of the interveners were more interested in raising minimum programs than in establishing an equitable system.

At one point in the state court trial, a spokesperson for the intervening school districts described existing inequities as desirable in that it forced the state to pump in new money each year. He compared the poor school districts to rabbits in a dog race serving an important purpose in giving the dogs something to chase.

Another reason for the lack of school district participation in school finance reform efforts was fear of retaliation by the defendant Texas Education Agency. There is no question that during my four years as superintendent of the Edgewood school district, which were the four years of the *Rodríguez* court case, I, and the school district, were subjected to extensive harassment by the state agency. TEA audits relatively unknown in other school districts, were frequent and meticulous, although they consistently proved fruitless. Due to a superior accounting system and good management, not a single penny in disallowances was ever identified during the four-year period. The inconvenience of surprise audits was greatly offset by a sympathetic supporter at the Texas Education Agency who consistently warned me of such surprise audits, as well as what the agency was looking for. In every case, the information that was requested for these audits was researched and prepared well in advance.

Minor infractions of the school district were magnified during the *Rodríguez* court case. For example, I received notification that an employee of the Texas Education Agency traveling through the Edgewood district had noticed that the state flag was not flying on a school day. I was informed that under state law, funds for the operation of that school would be disallowed if not remedied by the next day. An investigation revealed what I had already suspected: flagpole ropes make good clotheslines, and some nearby resident had appropriated the school's. To prevent further threats of loss of funds it was eventually necessary to use wire welded into a loop to keep the Texas flag flying.

A large disallowance in Title I funds in incurred by a previous administration and never settled was similarly used as a threat by the Texas Education Agency against Edgewood's participation in school finance reform. Several times, I received calls from the agency informing me that the debt could be eliminated if I would quit my foolishness and stay out of school finance matters.

Edgewood and other very low wealth districts became the training ground for school personnel who could then be hired in other parts of the city. If they performed well, they were motivated to apply for a position in a nearby higher-paying school district.

The fear of retaliation by the Texas Education Agency for school finance reform advocacy was such that it prompted my resignation from the school district in order to participate in the design of a new system of school finance. It was obvious that my continued employment by a school district subject to TEA regulation placed me in too precarious a position to be really effective in bringing about change in the system. James Vasquez, the dynamic superintendent of the Edgewood district during the *Edgewood* litigation, frequently reported similar harassment.

I believe then, and I believe now, that the effect of wealth disparities between school districts did not receive the attention it deserved during the entire reform period from the defendants, the courts, educators, the media, the general public, or even the plaintiffs. Edgewood is one of 12 independent school districts in metropolitan San Antonio. It does not exist in isolation, but rather in competition with the other 11 school districts. All 12 districts recruit teachers, special service personnel, supervisors, administrators and other staff from a common labor pool. Since Edgewood was the poorest of the 12 school districts, it was limited in the amount of enrichment funds that could be utilized to supplement the state minimum salary. During my tenure as a teacher and principal in Edgewood, the state minimum salary was the salary schedule used. There was no supplement. As a result, Edgewood and other very low wealth districts became the training ground for school personnel who could then be hired in other parts of the city. If they performed well, they were motivated to apply for a position in a nearby higher-paying school district. Since few of the Edgewood professional personnel came from the school district itself, moving to another district meant working closer to home, with a higher salary, better fringe benefits and superior working conditions. Edgewood was forced to hire emergency non-certified teachers. If they completed their certification requirements, jobs were readily available elsewhere. This led to a trend of a constant outward flow of the best performing personnel. When I became school district superintendent in 1969, more than half of the teachers in the school district did not meet the minimum requirements for certification and were teaching on emergency permits. The annual teacher turnover rate was 33 percent. One-third of the instructional staff had to be employed and trained each year.

In some cases, the training and experience of emergency certified teachers were exceptionally bad. When I was teacher certification officer at St. Mary's University, I was almost sued by a math secondary school teacher in Edgewood for not recommending an extension to his emergency certificate. The case was dropped when I reviewed his transcripts with his attorney. Not only had the math teacher in question never taken a math course in college (he was a music major and an excellent musician), but he had been admitted to college on a probationary status because he had failed all of his math courses in high school.

Although the handicap in recruiting and keeping teachers was the most obvious hardship in the competition among school districts, there were other more subtle competitions, not generally recognized, but psychologically detrimental the students. For instance, Edgewood participated in the University Interscholastic League activities. In each of the three high schools, the football, basketball and baseball teams were each coached by a single individual. If the coach in one sport needed assistance, he could be helped by one of the coaches from the other sports, provided that it did not interfere with the other sport's season. The Edgewood teams competed against teams that had as many as six coaches – offense, defense, line, receivers, quarterback and other coaching specialties. It was heartbreaking for me, as well as for the students and coaches, to see the Edgewood teams consistently defeated by other teams with superior coaching, along with superior equipment and practice fields. In spite of a lack of financial resources, Edgewood did produce some outstanding coaches, but these successful coaches moved on to better paying positions in wealthier school districts.

Neither educators nor the general public appear to have given extensive thought to the psychological implications of kids being consistent losers, not necessarily because of a lack of talent, but because the system does not provide adequate resources for the development of talent.

The effect of these inequities can best be demonstrated in football or basketball competition, but the effect is present in all interscholastic activities and to the same extent in the academic program.

One time when I was vice principal at Edgewood High School and prior to the desegregation of schools following the U.S. Supreme Court *Brown* decision, I was asked by the superintendent to provide some type of assistance to the principal of the school district's segregated Black school. As I was walking through the campus, I heard a strange sound, as if many persons were simultaneously drumming their fingers on a flat surface. Curiosity got the best of me, and I peered into the classroom. What I saw made an effect on me that has lasted a lifetime. I was looking at a typing class with some 20 African American students. The students had drawn typewriter keyboards on pieces of cardboard and were practicing their typing on non-existing typewriters, their fingers hitting the place in the cardboard where the letters were depicted. This experience came to mind just a few years later when the personnel director of one of San Antonio's military bases stated that they had very few African American employees in secretarial positions because they had found that African Americans had poor typing skills. I would imagine so. If typing instruction was provided on pieces of cardboard rather than on real typewriters, in the absence of a strong affirmative action program, African American applicants for competitive civil service positions would be hard pressed to land a job.

It is strange that so many educators did so little to bring about school finance reform in Texas. The argument that funds should be focused on raising minimums rather than on achieving equity has always seemed an admission that their students are less than equal and should be treated as such in the educational system.

In the October 1973 issue of the *TEE Newsletter*, I presented a plan for a state program of construction assistance to Texas school districts (Cárdenas, 1973). Since the state did not include facilities in the minimum foundation program, this aspect of school finance was the most inequitable part if the Texas system. In the article, I mentioned that 30 states had such programs, and I warned that the local property tax provided too narrow a base to continue supporting the cost of school construction. Shortly after the publication of this article, I met with Camila Bordie from the Texas Legislative Council, and we worked out a bill to provide state construction aid to Texas school districts. Such aid was to be provided to school districts with low wealth and high tax effort rapidly growing districts and to school districts with old and obsolete facilities. Camila Bordie obtained a sponsor for the bill it was introduced in the legislature, and it was referred to the House Education Committee. A hearing was scheduled, and I disseminated the date, time and place. On the day of the hearing, not one single school superintendent, not one single school board member, not one single educator from a school district in the entire State of Texas showed up to testify in support of the bill. Needless to say, the bill died in committee.

It is strange that so many educators did so little to bring about school finance reform in Texas. The argument that funds should be focused on raising minimums rather than on achieving equity has always seemed an admission that their students are less than equal and should be treated as such in the educational system.

Myth #4. Disparities in spending should be corrected only by upward leveling

During the entire 25-year school finance reform effort, educators from high wealth school districts purported to be sympathetic to the plight of low wealth districts but insisted that it would be detrimental to equalize by taking away the privileged positions that they held. Instead, their consistent argument was that it was the responsibility of the state to increase funding for low wealth districts in order to raise their revenues to the status of high wealth districts.

The apex of this argument came about when the state courts had found the state system of school finance unconstitutional, and it was no longer a question of whether the system should be equitable, but rather, how the system was to be made equitable.

The argument that equity can best be achieved by leveling upwards sounds reasonable until one considers the resources involved. In the October 1991 issue of the *IDRA Newsletter*. I presented arguments showing that leveling upwards was not a feasible solution:

> "Everyone in Texas would be extremely happy if disparities were removed and no school district would have less money under the new system than they had under the old system.
>
> "This goal may be admirable in theory, but it is indefensible in practice. To bring all school systems in the state to the level of the highest expending school district in Texas this past year would require an additional state appropriation of $45 billion. Considering that the state legislature turned catatonic at the prospect of having to provide $4.5 billion in additional appropriations to address the state deficit, it is inconceivable that it would consider a massive leveling up as recommended by high wealth school districts. Nor would the general public react favorably to or support a $45 billion increase in school taxes.
>
> "High wealth districts concede that the state has limited resources to eliminate existing disparities, therefore the disparities can be slowly eliminated over a period of time. Leveling up would consist of the allocation of additional state money on the basis of low wealth until all districts are on a par with the wealthiest. Unfortunately, this will never come to be. Not only is the disparity so great that several generations of children would finish school under the preset inequitable system prior to parity being achieved, but the failure to provide a practical cap for high wealth districts allows them to continue to increase disparities at the high end of the expenditure range as the state pours money in at the low end.
>
> "In the past 40 years since the implementation of the current system of school finance, each attempt by the legislature to narrow disparities with the infusion of huge sums of money for low wealth districts

has resulted in an increase in expenditures by high wealth districts which has actually increased the disparities in wealth. The appropriation of $4 billion in 1984 through House Bill 72 was completely eroded by the time of the *Edgewood vs. Kirby* trial in 1986, with disparities in school district spending being greater than prior to the infusion of the massive amounts of funding." (Cárdenas, October 1991)

Myth #5. Reform efforts result in loss of funds of rich districts

Every time that an attempt was made to reform the system to provide increased equity, the cost effects of the proposed change were estimated by the Texas Education Agency and reported in the public media. Inevitably, the projections in the reported data failed to take into consideration existing inequitable tax rates, and thus high wealth school districts were depicted as losing huge amounts of funds. In each case, the amount reported as a loss was contingent upon a continuation of inequitable and low tax rates for the high wealth school districts, a condition seldom or never mentioned in the report.

For example, a rich school district would have a tax rate of $0.50 per $100 of valuation, when the average tax rate for districts in the state was $0.75, and some of the poorest school districts had rates of $1.50. A proposed equity change that would reduce the state subsidy for the rich school district would mean a reduction of revenues only if the rich school district continued its privileged tax rate of $0.50. In many cases, an increase of 10 cents in the tax rate, which would still be 15 cents lower than the state average, would continue to produce more revenues than in poor school districts with a $1.50 tax rate.

Projections released by the state and reported in the media as losses of millions of dollars in school funds for wealthy school districts without indicating that it was assumed that the low tax rate would remain constant, provided a distorted picture of the effects of the proposed change with extensive concern and sympathy for the children in high wealth school districts.

Myth #6. Caps on school expenditures are unfair

Since its inception, the Texas system of school finance has always provided limitations on the amount that can be expended for education at both the state and local levels. Throughout its history, there has been a limitation on the maximum tax rate that may be enacted to supplement with local enrichment funds the inadequate provisions of the minimum foundation program.

In middle wealth school districts, the cap on the tax rate has served as a mild limitations on how much can be expended in support of the educational program. In low wealth school districts, the limitation on the permissible tax rate has served as a severe constraint on the quality of education. Even at the highest tax rate permitted by state law, low wealth school districts could not compete for the acquisition of personnel and material resources. The disparities in revenues for school districts with varying wealth resembled a traveling worm. As more money was allocated for the low wealth school districts, a slight increase in the tax rate in high wealth school districts was re-established, and in most cases, exacerbated the disparities.

Since the state revenues available for equalization were finite, it was evident very early in the reform period that low wealth school districts would never catch up unless the limitation on tax rate was extended or replaced with a limitation on revenues. Each time such a recommendation surfaced, there was a loud cry from educators and patrons in high wealth school districts that it was detrimental to place a limit on the quality of education in the state.

Until such time as these local wealth disparities are neutralized, there can never be an equitable system of school finance in the state.

It is difficult not to accept this argument, but it was evident that, without such a limitation, all efforts for the creation of an equitable system were doomed. As stated previously, it was extremely unfair to place a cap on local enrichment that served as a constraint on only the low wealth school districts. A better alternative is to place feasible constraints on all school districts and to pace no limitation on the amount that the state can expend on education with all school districts receiving equal benefits.

For all practical purposes, limitations on the quality of education have always existed, even in the wealthiest school districts. Regardless of the amount expended for education in high wealth districts, local school campuses within a school district have never had the prerogative of outspending other campuses within the district. It is difficult to accept the concept of unlimited disparities in interdistrict expenditures, when school districts observe rigid limitations on intradistrict disparities.

Expenditure disparities are caused by unlimited local enrichment, which in turn is extremely inequitable because of large disparities in local wealth. Until such time as these local wealth disparities are neutralized, there can never be an equitable system of school finance in the state.

Myth #7. Money does not make a difference

As the threat of fiscal equalization arose, there was a consistent reaction from high wealth school districts asserting that there was no need for an equitable system since "money does not make a difference."

This argument first surfaced during the *Rodríguez* trial. When the federal court noted a much higher level of expenditures in the high wealth school district than in the low wealth district documented in the court case, the immediate response by defendants was that the different levels of expenditures did not necessarily indicate a better educational program in the high wealth school district. At one point, defendants argued that the excess wealth was used for the development of curricular materials that were then made available to low wealth school districts, thereby nullifying the advantages of wealth.

This argument would have been difficult to accept even if it were true. Curriculum developed for affluent students in high wealth school districts is usually not appropriate for use in low wealth districts with high concentrations of economically disadvantaged, minority, migrant, immigrant and limited-English-proficient students. Actually, many of the educational problems of such atypical students can be attributed to the failure of the elitist U.S. educational system to develop and implement materials and methodologies compatible with the characteristics and needs of atypical school populations.

In the Texas system of school finance, the rationalization of the advantages of wealth with a trickle down concept of benefits accrued was moot. The additional funds available to high wealth school districts were not allocated to curriculum development, shared or unshared. The bulk of the additional funds were used in augmenting personnel salaries and fringe benefits to attract and retain the best trained, experienced and most successful school personnel. The next highest priority for enrichment funds was for the purchase of instructional materials, equipment and facilities to augment the meager supply provided or completely absent in the foundation program.

My fundamental question during the school finance effort was, "If money does not make a difference, why are the rich school districts fighting so hard to retain it?"

The defendant's argument that money does not make a difference reminds me of the time when President Abraham Lincoln was intending to sign the Emancipation Proclamation that would free the slaves. Prior to his signing the proclamation, he was visited by a pro-slavery delegation that went to great lengths to extol the advantages of slavery. Their arguments in behalf of slavery were not found very convincing by Lincoln, who could not help but note that slavery could not be all that desirable considering that none of the speakers would wish it upon themselves.

My fundamental question during the school finance effort was, "If money does not make a difference, why are the rich school districts fighting so hard to retain it?"

Myth #8. Robin Hood is evil

Under strong pressure from the state courts, the legislature enacted a new school finance system in 1991 based on the creation of County Education Districts that provided an equalization within 188 county and multiple-county taxing entities which eliminated most of the expenditure disparities at a very low cost to the state. Both in efficiency and in cost to the state, this plan, enacted as Senate Bill 351, was the best response to state inequities in school finance developed during the entire reform period, even vastly superior to the current law finally found acceptable by the courts.

Once the courts had established that the old system of school finance was unconstitutional, the goal of the reformers was to conceptualize a new system that would provide total equity and be affordable. One of the salient problems of the old system was that there were many very high wealth school districts with extremely low tax rates. In some, the tax rates were so low that they were commonly referred to as "tax haven" school districts.

Albert Kauffman, lead attorney from the Mexican American Legal Defense and Educational Fund (MALDEF), who represented plaintiff districts in the *Edgewood* suit, and José A. Cárdenas, executive director of IDRA, independently undertook the task of designing a new and equitable system. Both efforts resulted in a similar design, the use of counties as the base unit for the assessment, collection and distribution of local enrichment funds. With assistance from Dr. Albert Cortez of IDRA, the concept was presented to state Sen. Hector Uribe from Brownsville and Rep. Gregory Luna from San Antonio, both strong advocates of school finance reform.

The two legislators introduced the bill for the creation of the county districts. Subsequently, Sen. Carl Parker submitted a similar bill in the senate. After much change and compromise, the proposed legislation emerged as Senate Bill 351, and it was signed into law by Gov. Ann Richards in May 1991.

The concept of various districts with varying wealth sharing tax bases was immediately labeled and addressed by the media as the "Robin Hood" plan. It was called such because it appeared to take tax revenues from rich school districts and gave them to poor school districts. All of a sudden, Robin Hood changed from a boyhood hero into a Texas villain. In response to the negative publicity being given Senate Bill 351 as the Robin Hood legislation by high wealth school districts and the public media, the following article by José A. Cárdenas appeared in the September 1991 issue of the *IDRA Newsletter*.

> "During the formulation of the new law, Senate Bill 351, and subsequent to it passage, this piece of legislation has been identified in the local, state and national media as the 'Robin Hood' plan for school finance equity. This sobriquet is invariably accompanied with the explanation that the new system of school finance takes money from rich school districts and gives it to the poor.
>
> "This stigmatization of the new system of school finance is unfortunate, since it is erroneous. Senate Bill 351 does not take money from rich school districts and gives it to poor school districts. Senate Bill 351 does create a new taxing entity. If the new school taxing entity is based on a Robin Hood model, then so are the tax and spend characteristics of all taxing entities.
>
> "Prior to the enactment of Senate Bill 351, each of the 1,056 school district enacted a mandated tax rate. If the local yield produced less money than what was needed to finance the foundation school program, the state made up the difference. If the local yield in high

wealth school districts produced more money than what was needed to finance the foundation school program, a school district could use the additional revenue to enhance the district's school program and/or lower the tax rate.

"In some very high wealth districts, a tax rate at 15 percent of the average school tax rate for the state provided more money than what the school district could effectively utilize. Unfortunately, low tax rates in high wealth districts provided a tax shelter, or very low taxation of high wealth property, at a time when the state was experiencing a crisis in providing funds to augment low wealth district tax collections.

"The creation of the 188 county taxing units provides for the revenue from a set tax rate to be distributed equally among all districts in the county, with the state still augmenting local revenues if the county education districts fail to raise sufficient funds for the basic school program. The use of the county units provides an equal tax effort for rich and poor districts alike, with the amount of the state subsidy for poor school districts being reduced by the excess revenues in high wealth districts. The county district makes no impact on low wealth districts other than some of the support coming from the high wealth district revenues rather than from the state.

"The sole beneficiary of the county system is the state rather than the low wealth district. Naturally this benefit will be passed along to the average taxpayers of the state who will not have to pay high taxes in support of low wealth school districts while high wealth goes relatively untaxed. Under the new system, the previously untaxed wealth is now being tapped so that all taxpayers share more equally in supporting area schools." (Cárdenas, September 1991)

Myth #9. Consolidation is the solution

Prior to the enactment of the *Gilmer-Aiken* legislation in 1949, there were about 6,000 school districts in Texas. Many of these districts were "dormant" districts, school districts that had no students but continued as political entities without a need for taxation since no schools were operational. *Gilmer-Aiken* eliminated all dormant districts and provided for the elimination of school districts that lost their enrollments. Since no minimum number of students was stipulated in the legislation, as long as a school district had at least one student it remained functional.

Gilmer-Aiken was contradictory since it forced the consolidation of dormant districts, but at the same time provided incentives for the continuation of small, dysfunctional districts. The legislation provided a special stipend for "smallness." According to a February 1988 article in the *IDRA Newsletter*, 730 of the state's 1,061 school districts (69 percent) were receiving this special stipend provided to small districts with less than 1,600 students. The article cites another reward for smallness:

"In addition to the financial subsidy to school districts with less than 1,600 students, the foundation school program provides further subsidies in support of smallness. In computing the amount of state assistance to be provided under the program, districts report either the number of students in average daily attendance or 130 students, whichever is greater, The foundation program provides minimum support for 130 students, even if the number enrolled is less.

"This subsidy and financial incentive for smallness applies to 99 school districts in Texas, enrolling 7,506 students, but receiving funds for 12,870 students. Multiplying the number of non-existing students by the average operating cost of the foundation program produces an expenditure of $16,564,032, with the state paying its share of this cost in support of 5,364 students who do not exist.

"Two important questions surface in the light of these data. First, what is the quality of educational opportunity afforded to the students in such small groupings? And second, what is the cost to the state of Texas in support of such an extensive number of financially inefficient small school districts?" (Cárdenas, 1988)

In most cases, the small, inefficient school districts were perpetuated because they provided a tax haven for the property owners. A favorite, but extreme, example was the Provident City School District in Wharton County. According to the IDRA publication, *Texas School Finance Data*, the school district had $7,723,507 in taxable property, a tax rate of $0.21 on market value and a 1973-74 enrollment of only one student (Cárdenas & Brischetto, 1974). The nearby Wharton school district had $57,844 to taxable property per student, a tax rate of $1.05 and an enrollment of 2,853 students. The consolidation of the two school districts with the Wharton tax rate would lead to a Provident City tax bill of $78,780. Maintaining the Provident City school district for one student cost property owners in Provident City $16,220, an annual property tax savings of $62,560. The last year that Provident City was operational, it had one student who was in attendance only three-fourths of the school days, producing an annual average daily attendance of 0.75. Eventually, Provident City lost its one frequently absent student and was merged with another school district, losing its privileged position as a tax haven.

During the legislative battles for school finance reform, a number of such small school districts formed a lobbying group for the preservation of small, tax haven districts. Its name was "The Committee for the Preservation of the Little Red Schoolhouse."

On the other hand, consolidation has never been perceived by IDRA as a panacea for solving the school inequity problem in Texas. Research in school administration has shown that there is an optimum size for school districts, with a tendency for school districts with a smaller number of students to be inefficient and ineffective. There is also evidence that there is also an optimum size on the large end of the scale, with school districts with excessive number of students tending to be bureaucratic, unresponsive, inefficient and ineffective.

Segments of the school finance reform movement in Texas focused early and exclusively on consolidation as a solution to existing inequities. I believe that the concept of huge tax savings by extensive consolidation is a myth. Wealth is distributed very unevenly throughout the state. In many communities, the consolidation of adjoining school districts would produce one large poverty-poor school district with a low tax base, a high tax rate and a low tax yield, the very characteristics that both the *Rodríguez* and *Edgewood* court cases were attempting to eliminate. As evidenced in the creation of the County Education Units in Senate Bill 351, the 254 counties in Texas had to be collapsed into 188 county and multiple-county units to achieve a semblance of wealth uniformity. Although this legislation did create some very large entities, their function was only for the collection and distribution of taxes, and they have no role in the administration of the schools in the various districts involved.

As pointed out in the February 1988 IDRA article on consolidation:

> "The merger [of all Bexar County district] would result in a large, bureaucratic school district with some 250,000 students which would immediately start to seek ways in which it could decentralize in order to be more responsive to the unique needs of the various segments of the community. As the size of a school district increases, it reaches a point where largeness starts to become a liability rather than an asset. Certainly the continuous efforts of the nation's large urban school districts to find ways to decentralize and be responsive to the varying community characteristics would indicate so.
>
> "Research in school finance indicates that the creation of a large school district does not result in significant savings in administrative costs. The need for a large bureaucratic administrative structure to operate the large district results in increased costs rather than savings. The elimination of a dozen school district superintendents would demand the creation of a dozen new positions in the new systems at a similar cost.
>
> "Past administrative assumptions that bigger is better have not proved true in contemporary research. Effective schools research has shown that very large schools are detrimental to student adjustment and performance." (Cárdenas, 1988)

The nine myths described above did not appear in any special order or sequence but appeared continuously in public opinion, legislation and litigation. Some of them were the results of public ignorance about the system of school finance and mistaken notions about the reasons for the existing inequities. The myths were commonly presented in the public media, which tended to give them undeserved creditability. In retrospect, it appears that no sooner had a specific myth been addressed and refuted by advocates of school finance reform before another myth surface or resurfaced in opposition to reform.

The myths were widely disseminated by educators in high wealth districts as well as the defendant state agencies in Texas. This was surprising because both educators and agency personnel knew better. Professionalism was quickly and easily compromised in behalf of the preservation of the elitist system of education in Texas.

Resources

Cárdenas, J. "Economic Index and Enrichment Funds," *TEE Newsletter* (San Antonio, Texas: Texans for Educational Excellence, October 1973).

Cárdenas, J. "Is School Consolidation the Solution to Achieving School Finance Equity," *IDRA Newsletter* (San Antonio, Texas: Intercultural Development Research Association, February 1988).

Cárdenas, J. "Myths and Issues in School Finance: Parts I and II," *IDRA Newsletter* (San Antonio, Texas: Intercultural Development Research Association, September 1991).

Cárdenas, J. "Myths and Issues in School Finance: Parts III and IV," *IDRA Newsletter* (San Antonio, Texas: Intercultural Development Research Association, October 1991).

Cárdenas, J., and R. Brischetto. Texas School Finance Data, Texans for Educational Excellence and the Southwest Schools Study Project (San Antonio, Texas: Texans for Educational Excellence, March 1974).

Cárdenas, J.A. *Texas School Finance Reform: An IDRA Perspective* (San Antonio, Texas: Intercultural Development Research Association, 1997).

Originally published in *Texas School Finance Reform – An IDRA Perspective*, 1997

Chapter Five – School System Indicators

Clues for Change

Aurelio M. Montemayor, M.Ed.

To check a school system with rigor
We need crucial clues and indicators:
Observable evidence for sharp-eyed raters.
Facts and data to analyze with vigor.

Singularly and in tandem, focus
On engaged families and students.
For teachers, no wouldn'ts, couldn'ts:
Quality curriculum, no hocus-pocus.

As referees we must keep score.
If indicators in all crucial realms
Feels complex and data overwhelms,
Remember we need data, more and more.

Life is complicated and so are schools:
Making it too simple, you'd call us fools.

Chapter Preface

The future of this country is inextricably linked to the quality of education of its citizens. This maxim has profound implications for our education system and its ability to prepare our citizenry to continue the leadership role that this country has enjoyed for so long. When we look at how U.S. students are performing among students worldwide, we are looking at a dismal and not very encouraging picture.

Uprooting current efforts to address these challenges is the lack of equity in many of our schools that is fed by a pervasive and subtle form of racism that negatively influences the quality of education that many of our fastest-growing student populations receive. As a nation we can face this challenge with accountable leadership, enlightened public policy, and engaged citizens dedicated to making schools work for *all* students.

An effective school is one where *all* students feel welcomed, valued and above all achieve both academically and socially. This effective school is characterized by having strong leadership and advocacy for equity and excellence of education for all students, a strong partnership with parents and community, a cadre of caring and qualified teachers and support staff, engaged students in learning, an inclusive program of extracurricular activities that provide students with opportunities to develop their talents, and a relevant and rigorous curriculum that provides the blueprint of a quality education.

This chapter includes articles that primarily focus on what schools must do to become the vehicles for change that will drive this nation to a more perfect union and re-energize its position as a world leader.

Access to quality curriculum and instruction, teaching quality, engaged students, and involved parents and communities – these are the four critical indicators in IDRA's Quality Schools Action Framework of what is needed to strengthen schools.

- To have students excel and graduate, schools need competent caring teachers who are well-paid and supported in their work. Kristin Grayson, M.Ed., provides IDRA's values that underscore the concept of teaching quality in "Defining Teaching Quality Beyond the Certificate."
- Bradley Scott, Ph.D., writes of the need for *teaching quality* to work for all students in "Teaching Must Be Culturally Relevant to be Quality."

- In "Aligning School-Based Factors for Student Success – Using Contextual Data to Inform Science Professional Development," Kristin Grayson, M.Ed., shares how a contextual analysis of school-based factors can inform professional development.

Schools also need consistent ways in which to partner with parents and engage the communities to which they belong. Effective *parent and community engagement* builds partnerships based on respect and a shared goal of academic success for every child.

- Aurelio Montemayor, M.A., debunks myths about parents of underserved children in "Getting 30 Warm Bodies to the Meeting? – Parent Engagement is More than This!"
- He then provides IDRA's principles for family leadership in education in "The Lens for Viewing the Full Dimensions of Families."
- Rosana Rodríguez, Ph.D., reviews the research base for effective parent and community engagement in "What Parent and Community Engagement Means for Quality Schools."

Student engagement is integral to any quality school reform plan. Schools need the capacity to create environments and activities that value students of all backgrounds and to incorporate them into the learning process and other social activities within the school, with academic achievement as a result.

- Kristin Grayson, M.Ed., and Veronica Betancourt, M.A., speak to the power of student engagement in mathematics achievement in "The 'Fourth-Grade Slump' and Math Achievement – Addressing the Challenge with Student Engagement."
- Adela Solís, Ph.D., and Kristin Grayson, M.Ed., provide an overview of IDRA's Engagement-Based Sheltered Instruction model as an example of an effective means of engaging students in "You Can't Win if You Don't Get to Play – Effectively Engaging All English Language Learners."
- In "Mentoring New Teachers for First-Day, First-Year Success," Adela Solís, Ph.D., provides suggestions for effective teacher mentoring based on research and experience.

School systems that strengthen holding power depend on a *high quality, enriched and accessible curriculum.* Curriculum quality and access encompasses the educational programs of study, materials and other learning resources – such as technology – and their accessibility. It also relates to the fair and unbiased assessment of students and the degree to which schools take responsibility for the academic success of all students.

- Abelardo Villarreal, Ph.D., and Bradley Scott, Ph.D., provide school administrators and communities a series of questions critical to school improvement in "IDRA's Community of Learners Approach to Instructional Quality – Three Critical Questions that are Rarely Asked in a Curriculum Audit."

- In "Successful Bilingual Education Programs – Criteria for Exemplary Practices in Bilingual Education," María Robledo Montecel, Ph.D., and Josie Danini Cortez, M.A., introduce the 25 common characteristics IDRA found that contribute to the high academic performance of students served by bilingual education programs.
- And lastly, in the article: "Integrating Technology for Quality Curriculum… Widening the Lens of Student Engagement," Kathryn Brown challenges us to expand our idea of what curriculum is and how it is developed.

Teaching Quality

Defining Teaching Quality Beyond the Certificate

by Kristin Grayson, M.Ed.

A successful school reform effort cannot ignore the fact that improving teaching quality is of the utmost importance. Dr. María Robledo Montecel, president and CEO of IDRA, describes IDRA's Quality Schools Action Framework by defining the critical components that must be addressed in any comprehensive school reform effort that will be sustained over time. This article will define teaching quality within this framework and will clarify this concept along with similar terms, such as *teacher quality*, that are used in federal and state legislation, teacher preparation and development, and current academic research. This will serve as a source of information to guide school leaders, administrators and teachers as they make critical decisions in areas of hiring, curriculum and professional development.

What is Teacher Quality?

There is great emphasis today, in part due to the *No Child Left Behind Act* (NCLB), on teacher quality in schools. NCLB has given impetus to states to improve teacher quality by requiring schools to have a qualified teacher in every classroom. This requirement is one step in addressing inequities in schools that occur when a high percentage of teachers in a given school are teaching out of their areas of certification. For example, 1993-94 federal government data show that high minority schools had higher levels of teachers teaching out of the field in which they had certification, with percentages ranging from 27 percent of teachers in high minority schools teaching out of area as opposed to 13 percent in low minority schools (Ingersoll, 2000).

The term *quality teacher* is defined by NCLB and used for state implementation as a teacher who: (1) has, at a minimum, a bachelor's degree; (2) has full state certification or licensure; and (3) demonstrates subject area competence in all the subjects that he or she teaches. State governments, in addition to certification criteria, also are required by Title I to improve teacher quality through professional development and other initiatives.

Sadly, however, inequities in teacher quality continue to persist as they have over the past 23 years. When schools have greater numbers of teachers teaching out of the field in which they are qualified, there are large numbers of students underachieving and leaving school before graduation.

A 2007 study of 14,000 students in 197 elementary schools found that collective teacher quality is related to greater school effectiveness, equity outcomes, and student achievement in math and reading, in particular where student subgroups (English language learners, low-income, etc.) were clustered (Heck, 2007).

A specific Texas example that illustrates the possible attrition relationship is in the low minority Highland Park High School in Dallas where the percent of teachers teaching out of field is 11 percent and its student attrition rate is only 6 percent. In contrast, at Edgewood Memorial High School in San Antonio, the out-of-field and attrition percentages are 22 percent and 40 percent, respectively. While there are other variables, schools that have teachers teaching within their areas of certification are correlated with higher student achievement.

Teaching quality refers not only to the teachers' credentials, but also to the perspective teachers bring to the classroom, the instructional strategies that they use, and the surrounding organization of the school and community.

Today, schools continue to lose high numbers of students when teachers do not meet the minimum criteria. Unfortunately, schools also are losing high numbers of students even when taught by "highly qualified" teachers. The rate at which Texas students leave high school before graduation is 33 percent, which is the same rate that it was more than 20 years ago when IDRA began its attrition studies.

Additionally, the gaps between attrition rates for White students and Hispanic students and between White students and African American students have grown. Since 1985-86, the attrition rate gap for Hispanic students has increased from 18 percent to 26 percent. For African American students the gap has increased from 7 percent to 20 percent. (Johnson, 2007)

Clearly, the dreams of the *Brown vs. Board of Education* and the *Mendez vs. Westminster* court cases have not been fulfilled. There are still many children who are being left behind. It is apparent that IDRA's mission of "creating schools that work for all children" is far from being realized. Many students are leaving schools unprepared to support themselves, their future families and the larger communities in which they live. There is work yet to be done.

IDRA's work emphasizes that *teacher quality* must accompanied by teaching quality within the context of a supportive organizational school and community structure as exemplified in the Quality Schools Action Framework.

What is Teaching Quality?

For IDRA, teaching quality refers not only to the teachers' credentials, but also to the perspective teachers bring to the classroom, the instructional strategies that they use, and the surrounding organization of the school and community. This multi-layered approach is supported by research, including the previously discussed study by Heck (2007).

Another study by Okoye, Momoh, Aigbomian and Okecha (2008) shows that the combined variables of teacher quality and instructional strategies are correlated with student achievement. Torff (2005) purports that lack of pedagogical skill and knowledge is a bigger threat to teacher quality than are certification issues.

Berliner (2005) describes teacher quality as a teacher who shows evidence of certain qualities of teaching in the lives of students. These qualities include more than assessing knowledge on a certification test. Teacher qualities also must include: "the logical acts of teaching (defining, demonstrating, modeling, explaining, correcting, etc.); the psychological acts of teaching (caring, motivating, encouraging, rewarding, punishing, planning, evaluating, etc.); and the moral acts of teaching (showing honesty, courage, tolerance, compassion, respect, fairness, etc.)." IDRA's construct of teaching quality encompasses this current research.

IDRA's framework for teaching quality guides IDRA professional development and its mentoring and coaching work. At its core is an underlying set of beliefs and values that include:

- All students bring assets to the learning environment that must be used as their educational foundation;
- All teachers also bring assets to the learning environment that must be used as a base to enhance professional growth and skills;
- Professional development and/or mentoring and coaching is best done by building a community of learners where all stakeholders collaborate, create and initiate changes; and
- The guiding vision of student engagement encompasses the classroom, the school, the family and the community.

What is IDRA Doing to Improve Teacher Quality and Teaching Quality?

IDRA works tirelessly on many initiatives to support students not only through schools but also with families, communities, higher education, and education research and policies that impact students.

Contextual Analysis – When working directly with schools and teachers, IDRA begins with a contextual analysis in order to understand the organizational and sociological influences that affect the teachers' and schools' strengths and opportunities for change and growth. Without an understanding of the context, a plan for growth cannot be implemented.

Community of Learners – The context also is essential to building a community of learners (Villarreal & Scott, 2008; see also Page 153). IDRA works to foster this community through online communication and planning, showcasing teachers and schools in workshops and online, valuing their input and opinions, and listening to what they and their students say they need.

The contextual analysis also includes student feedback about their linguistic and background experiences, their learning preferences, and their level of self-efficacy for learning specific subject material. All students are recognized as bringing assets to the learning environment, and students learn best when empowered to be partners in the learning process. Students are part of the community of learners.

In-Class Assistance – Within IDRA professional development programs, a model of coaching and mentoring is used to provide in-class assistance as an essential step following workshops. This coaching and mentoring process is individualized to supplement the teacher's strengths by modeling and demonstrating strategies and content that can enhance the teacher's instruction. Steps of this process might evolve from an in-class lesson demonstration by the consultant or a specific strategy demonstration that is followed by a teacher demonstration with supportive coaching. All of the in-class assistance is followed by a collaborative reflection over accomplishments, lessons learned and goal setting. IDRA acknowledges that professional development is not a "one size fits all" solution but has to be specific to the teacher, student, school and district.

Student Engagement in the Larger Context – Quality teaching cannot happen in isolation. Engaging the student in the classroom and classroom instruction cannot happen unless there is engagement in the larger context. It only happens when all the surrounding pieces of the larger system are in place. The structure of the school, the school leadership and the community also are essential to quality teaching. These components are addressed elsewhere in this book.

The non-negotiable in the IDRA vision of teaching quality is that schools must work for all students. All students must be prepared to meet necessary academic goals so that none drop out, none is left behind, and the dream of an equitable education for all can be achieved.

Resources

Berliner, D.C. "The Near Impossibility of Testing For Teacher Quality," *Journal of Teacher Education* (2005) 56 (3), 205-213.

Heck, R. H. "Examining the Relationship Between Teacher Quality as an Organizational Property of Schools and Students' Achievement and Growth Rates," *Educational Administration Quarterly* (2007) 43 (4), 399-342.

Ingersoll, R.M. "Teacher Quality, The Inequity," Student Achievement and School Accountability Conference presentation, unpublished (University of Georgia, 2000).

Johnson, R.L. Texas Public School Attrition Study, 2006-07 – Texas School Holding Power Worse than Two Decades Ago," *IDRA Newsletter* (San Antonio, Texas: Intercultural Development Research Association, October 2007).

Okoye, N.S., and S.O. Momoh, D.O. Aigbomian, R.E. Okecha. "Teachers' Quality, Instructional Strategies and Students' Performance in Secondary School Science," *Journal of Instructional Psychology* (2008) 34 (4), 204-211.

Torff, B. "Getting it Wrong on Threats to Teacher Quality," *Phi Delta Kappan* (2005) 87 (4).

Villarreal, A., and B. Scott. "IDRA's Community of Learners Approach to Instructional Quality-Three Critical Questions that are Rarely Asked in a Curriculum Audit," *IDRA Newsletter* (San Antonio, Texas: Intercultural Development Research Association, February 2008).

Originally published in the *IDRA Newsletter*, February 2009

Teaching Must be Culturally Relevant to be Quality

by Bradley Scott, Ph.D.

IDRA has taken a stand on the importance of building quality schools to support student success and increase graduation. Our Quality Schools Action Framework presents a way of looking at systems change to produce student success and increased graduation (Robledo Montecel, 2005).

This article makes the case that one of the important areas of focus for change – teaching quality – must embrace cultural relevance as a necessary and absolute component. In fact, teaching in public schools cannot and should not be considered high quality if it is not culturally relevant. Why is that so?

I have previously described the Six Goals of Educational Equity and School Reform (Scott, 2000) that are a guide for ensuring that public schools work for all students regardless of their diversity. Systemic equity is defined as "the transformed ways in which systems and individuals habitually operate to ensure that every learner – in whatever learning environment that learner is found – has the greatest opportunity to learn, enhanced by the resources and support necessary to achieve academic competence, excellence, independence, responsibility and self-sufficiency for school and for life" (Scott, 2000).

At the onset and throughout every aspect of creating quality schools is the regular work to ensure success and graduation for all diverse learners. The Quality Schools Action Framework would have, as an added dimension at its entrance point, the Six Goals of Educational Equity and School Reform.

This is important because when education stakeholders want to create success for all learners, then those who provide high quality education do so with the learners in mind. If one accepts that learners are diverse, they do not necessarily learn in the same way, and all can achieve and excel, then one also must accept something else. While good teaching can be effective for all learners, it may not be if it is approached in a rigid, fixed, non-responsive way for students who are diverse in language, culture, socialization and many other dimensions.

Diverse students do learn in many ways. The way they learn, the way they bring skills to bear in the learning process, their manner of engaging the learning process, and how they interact with teachers and other students are all cultural in nature.

Teachers need to understand this about their students, and students must come to know this about their teachers. The encounter of teaching in the classroom is not just intellectual; it is also cultural. It needs, therefore, an approach that is culturally competent requiring powerfully dynamic and responsive pedagogy.

Many scholars have made similar assertions in some form (Ladson-Billings, 1995; Wortham & Contreras, 2002; Howard, 2003; Trumbull & Pacheco, 2005; Hill & Flynn, 2006). It appears that many teachers, however, are still not prepared to provide educational experiences that effectively serve diverse students in ways that move them to high achievement and other positive outcomes.

The encounter of teaching in the classroom is not just intellectual; it is also cultural. It needs, therefore, an approach that is culturally competent requiring powerfully dynamic and responsive pedagogy.

Goe, Bell and Little note in *Approaches to Evaluating Teacher Effectiveness*, "Given that teachers' roles involve much more than simply providing subject-matter instruction, it is appropriate to consider a broader and more comprehensive definition of effective teachers consisting of five points and formulated by evaluating discussions of teacher effectiveness in the research literature as well as in policy documents, standards and reports" (2008).

They provide a five-point definition of effective teaching based upon the current research. One should note that within the five points, three speak specifically to culturally relevant pedagogy.

- Effective teachers have high expectations for all students and help students learn, as measured by value-added or other test-based growth measures or by alternative measures.
- Effective teachers contribute to positive academic, attitudinal and social outcomes for students, such as regular attendance, on-time promotion to the next grade, on-time graduation, self-efficacy and cooperative behavior.
- Effective teachers use diverse resources to plan and structure engaging learning opportunities; monitor student progress formatively, adapting instruction as needed; and evaluate learning using multiple sources of evidence.
- Effective teachers contribute to the development of classrooms and schools that value diversity and civic-mindedness.
- Effective teachers collaborate with other teachers, administrators, parents and education professionals to ensure student success, particularly the success of students with special needs and those at high risk of failure.

Teaching quality that works just for some cannot be the goal or outcome of schools. Teaching quality has to be effective in supporting all students in realizing academic, civic, social and life success. Teaching quality is absolutely necessary to move all diverse students to high outcomes. And teaching must be culturally relevant for the learners who encounter it to be high quality.

Resources

Goe, L., and C. Bell, O. Little. *Approaches to Evaluating Teacher Effectiveness: Research Synthesis* (Chicago, Ill.: National Comprehensive Center for Teacher Quality, 2008).

Hill, J.D., and K.M. Flynn. *Classroom Instruction that Works with English Language Learners* (Alexandria, Va.: Association for Supervision and Curriculum Development, 2006).

Howard, T.C. "Culturally Relevant Pedagogy: Ingredients for Critical Teacher Reflection," *Theory Into Practice* (Summer 2003). pp. 43-51.

Ladson-Billings, G. "But That's Just Good Teaching! The Case for Culturally Relevant Pedagogy," *Theory Into Practice* (Summer 1995). pp. 159-165.

Robledo Montecel, M. "A Quality Schools Action Framework – Framing Systems Change for Student Success," *IDRA Newsletter* (Intercultural Development Research Association, November-December 2005).

Scott, B. "We Should Not Kid Ourselves: Excellence Requires Equity," *IDRA Newsletter* (Intercultural Development Research Association, February 2000).

Trumbull, E., and M. Pacheco. *Leading with Diversity: Cultural Competencies for Teacher Preparation and Professional Development* (Providence, R.I.: The Education Alliance at Brown University and Pacific Resources for Education and Learning, 2005).

Wortham, S., and M. Contreras. "Struggling Toward Culturally Relevant Pedagogy in the Latino Diaspora," *Journal of Latinos and Education* (2002) Volume 1, Issue 2).

Originally published in the *IDRA Newsletter*, May 2009

Aligning School-Based Factors for Student Success

Using Contextual Data to Inform Science Professional Development

by Kristin Grayson, M.Ed.

The success of a professional development program for science teachers depends on the interplay of many school factors. Such factors include leadership advocacy and support for the academic success of all students, curriculum quality and accessibility, partnership with parents and community, demographics and history of achievement, a culture of high expectations for teachers and students, and quality of teaching personnel as defined by certification, teaching in fields, knowledge, beliefs, and experience. Consequently, before embarking with professional development in any school district or campus, IDRA conducts a contextual analysis mini-study to inform planning with school administrators.

A contextual analysis is especially important in the area of science because effective science teaching is a critical concern of many public schools today. This concern stems in part from statistical studies that show the United States is behind other countries in student achievement in science. Compounding the issue is the increasing diversity of student demographics in public schools, meaning more and more teachers are called upon to teach diverse student groups in their classrooms (Capps, et al., 2005). Diverse student groups (Hispanic, African American, English language learner) have not achieved at the same levels as White students (IES, 2005). Recently, U.S. Secretary of Education Arnie Duncan said to the National Science Teacher Association, "Science education is central to our broader effort to restore American leadership in education worldwide" (U.S. Department of Education, 2009).

This article discusses ways a contextual analysis of school-based factors can be used to inform the success of a professional development program by citing current research, disclosing experiences, and sharing activities that IDRA has used in conducting a contextual analysis mini-study.

Literature Review about Contextual Analysis

In a literature review of general professional development research, Klinger (2004) states that all of the factors concerning teachers and their diverse environments must be considered in order to effectively plan and conduct professional development. Klinger concludes that implementation of new practices into the classroom learned in professional development is heightened when the practices learned are flexible enough to fit with the needs of teachers and students and when the support for implementation in the classroom is adapted to the level needed by each teacher. Hence, awareness of the needs of teachers and students is an essential outcome of the IDRA contextual analysis before professional development is initiated.

> All of the factors concerning teachers and their diverse environments must be considered in order to effectively plan and conduct professional development.

Research about teacher knowledge, beliefs and practice has been conducted in other studies to inform the course of science professional development interventions. Lee, Lewis, Adamson, Maerten-Rivera and Secada (2007) conducted a five-year study and recapped it in an article titled "Urban Elementary School Teachers' Knowledge and Practices in Teaching Science to English Language Learners." Zohar (2006) stated in another article that by assessing teacher preexisting knowledge and beliefs about teaching, learners, learning and the subject matter, one can begin to understand the context that teachers bring to professional development. Sweeney (2003) supported a methodological approach to analyzing teachers' behaviors and rationales in particular as a basis for mentoring within professional development.

Yet despite research such as this, reform efforts often have failed to acknowledge teachers' existing knowledge, beliefs and attitudes, according to Gray and Bryce (2006). IDRA, however, does follow the research and supports using a contextual analysis as an important initial step in professional development.

In determining what teachers need to know, Shulman (1987) describes four areas as essential: general pedagogical knowledge (how to teach), content knowledge (science), pedagogical content knowledge (how to teach science), and disciplinary knowledge (inquiry and scientific processes). In a paper commissioned by the National Academy of Sciences, Windschitl defines in more detail what the specific knowledge is in these four areas. Knowing what knowledge teachers possess in these areas, according to Zohar and Schwartzer (2005), affects what teachers will learn during professional development and what they might use in the classroom as a result of the professional development.

Teacher efficacy is an important part of teacher beliefs. Tshannen-Moran, Woolfok, Hoy and Hoy (1998) define teacher efficacy as "the teacher's belief in his or her capability to organize and execute courses of action required to successfully accomplish a specific teaching task in a particular context." Higher levels of teacher self-efficacy are well correlated to higher levels of student achievement in education research. This is noted in recent research for mathematics and science (Uekawa, Borman & Lee, 2007).

In an article titled, "Teacher Beliefs and Cultural Models: A Challenge for Science Teacher Preparation Programs," Bryan and Atwater (2002) emphasize that teacher beliefs affect the learning that occurs in the classroom. It is important to be aware of teacher beliefs about student characteristics (race, culture, ethnicity, language, social class), beliefs about external factors that influence student learning, and beliefs about appropriate responses to diversity. It also is important to be aware of how different cultural models might impact a teacher's instruction and interaction with students of diversity.

Similarly, Saam, Boone and Chase (2000) found an interesting result while comparing the self-efficacy of "local" (mostly White) science teachers with the demographic variables of their students. Teachers' self-efficacies were not dependent on the students' level, geography or ethnicity. However, researchers did find a significant difference between the self-efficacies reported by teachers who mostly had students of middle- and upper-income backgrounds and those who mostly had students of a poverty or low-income background.

IDRA Contextual Analysis for Science Teaching Quality

In conducting a contextual analysis prior to initiating science professional development, IDRA collects data from several sources: assessment of curriculum quality and school culture (high expectations, vision, experience with success, school safety); teacher demographic and certification data; self-assessment survey for proficiency in science content knowledge and pedagogy of diverse student learners, including English language learners; success in partnering with parents and community; survey for science self-efficacy for diverse students; and onsite observations.

In order to assess teacher knowledge and beliefs, IDRA uses and/or modifies a combination of surveys obtained from current research. Using these surveys helps inform the professional development so that specific teacher content knowledge that aligns with state standards, such as the Texas Essential Knowledge and Skills, is targeted and strengthened.

Teacher beliefs and attitudes toward their ability to effectively teach science, especially to diverse students also can guide the professional development process. Numerous studies document the positive correlation of teacher self-efficacy to student achievement. Therefore, during the contextual analysis, IDRA assesses teachers' science self-efficacy for diverse students using the equity lens to ensure that all teachers are prepared in attitudes, knowledge and practice so that "no learner is denied the fair and equitable benefit of a quality, sound educational experience afforded to all other students regardless of race, gender, national origin, economic level and handicap" (Scott, 2009).

When observing science classroom instruction, IDRA uses the *Reformed Teaching Observation Protocol*. This is a science and mathematics classroom observation instrument (Sawada, et al., 2002) developed by the Arizona Collaborative for Excellence in the Preparation of Teachers. It details observable features of quality science teaching within categories of lesson design and implementation, content knowledge, and pedagogical and pedagogical content knowledge. Pedagogical content knowledge is further divided into propositional knowledge and procedural knowledge. These types of knowledge have to do with teachers not only knowing their content but also being able to promote students' deep conceptual understanding and connections to other subject areas by making predictions, stating hypotheses and reflecting on their own learning. Additionally, student-centered instruction, standards-based, and inquiry focus are key components of quality science teaching within this framework. This framework supports the goals of the four strands of scientific proficiency detailed by the National Academic of Sciences that all learners need to acquire.

The observation protocol has additional indicators included to assess the teachers' use of strategies that engage English language learners, something stressed by language acquisition expert Dr. Jim Cummins. Cummins (2001) emphasizes the importance of teachers engaging English language learners by using a variety of instructional strategies that connect the learning to the students' own experiences or past learning and that develop academic language.

Echevarria, Vogt and Short's research (2004) into sheltered instruction emphasizes that teachers must make the academic content comprehensible while using systematic methods to build and practice English language proficiency within the academic language of science. Kinsella (2006) further defines English language learner active engagement and the structuring of academic language. Indicators that reflect these English language learner strategies are included in the observation protocol used by IDRA.

The resulting information about teaching quality along with data collected about other important school-based factors is used by IDRA in conjunction with school districts to inform the plan for transformational change. This contextual analysis provides information about the condition or level of functioning of the various key school-based factors that influence the impact that professional development can have on teacher practices and student achievement. In other words, it provides administrators with information on maintaining or improving the condition of these school-based factors and aligning them to support the teacher and a professional development effort in increasing teaching effectiveness and student success.

For more information about IDRA professional development models that incorporate a contextual analysis component contact IDRA (210-444-1710; contact@idra.org) or visit http://www.idra.org.

Resources

Bryan, L., and M. Atwater. "Teacher Beliefs and Cultural Models: A Challenge for Science Teacher Preparation Programs," *Science Teacher Education* (2002) 86 (6), 821- 839.

Capps, R., and M.E. Fix, J. Murray, J. Ost, J.S. Passel, S. Herwantoro. *The New Demography of America's Schools: Immigration and the No Child Left Behind Act* (Washington, D.C.: Urban Institute, 2005).

Cummins, J. Understanding Academic Language Learning: Making It Happen in the Classroom (Chapter 5), *Negotiating Identities: Education for Empowerment in a Diverse Society*, second edition (Los Angeles: California Association for Bilingual Education, 2001).

Echevarria, J., and M.E. Vogt, D.J. Short. *Making Content Comprehensible for English Learners: The SIOP Model*, second edition (Boston: Pearson, Allyn and Bacon, 2004).

Gray, D.S., and T. Bryce. "Socio-scientific Issues in Science Education: Implications for the Professional Development of Teachers," *Cambridge Journal of Education* (2006) 36 (2), 171-192.

Institute of Education Sciences. "Indicator 17: International Mathematics and Science Achievement," *Youth Indicators, 2005 – Trends in the Well-Being of American Youth* (Washington, D.C.: National Center for Educational Statistics, 2005).

Kinsella, K. "Structured 'Academic Talk' for English Learners: A Key to Narrowing the Verbal Gap in K-12 Classrooms," presentation at OELA Fifth Annual Celebrate Our Rising Stars Summit (Washington, D.C.: Office of English Language Acquisition, October 2006).

Klinger, J.K. "The Science of Professional Development," *Journal of Learning Disabilities* (2004) 37, (3), 248-255.

Lee, O., and S. Lewis, K. Adamson, J. Maerten-Rivera, W.G. Secada. "Urban Elementary School Teachers' Knowledge and Practices in Teaching Science to English Language Learners," *Science Teacher Education* (2007).

Saam, J., and W.J. Boone, V. Chase. "A Snapshot of Upper Elementary and Middle School Science Teachers' Self-Efficacy and Outcome Expectancy," ERIC Document 443685 (2000).

Sawada, D., and M. Piburn, E. Judson, J. Turley, K. Falconer, R. Benford, Russell, I. Bloom. "Measuring Reform Practices in Science and Mathematics Classrooms: The Reformed Teaching Observation Protocol," School Science and Mathematics (October 2002) Vol. 102 Issue 6.

Shulman, L. "Knowledge and Teaching: Foundations for a New Reform," *Harvard Educational Review* (1987) 51, 1-22.

Scott, B. "The Role of School Governance Efficacy in Building an Equity Context for School Reform," *IDRA Newsletter* (San Antonio, Texas: Intercultural Development Research Association, June-July 2009).

Sawada, D., and M. Piburn, E. Judson, J. Turley, K. Falconer, R. Benford, I. Bloom. "Measuring Reform Practices in Science and Mathematics Classrooms: The Reformed Teaching Observation Protocol," *School Science and Mathematics* (2002) 102, 245-253.

Sweeney, A.E. "Articulating the Relationships Between Theory and Practice in Science Teaching: A Model for Teacher Professional Development," *Teachers and Teaching: Theory and Practice* (2003) 9(2), 107-132.

Texas Education Agency. Academic Excellence Indicator System 2007-2008 (Austin, Texas: Texas Education Agency, 2009).

Tschannen-Moran, M., and A.W. Hoy, W.K. Hoy. "Teacher Efficacy: Its Meaning and Measure," *Review of Educational Research* (1998) 68 (2), 202-248.

U.S. Department of Education. "Secretary Arne Duncan Speaks at the National Science Teachers Association Conference," speech (Washington, D.C., March 20, 2009).

Uekawa, K., and K. Borman, R. Lee. "Student Engagement in U.S. Urban High School Mathematics and Science Classrooms: Findings on Social Organization, Race and Ethnicity," *The Urban Review* (2007) 30 (1).

University of Louisville. "Middle School Science Content Summary Chart," Diagnostic Science Assessments for Middle School Teachers web site (Louisville, Ken.: University of Louisville, College of Education and Human Development, nd).

Windschitl, M. "What Types of Knowledge do Teachers Use to Engage Learners in "Doing Science"? – Rethinking the Continuum of Preparation and Professional Development for Secondary Science Educators," paper commissioned by the National Academy of Sciences (2004).

Zohar, A. "The Nature and Development of Teachers' Metastrategic Knowledge in the Context of Teaching Higher Order Thinking," *The Journal of the Learning Sciences* (2006) 15 (3), 331-377.

Zohar, A., and N. Schwartzer. "Assessing Teacher's Pedagogical Knowledge in the Context of Teaching Higher-Order Thinking," *International Journal of Science Education* (2005) 27 (13), 1595-161.

Originally published in the *IDRA Newsletter*, September 2009

Parent and Community Engagement

Getting 30 Warm Bodies to the Meeting?

Parent Engagement is More than This!

by Aurelio M. Montemayor, M.Ed.

As a trainer was preparing his presentation on meaningful parent engagement to meet Title I requirements, he overheard several parent liaisons talking about their work: "I've got to get food and door prizes, otherwise they won't come!" "We sent bilingual notices with the children, and only 10 showed up." "If I get the kids to perform, the parents show up, but if we have a meeting afterwards… the children running up to the families are a great distraction." "I feel I really succeed in parent involvement if I get 30 warm bodies in the room for the meeting."

Not only are these opinions passé, the intentions reflected in them do not help parent involvement staff meet the requirements of the law.

For purposes of illustration below, two major points of view are divided into the old and the new paradigm of parent engagement.

The Old Paradigm

Certain traditions and regularities have become part of school parent involvement. These are not necessarily negative or damaging, but they do cluster together under certain unifying views. Parent participation can be organized around several concepts:

- Volunteers and free labor for an understaffed, under funded and over-extended school;
- Participants in hobbies and enjoyable activities such as crocheting, decoupage and aerobics; and
- Course attendees for self-improvement, such as English as a second language, citizenship class and driver's license preparation.

We have several generations of professionals who are parent involvement specialists. Their positions are mostly funded through the federal *No Child Left Behind Act*. Many come from having been parent volunteers who were rewarded by the school by hiring them as parent liaisons.

The traditions mentioned above are part of the weekly tasks and activities of many family liaisons. They set-up craft groups that knit, collage or otherwise create objects for raising funds or simply for personal enjoyment. Fundraising for the school, inherited from older parent organizations, continues to prevail.

In all these activities, family participation has reflected community interests, priorities, accessibility and affordable time. Many of the very successful family involvement personnel in this mainstream are dynamic, go-getting and charismatic. These family involvement leaders create a strong following and dependence from poor and minority families. Sometimes these same popular leaders are patronizing and condescending toward families, especially families that are poor, minority or speak a language other than English.

These points of view have little room for perceiving the parent as co-constructor of an excellent education for all children. Even loving statements about parents, from these traditions, cast them as naïve, child-like and in need of guidance and correction.

The New Paradigm

Parent engagement as proposed and carried out by IDRA (and that coincides quite well with the spirit of Section 1118 of the Title I regulations) is in a different realm than the traditions listed above. Effective parent engagement to meet the letter of the law presumes a very different view of parents and their role in education.

> Each NCLB parent involvement policy point requires a parent engagement approach that recognizes intelligence, critical thinking, informed decision-making and assertiveness in demanding the highest quality of education for children.

This difference is dramatically highlighted in the key parent pieces in the statute: (1) School Parent Involvement Policy; (2) Parent-School Compact; (3) District-wide and Campus Policy; (4) Report Cards; (5) Public School Choice and Supplemental Educational Services; and (6) State Review of Parent Involvement Compliance.

Each of the above requirements attests to the change in direction for parent involvement. None of these can be complied with by increasing the traditional parent volunteer and fundraising activities. Evening classes for parents, though beneficial, will not meet the requirements unless the topic is the requirements themselves.

All of the Title I mandates are focused directly on the *academic success of children*. They rightly recognize that parents are vitally interested in that topic. Below are examples.

- Developing and approving *policy* requires dialogue and critical thinking. A meeting for this purpose must have parents present and participating.
- *School-family compact* requires parents coming together to determine their responsibilities and agreements with the school to ensure the academic success of their children, while also listing what is expected

of the school.

- *Report cards* present critical information to parents and engage them in the status of their children in school.
- *Public school choice and supplementary educational services* empower parents to make informed decisions about their children's effective instruction.
- Inviting the state educational agency to ensure parent involvement *compliance* is a dramatic opportunity for parents to request that the state monitor the school district and their children's schools.

New Paradigm Requirements

Each of these examples necessitates school personnel – and very specifically parent liaisons – to communicate directly and effectively with families. The locus is the family and, therefore, requires personal outreach, home visits, multiple settings for meetings and seeking creative ways to inform families who, because of work and other circumstances, are not able to attend an evening meeting on campus.

As stated by López, et al.: "A home-school relationship should be a *co-constructed* reciprocal activity in which both the agency and sense of efficacy of parents, and the involvement opportunities provided by schools and other institutions that work with children are important" (2004-2005).

In a Latino neighborhood, it might be that the key parent volunteers are the center of a *comadre* network, with each one acknowledged and validated for the number of other families they communicate directly with about school matters and events. These secondary contacts are in turn encouraged and supported in developing their own networks of parents for the same purposes.

From "Some" to "All"

Each NCLB parent involvement policy point requires a parent engagement approach that recognizes intelligence, critical thinking, informed decision-making and assertiveness in demanding the highest quality of education for children. And though this policy is aimed at economically disadvantaged parents, these assumptions are already made about middle-class, professional and formally educated parents. These assumptions, applied to all parents, are the paradigm shift.

Resources

López, M.E., and H. Kreider, M. Caspe. "Evaluating Family Involvement Programs. Theory and Practice. Co-Constructing Family Involvement," *The Evaluation Exchange* (Volume X, No. 4, Winter 2004-2005).

Montemayor, A.M. "IDRA's Family Leadership Principles," *IDRA Newsletter* (San Antonio, Texas: Intercultural Development Research Association, September 2007).

Montemayor, A.M. "Every Family Engaged = Every Child Ahead: Building School Capacity through NCLB Parent Participation Requirements," *IDRA Newsletter* (San Antonio, Texas: Intercultural Development Research Association, January 2007).

Wilson, B., and D.H. Corbett. *"I didn't know I could do that": Parents learning to be leaders through the Commonwealth Institute for Parent Leadership* (Lexington, Ken.: Commonwealth Institute for Parent Leadership, 2000).

Originally published in the *IDRA Newsletter*, November-December 2007

The Lens for Viewing the Full Dimensions of Families

by Aurelio M. Montemayor, M.Ed.

The 3D Glasses

I'm old enough to remember the first 3D movies with the special glasses that were given out to viewers. Whether it was Bwana Devil or House of Wax, the screen was blurry without the Polaroid plastic lenses. You just couldn't get the full effect without them. In fact, when the film was shown later on TV, the scenes that were meant to jump out at you were uninteresting and made little sense in terms of the story line. You totally missed the novelty of a ball leaping from the screen straight at you. Similarly, if you want to get the full effect of IDRA's family leadership activities, you need to see them through the lens of our principles.

Live Action: Families and their Children

The broad umbrella of families' connection to the education of their children has many strands, each with its own goals. For newborns and very young children, the focus of services is primarily information and support around health and safety. New parents need and want this support.

As the child develops, the early stages of child growth and development become the focus. Discipline, limits and social behaviors are of concern, as are language development and communication. When the child is of school age, education becomes the center focus for most families.

The Root Beer Bottle Bottom Lens

We can choose to gaze at families dealing with their children during these stages and look through the lens of limitation and ignorance to see the families as needing and the children as hurting. We can list, as some popular writers and consultants do, the assumed characteristics of poor families and see the families and children through that lens. This chosen lens colors the viewer's attitude and dictates his or her actions. If something is seen as broken, then the action is to fix it; if lacking, then fill that void.

This deficit stance has been present in our schools for many generations and is reborn for each new generation with perhaps new colors and shiny gloss. But it is still the same old same old. Twenty years ago, a well-known and respected research firm approached IDRA about a survey on dropouts they were conducting. The survey instrument was a long catalog of the many deficits the students might have that were considered possible reasons they had dropped out of school. Might a set of questions about the *institution* have revealed a different set of data?

It can be termed as common sense, pointing out the obvious, quoting the internalized self-recrimination of some families, getting children from poor neighborhoods to attest to the horribleness of their existence, etc. Sadly, this point of view is held and nurtured across the political and class spectrum.

In addition to being a distorted and inaccurate (and certainly unfair) view, it also isn't practical. It doesn't work.

When families partner with school people and the broader community participates, there is a greater possibility for a sustained and positive reform of a school.

So some consultants get hurrahs and hosannas from educators as they reap such high-paid contracts. Why not? Their presentations and advice echo what was already suspected by the participants and is artfully reinforced by the presenter. And all because we care so much about these poor, abused, needy and scarred children. "These poor parents, they've been a mess, but what do you expect? They're poor, not just economically, but in spirit, in language, in culture, in civility, in social skills, in their limited expectations for their children." Ad nauseam.

Another Set of Glasses

IDRA has used a valuing point of view and with dramatically different results. Our constant challenge has been to get the teachers of the students in the program to change glasses… to view the students as they really are: valuable assets rather than as at-risk, close-to-being-lost-by-the-school problems.

This is why our principles are so important. Each one is interrelated with the others but also stands by itself as an important premise and undergirding of our actions in support of parent leadership in education. Following is an overview of IDRA's principles for family leadership in education.

1. Families can be their children's strongest advocates. This premise is based on the natural almost universal inclination in families to defend their children. It points to the potential that all families have in speaking for, defending and supporting their children. The advocate role requires little explanation or rationale when addressing any group of families. The conversation usually shifts to *how* and *when* to advocate effectively. Just as all children are valuable and none is expendable, so is our view of families that each must be respected and treated as the crucial defender and protector of their children.

2. Families of different races, ethnicities, languages and classes are equally valuable. Each group has assets, traditions and a language that is worthy of respect. Our most effective and impactful work with families and their schools happens when this principle is evident in the outreach and work done with families. Families engage with their children's schools and the children blossom.

3. Families care about their children's education and are to be treated with respect, dignity and value. Latinos and other groups consider education of their children a priority. This almost universal concern is the critical connection between families and schools and is a most useful basis for beginning a dialogue and a project that engages families more fully in the education of their children and that underlies effective outreach efforts.

4. Within families, many individuals play a role in children's education. There are many key caretakers of children who are not genetic parents. The combination of all who live within a home are important influences on children and can be a collective force for creating excellent schools. For educators, this means rather than developing activities that assume a biological parent be present, design activities for whomever arrives and rejoice in the presence of whomever the family members are.

5. Family leadership is most powerful at improving education for all children when collective efforts create solutions for the common good. The power that families have in a neighborhood public school is in their numbers. Assertive individuals are good sparks and energizers, but the staying power resides in the network of families. When families connect around the education of their children and move to the group consciousness, they are drawing on the combined intelligence, energy and power to transform a school and to catalyze administrators to raise their hopes, standards and expectations for all children. When families operate out of optimism, draw on individual and neighborhood assets, and move a school to achieve new heights, all children benefit.

6. Families, schools and communities, when drawn together, become a strong, sustainable voice to protect the rights of all children. Transformation and improvement of schools lasts if it is only led from within. Families attempting to reform schools, when only acting as an external force, no matter how strong, rarely last beyond a few years. When families partner with school people and the broader community participates, there is a greater possibility for a sustained and positive reform of a school.

Are We Facing Reality?

A criticism could be made that these principles are romanticizing who families are and what they can accomplish. It's almost the mirror image of the negative deficit model critiqued above.

These premises don't assume all families are perfect or models of virtue or childrearers of the highest order. What these points of view bring is a different set of rules for effective work with parents. They discard "banking" notions of education for parents, that is, that the parents who happen to be poor and/or minority have empty little heads into which we will deposit coins of knowledge.

Under these assumptions, the reason for reaching out to families is to find out what they think, what they expect for their children and from the school, and what critical questions they have.

The reason for bringing parents together in a meeting, session, workshop or any other gathering is to have them analyze, synthesize and evaluate critical pieces of information. The idea is not to make them little lawyers and have them memorize large amounts of data, but to know that key data means and to seek more if it is important and relevant.

An asset-based model of operating doesn't validate what precious knowledge and skills are present in the community because we want to improve their self-image and concept, but because those assets are the strength and power that will transform a school and a neighborhood.

Consultation, for Real, if You Follow Our Drift

For all the criticisms of the *No Child Left Behind Act*, some pieces have been very useful in carrying out our valuing model. Every requirement for a consultation on a Title I campus has been an opportunity to engage families in meaningful conversation and to enlighten teachers and administrators about the validity of our vision and principles.

So whatever changes or is reformed in the new federal education policy, we expect, we wish for, we are prepared to move on to school data presented in meaningful and disaggregated forms; families made partners and co-discussants of the standards; curriculum and instruction happening on a campus; and outreach and connection with the families being real, being personal and being a means to inquire what families think, invite and welcome to the table.

We Knew it Would Happen

It's been heartwarming to see families and their children engaged in seeking and discussing online information, as well as families participating in dynamic dialogues about curriculum and instruction. Yes, it's been positive and motivating, but given our point of view, not surprising.

Originally published in the *IDRA Newsletter*, April 2009

What Parent and Community Engagement Means for Quality Schools

by Rosana G. Rodriguez, Ph.D.

President Barack Obama has said that the chance to get high quality schooling and a college education must not be a privilege of a limited few, it should be a birthright of every single American. This mantra should be adopted by every school. Parent involvement and community engagement are critical vehicles through which the promise of a quality education will be fulfilled. Our definition of engagement must extend far beyond a narrow catch phrase toward a genuine partnership of parents and teachers working together and making decisions together within the teaching and learning process that will have a lasting impact on the future of students.

Current theories regarding the relationship between community involvement and increased school efficiency and student learning are based on the premise that in traditional society, the community is often the provider of children's education (Bray, 2000; Williams, 1997) and therefore, the public owns its schools.

When considering public education, the literature on community participation provides many theories of participation that shed light on the relationship between community involvement and increased school efficacy and student success. Some of the models, such as IDRA's Parent Leadership Model (Montemayor, 2000), offer dimensions around which a community can positively impact its schools: parents as teachers, as resources, as decision makers, and ultimately leaders and trainers of other parents. Within these domains of community participation, the impact of parent involvement can be felt beyond the classroom.

Swift-Morgan (2006) suggests that there are at least six domains for community participation in schools: infrastructure and maintenance, management and administration, teacher support and supervision, pedagogy and classroom support, student supervision, and student recruitment. Jimenez (2002) underscores the importance of the community's role in school administration and management. Muskin (2001) considers the advantages of the community's role in participation in school curriculum. IDRA's President, Dr. María "Cuca" Robledo Montecel (2005), presents the Quality Schools Action Framework where parents and communities play "vital roles in every school reform effort – from fighting for fair funding to making sure that students are not ignored or punished because of the language they speak. As partners in education and catalysts for education policy and funding reform, their role can be critical to helping local neighborhood schools turn the tide of student attrition."

Some theorists develop categories of involvement in education, such as Shaeffer (1994) who offers a ladder of involvement that ranges from the lowest, being the mere use of a service in a school, to the highest, representing true responsibility and power that is described as participation in real decision making at every stage of education. This decision making includes problem identification, feasibility studies, planning, implementation and evaluation. And Williams (1997) makes the important distinction between who in the community is participating: Are only the officials involved or "only the rich with the clout, time and means to participate?"

Administrator and teacher attitudes are key to establishing a culture of engagement that encourages full participation by all the community members

Swift-Morgan (2006) reminds us that the international community recognizes the importance of community participation as a critical ingredient for educational access and quality. Viewing engagement from an international perspective offers worthwhile insights into the scale of community participation as well as potential domains of engagement where parents and community can have greater impact working with schools to ensure they are responsive to all children. Throughout the world, just as in our nation, under-resourced communities are calling for financial incentives as well as technical assistance to assist in learning how to encourage broader based community participation that can lead to improved high school graduation rates and higher access, persistence and graduation rates in higher education.

The international research done by Swift-Morgan (2006) with rural communities delves further into what constitutes community participation and the impact on schooling. In her extensive focus group discussions, she proposes forms of engagement for the future that include the following, which are certainly relevant within the U.S. context:

- participation in ongoing dialogues with school staff on issues of enrollment, academic performance and general school improvement;
- participation in awareness-raising and community participation; and
- assisting with teaching on topics such as culture and language.

Emerging forms of participation include advocacy work, such as parent leadership training, that seeks to identify key issues that relate to quality schooling and raising awareness for changes in policy and practice at the school or state level.

In its advocacy work over the past 35 years, IDRA's parent engagement model and parent leadership training makes the case for all parents – particularly those whose voices are most often not heard – to fully participate in the decision making process. This is especially true in the highest form of parent engagement where parents serve as advocates and trainers of other parents. On this level, parents see the importance of their participation not only for their children, but for themselves, their schools and for the entire community.

Throughout her extensive focus groups with multicultural and multilingual communities in southern Ethiopia, the factors cited by Swift-Morgan (2006) that encourage parent and community engagement in school include the following:

- Encouragement from staff to welcome parent participation;
- Staff expressing their respect for parents and the valuing of different community contributions;
- More meetings among school, parents and community;
- Financial resources allocated to support school expenses and improvement projects; and
- Technical assistance to help formal and informal parent groups manage schools better and facilitate parent and community involvement.

In Swift-Morgan's research, throughout all types of communities, parents expressed a desire for "co-ownership" of the school in partnership with school officials and governments. She found universal parent and community member willingness to contribute in-kind with their time, talent or personal knowledge.

Administrator and teacher attitudes are key to establishing a culture of engagement that encourages full participation by all the community members (Rodríguez & Villarreal, 2003a; 2003b). In areas of advocacy and awareness raising, the involvement of parents, communities and teachers working together through dialogue and action planning can positively impact teaching quality, access to resources for all students, governance and policy at the school and district levels.

In order to ensure that community and parent engagement will be embraced for the wealth of knowledge and support it can provide toward improving the teaching and learning process, institutions of higher education and schools of education also need to partner in preparing a new cadre of teachers who are fully committed to emphasizing teacher-parent relationships. Stressing this aspect is important in the preparation and certification of teachers, in training and retraining teachers, through professional development and through additional research and resources.

The great Spanish philosopher Jose Ortega y Gasset pointed out that every generation "has its own theme, its own preoccupation" (Max-Neef, 1991). One hopes that ours is a relentless quest for quality education for all children through effective community-school partnerships.

The promise of fulfilling every child's birthright to a quality education will become reality only when we fully embrace a vision of teachers and parents as co-leaders, co-creators of a new reality for schools. True partners learn how to work together as significant change agents to implement the Quality Schools Action Framework and can have positive impact on schooling as well as on the quality of life in the surrounding community they serve for generations to come.

Resources

Bray, M. *Community Partnerships in Education: Dimensions, Variations and Implications* (Paris: United Nations Educational, Scientific, and Cultural Organization, 2000).

Jiménez, E. "Empowering Communities and Individuals to Improve Education," paper presented at the World Bank Empowerment Retreat (May 2002).

Max-Neef, M.A. *Human Scale Development: Conception, Application and Further Reflections* (New York: The Apex Press, Council on International and Public Affairs, 1991) pg. 109.

Montemayor, A.M., and A.A. Romero. "Valued Parent Leadership," *IDRA Newsletter* (San Antonio, Texas: Intercultural Development Research Association, June-July 2000).

Muskin, J. "Measuring Community Penetration into the School-Based Learning Process," presented at the annual conference of the Comparative and International Education Society (Washington, D.C.: Comparative and International Education Society, March 2001).

Robledo Montecel, M. "A Quality Schools Action Framework – Framing Systems Change for Student Success," IDRA Newsletter (San Antonio, Texas: Intercultural Development Research Association, November-December 2005).

Rodríguez, R., and A. Villarreal. "Community and Public Engagement in Education – Opportunity and Challenge," *IDRA Newsletter* (San Antonio, Texas: Intercultural Development Research Association, November-December 2003).

Rodríguez, R., and A. Villarreal. "Community-Based Education Reform – Increasing the Educational Level of Communities as an Integral Part of School Reform," *IDRA Newsletter* (San Antonio, Texas: Intercultural Development Research Association, June-July 2003).

Schaeffer, S. *Participation for Educational Change: A Synthesis of Experience* (Paris: UNESCO International Institute for Educational Planning, 1994).

Swift-Morgan, J. "What Community Participation in Schooling Means: Insights from Southern Ethiopia," *Harvard Educational Review* (Fall 2006) Vol. 76, No. 3, pp. 339-368.

Williams, J. H. "Improving School-Community Relations in the Periphery," *Quality Education For All: Community-Oriented Approaches*, H.D. Nielson and W.K. Cummings (Eds.) (New York: Garland Publishing, 1997) pp. 37-78.

Originally published in the *IDRA Newsletter*, April 2009

Student Engagement

The "Fourth-Grade Slump" and Math Achievement

Addressing the Challenge with Student Engagement

by Kristin Grayson, M.Ed., and Veronica Betancourt, M.A.

We've all heard about the fourth-grade slump in reading. Chall first defined the fourth-grade reading slump in 1983 as the time when students fall behind in reading. The premise is that the slump in reading occurs because of the change in academic language required to read grade-level content texts. Starting around the fourth grade, reading shifts from "learning to read" to "reading to learn" with the inclusion of a more extensive vocabulary, a heavier content load and a need for more background knowledge (Chall & Jacobs, 2003).

Coles states that this type of reading requires students to be familiar with less common words, employ wider reading and have a deeper comprehension of the content material (Coles, 2007).

Noted second language linguist and researcher Cummins further makes reference to the fourth-grade slump and English language learners in many of his articles. He spoke about it just last year in a speech at the California Teachers of English to Speakers of Other Languages conference in San Diego (Meteor, 2007).

But there is a comparable slump that occurs in math achievement. Achievement gaps in math increase as the grade level goes up. The National Center for Educational Statistics as cited by Freeman and Crawford finds that 82 percent of Hispanic students nationwide are below proficient in math in the fourth grade (2008).

For the state of Texas, an analysis of Texas Assessment of Knowledge and Skills scores for 2006 (Texas AEIS data) shows a steady decrease for all three major subgroups for White, African American, and Hispanic students beginning at the fourth grade and continuing through the ninth grade.

For English language learners, the *Biennial Report to Congress on the Implementation of the Title III State Formula Grant Program; School Years 2004-2006*, indicates that only one state showed that English language learners had met annual yearly progress (AYP) in mathematics. The report also found that achievement in reading and math for English language learners decreased as the grade level of the students increased (Zehr, 2008).

A Pew Research Center Report states that across the board English language learners are less likely to achieve in reading and math. In fact, achievement gaps are in the double digits in mathematics in the five states with the largest English language learner populations (Fry, 2007). Clearly, the achievement gap and math achievement is a matter of grave concern.

The Language of Math

Just like reading is related to academic language, math is reflective of a specific academic language. Math has two types of language, words and symbols. And although math might be considered a universal language, it can be difficult for any student to understand. Math has new terms, such as *coefficient* and *tessellation*, and common words that are used in a specific mathematical way, such as *scale* and *change* (Freeman & Crawford, 2008). Math uses terms that may be used in other subject areas with different meanings, such as *table, slope* and *run*. Additionally, there are multiple math terms that mean the same thing, such as *slope, rate of change, rise/run* and *delta y over delta x*.

> One approach to addressing the drop in math achievement scores, especially as related to the fourth-reading slump, is to consider student engagement during math instruction.

The academic language of math includes the ability to read, write and engage in substantive academic conversations (Freeman & Crawford, 2008).

Etsy states: "Like other languages, mathematics has its own vocabulary, grammar (principles that govern the correct use of a language), syntax (the part of grammar that concerns rules of word order), synonyms, negations, conventions, abbreviations and sentence structure… It is a specialized language with its own concepts and symbols that must be learned. Even if you can do some math, you might not be able to read math. Learning to read math takes work." (2007)

Student Engagement Affects Math Achievement

Math achievement is critical for all students. In fact, it is considered to be the strongest predictor of college success (Sciarra & Seirup, 2008).Thus, improving instruction and achievement in math for all students has been at the forefront of educational topics in recent years. The final report of the National Mathematics Advisory Panel has an array of recommendations for improving math achievement in U.S. schools, including strengthening teacher math preparation for elementary teachers (U.S. Department of Education, 2008). For instructional practices, the panel recommends a combination of "student centered" and "teacher directed" methods. Research also supports other instructional methods under specified circumstances.

One approach to addressing the drop in math achievement scores, especially as related to the fourth-reading slump, is to consider student engagement during math instruction. In a 2008 study of U.S. high school students, investigators conducted a two-way analysis of covariance to test for the interaction of race and three levels of engagement and the effect on math achievement (Sciarra & Seirup, 2008). Key findings showed that the overall combination of three types of engagement (behavioral, emotional and cognitive) was significantly related to math achievement for all racial groups. Emotional engagement was a more significant predictor for Hispanic students than for other groups. Student engagement and math achievement are related.

What is student engagement? What does it look like in the mathematics classroom? How can elementary teachers, especially, help students engage in the language and the content of mathematics?

The Sciarra and Seirup study describes three types of school engagement. *Behavioral engagement* has to do with effort and appropriate conduct. *Emotional engagement* concerns students' feelings and a sense of belonging. *Cognitive engagement* relates to the student investment in learning, the belief in the importance of doing well in school and doing what it takes to go beyond the minimum requirements for completion of coursework (2008).

> If students are not engaged or if assessment shows that students have not mastered the mathematical concept and language, the teacher can use the indicators for student engagement to guide his or her choice of the next instructional strategy to implement.

IDRA also has conducted an extensive review of the literature of student engagement and of English language learner engagement, in particular (Solís, 2008). IDRA has compiled a list of student engagement indicators that a teacher can use to observe students during class to help guide teacher decisions for strategy adjustment and implementation. These student indicators cluster around four areas of evidence showing:

- Students as part of a community;
- Student use of academic language, student concentration and focus;
- Student confidence in performance; and
- Students as active and participatory.

Strategies that teachers can use to help students, especially English language learners, engage in the learning around these cluster areas include:

- Making the classroom environment and learning context conducive for interaction;
- Ensuring that lesson preparation, delivery and plans integrate language and content with a variety of interaction modes (small group, pairs, large group) while addressing language proficiency levels;
- Building teacher-student relationships that promote trust and high expectations with a respect for student background, culture and native language;

- Using a sheltered instruction approach that makes content comprehensible while systematically and purposefully improving English language proficiency and skills; and
- Including active and interactive experiences that are structured, rigorous and accountable.

A Student Engagement Scenario

Following is an imaginary scenario to show application of observation for student engagement and teacher strategy adjustment.

***

Fourth grade students are completing a handout with math word problems involving multiplication and division. The teacher observes that at least half of the class is not engaged. Those students happen to be the ones who usually score poorly on classroom assessments. Some are daydreaming, some are fiddling with things in their desk, while other students are playing with their pencils and erasers and talking and laughing with other students around them. Students who are engaged are writing on the handout, mouthing numbers and gesturing procedures that they are mentally doing – in other words they are immersed in the task.

The teacher wants all students, especially struggling math students, to be engaged. She decides to take another approach the next day. Instead of having students individually work on handouts, she arranges the desks in pairs. Her initial presentation of the lesson is begun by asking students a question about a real-life situation where one might use the concept under study. A question that addresses multiplication might be, "How could you determine the amount of food to cook if you add six relatives coming to eat along with the six people already present in your household?" Students talk among themselves, and then the teacher presents the concept under study by using PowerPoint screens and real-life objects along with the mathematic numerical representation (visuals for comprehensibility).

She asks students to brainstorm words that she has used in the presentation that they might use in other situations or in other subject areas, such as the *words times, table* and *order* (systematic building of word knowledge). She asks students if any of the words are like words in their home language, pointing out words such as *division* and *multiplication* (awareness of cognates for language transfer).

Then the students work in pairs. She structures the work so that for each word problem only one student will see, read aloud and explain how to solve the problem to the other. The student is to use vocabulary words (academic mathematical language) that are specified by the teacher and posted in the front of the class. The other student is to record the solving of the problem according to the exact description by the first student (encourage both language comprehension and production skills). Discussion ensues among the pairs about the solution to the problem. Then the roles are reversed (encourage interaction), and another problem is read, explained and solution written.

In the final phase of instruction, pairs work together with another pair to compare their work and agree on a final solution to the problem (pairs to small group). The class, as a large group, then receives the final feedback from the teacher.

During the entire class period, the teacher is monitoring for student engagement and making adjustments to the process to maximize the engagement. At the end of the class period, the teacher briefly reflects and mentally notes strategies used that helped students engage conceptually and linguistically in mathematics.

***

Student engagement is one of the critical components of the IDRA Math Smart! professional development model. While there are other critical features to effective math instruction, the importance of student engagement in math achievement cannot be understated. Student engagement observation indicators can be the first step for a teacher to transform his or her approach to improving mathematics achievement starting at the elementary school level. This might be a paradigm shift for some teachers. The desired shift is to change the initial focus from, "What strategy should I use or try?" to "Are students engaged in learning with what I am already doing?"

If students are engaged, as evidenced by the indicators for student engagement, then the instruction can proceed with the approach being used. If students are not engaged or if assessment shows that students have not mastered the mathematical concept and language, the teacher can use the indicators to guide his or her choice of the next instructional strategy to implement.

Research is clear that increased engagement correlates with increased achievement in mathematics. By focusing on student engagement, teachers can help students improve in mathematics achievement.

Resources

Anthony, A. "Output Strategies for English-Language Learners: Theory to Practice," *The Reading Teacher* (2008) 61, 472-482.

August, D., and T. Shanahan (eds.). *Executive Summary: Developing Literacy in Second-Language Learners: Report of the National Literacy Panel on Language-Minority Children and Youth* (Mahwah, N.J.: Lawrence Erlbaum Associates, 2006).

Chall, J.S., and V.A. Jacobs. "Poor Children's Fourth-Grade Slump," *American Educator* (Spring 2003).

Coles, G. "The 4th Grade Slump: What's Wrong with the Brains of Slumping Children?," *District Administration* (October 23, 2007).

Etsy, E. *The Language of Mathematics* (Published by author, professor at Montana State University, 2007).

Freeman, B., and L. Crawford. "Creating a Middle School Mathematics Curriculum for English-Language Learners," *Remedial and Special Education* (2008) 29, pp. 9-19.

Fry, R. *How Far Behind in Math and Reading are English Language Learners?* (Washington, D.C.: Pew Hispanic Center, June 2007).

Meteor, B. "Jim Cummins Demolishes NCLB's Ideology and Practice," *Daily Kos Newspaper* (2007).

Sciarra, D., and H. Seirup. "The Multidimensionality of School Engagement and Math Achievement among Racial Groups," *Professional School Counseling* (2008).

Solís, A. "Teaching for Cognitive Engagement – Materializing the Promise of Sheltered Instruction," *IDRA Newsletter* (San Antonio, Texas: Intercultural Development Research Association, April 2008).

Texas Education Agency. Academic Excellence Indicator System, 2005-06 (Austin, Texas: Texas Education Agency, 2006).

U.S. Department of Education. The Final Report of the National Mathematics Advisory Panel (Washington, D.C.: U.S. Department of Education, 2008).

Zehr, M. "English-Learners Still Lag on Reading, Math Progress," *Education Week* (April 2008).

Originally published in the *IDRA Newsletter*, August 2008

You Can't Win if You Don't Get to Play

Effectively Engaging All English Language Learners

by Adela Solís, Ph.D., and Kristin Grayson, M.Ed.

Two English language learner youths talk about their school experience. One says: "Classes would be more interesting if teachers were excited, had us do interesting things and relate subjects to what's happening around us. I hate it when all we do is silly worksheets" (Walqui, 2000).

Another student says: "It was really bad… I was almost the only one… and there were no translators. So I was just sitting there, and they were speaking English to me, and I didn't understand anything" (Peitzman & Gadda, 1994).

From these statements, one thing is clear. These students are not engaged in learning. There are many reasons students are disengaged. For these English language learners, it appears that the irrelevancy of classwork and lack of access to comprehensible instruction cause them to disengage.

As maturing adolescents, it is likely they recognize the implications for not being in the game of learning. The academic learning process, in a way, is no different than participating in sports. To succeed, it is necessary to suit up and show up for the game and, more importantly, to be able to play. Just like the players in that all important ball game, English language learners cannot win if they do not get to play.

English language learners need to be cognitively engaged in the learning process. Regardless of their background or English language proficiency, they should have meaningful opportunities to succeed in school.

These authors, as IDRA professional development specialists, have been working for some time on a new professional development project that focuses on the engagement of English language learners in secondary English as a second language and content classes. The purpose of this initiative is to bring the literature on student engagement to bear on serving these students.

Guided by the literature and first-hand experiences working with teachers and students in sheltered instruction classrooms, IDRA has conceptualized a professional development model to refine and extend teachers' sheltered instruction expertise so they can strategically plan and deliver sheltered instruction for engagement. This model, Engagement-Based Sheltered Instruction (EBSI), and its related research-base are the topics of this article.

Literature Review

The literature on student engagement offers insights to help define engagement and elaborates on the nature and extent of the problem, its implications and solutions. From this literature, we know that engagement is a prerequisite of learning. That is, without engagement there is no learning. Further, there is a distinction between superficial, or procedural, engagement and substantive, or cognitive, engagement. It is only through the latter that learning actually occurs (McLaughlin, et al., 2005).

The condition for learning has two dimensions: *internal factors*, or things residing within the student, and *external factors*, typically recognized as the contexts in which learning occurs (Hall & Bissell, 2006).

Motivation and discipline often are cited as internal factors that influence engagement (Voke, 2002), as are students' socio-emotional readiness and level of skills, such as academic skills and English skills (Walqui, 2000). These sources on student engagement reveal specific characteristics of student behavior that serve as *evidence of student engagement* and are part of the Engagement-Based Sheltered Instruction model.

> There is a distinction between superficial, or procedural, engagement and substantive, or cognitive, engagement. It is only through the latter that learning actually occurs

Certainly, for English language learners, limited English proficiency and academic skills play a large part in their disengagement. Cummins (2001) contributes significantly to the understanding of engagement and the English language learner. He asserts that a connection exists between cognitive engagement and student identity. His premises are expressed like this: "Cognitive engagement is a prerequisite of academic success. For students dominant in a language other than English, cognitive engagement occurs in the language they understand. Negative teacher attitudes toward the student and his native language affects his identity (feelings about self) and inhibits engagement. The teacher then must affirm the student's identity. In doing so, the student then creates conditions for maximum identity investment in the learning process. There is a reciprocal relationship between cognitive engagement and identity investment: the more students learn, the more their academic self concept grows and the more academically engaged they become" (2001).

Besides (student) internal factors, cognitive engagement also is dependent on external factors. A good portion of the literature indicates that the school in general and the teacher specifically can influence students' willingness and ability to stay focused in the learning process. The number of suggestions in the literature on what teachers can do to engage students is extensive. This literature seems to be an important part of the pedagogical content knowledge base, or the knowledge of how to teach specific content areas. (University of Northern Iowa, 1999; Walqui, 2000)

The Sheltered Instruction Observation Protocol model (Echevarria, et al., 2004; Center for Applied Linguistics, 2004), the most recent of several sheltered instruction approaches, provides a framework for effectively instructing English language learners that promotes engagement. The authors stress the importance of lesson delivery for engagement and describe three aspects of engagement – allocated time, engaged time and academic learning time – as aspects of efficient and rigorous instruction (Echevarria, et al., 2004).

ESL literacy research (Kinsella, 2000 and 2006) similarly stresses rigorous student engagement. The author incorporates into her language and literacy training approach strategies for *structured learning engagement.*

The general and English language learner-specific sources cited above reveal contextual factors and teacher behaviors that are predictive of English language learner engagement that are pedagogical dimensions of English language learner instruction addressed in the EBSI model.

EBSI – Highlights of the Research-Base Model

IDRA's Engagement-Based Sheltered Instruction model focuses on student engagement within sheltered instruction. The model was developed based on the literature that stresses its importance and on first-hand experiences that reveal the absence of substantive cognitive engagement in the instruction of English language learners. It is designed to more rigorously and strategically bring about desired learning. Following are some key components of the model.

Tools for Observing Engagement

Observing for evidence of *student engagement* is a unique feature of the model. Observable student behaviors can be noted as evidence of student engagement. These have been organized into the following evidence categories: sense of community; use of language; concentration and focus; confidence in performance; and active involvement and independence. These behaviors are included in a set of indicators and are one part of the Student Engagement Observation Tool.

Observing for teachers making engagement happen is a second part of this observation tool. The sound pedagogy predictive of English language learner engagement was organized into dimensions containing specific indicators that can be observed as evidence of engagement-based instruction:

1. Classroom environment and learning context conducive to interaction;
2. Lesson preparation and delivery plans;
3. Teacher-student relationships that promote trust and high expectations;

4. Comprehensible content and language teaching (i.e., sheltered instruction);
5. Active-interactive experiences; and
6. Structured engagement tasks (or specific techniques for focused participation).

Training and In-Class Support

This dynamic professional development focuses first on assessment of the current status of ESL teaching and levels of student engagement. Training and support are then offered to extend teachers' knowledge of second language acquisition principles and sheltered instruction and to develop insight and expertise in structuring content teaching for maximum student engagement.

Technology and assessment tools for engagement-based sheltered instruction are interwoven into the training and assistance that are part of this model. Areas of training and support include:

- Serving English Language Learners and Current Levels of Engagement;
- English Language Learner Needs and English Language Proficiency Levels;
- Understanding the Language Demands of the Content Area Classroom, Texts and Tests;
- Understanding Cognitive Engagement;
- Strategies for Comprehensible Content and Language;
- Planning, Teaching and Observing for Maximum Cognitive Engagement of English Language Learners; and
- Technology as a Tool for Student Engagement.

The Engagement-Based Sheltered Instruction model is helping teachers feel empowered to make a difference for English language learners, build trusting relationships with English language learners and, very importantly, present content in a comprehensible way to all students to be sure they are engaged. These are teachers who understand and act on the notion that *you can't win if you don't play.*

The IDRA EBSI professional development model is designed to accommodate each district's or school's unique needs with a combination of training sessions and individualized in-class assistance.

Contact IDRA at 210-444-1710 or contact@idra.org to learn more about how EBSI can help your teachers and English language learners achieve academic success.

Resources

Center for Applied Linguistics. *Using the SIOP Model: Professional Development Manual for Sheltered Instruction* (Washington, D.C.: Center for Applied Linguistics, 2004).

Cummins, J. "Understanding Academic Language Learning: Making It Happen in the Classroom," chapter 5. In *Negotiating Identities: Education for Empowerment in a Diverse Society* (second edition) (Los Angeles: California Association for Bilingual Education, 2001).

Echevarria, J., and M.E. Vogt, D.J. Short. *Making Content Comprehensible for English Learners: The SIOP Model* (second edition) (Boston: Pearson, Allyn and Bacon, 2004).

Hall, D.M., and A.N. Bissell. "Who Are We Trying to Help? A Framework for Understanding the Nature of Academically Vulnerable College Learners and Implications for Practice," conference presentation (Durham, N.C.: Duke University, 2006).

Kinsella, K. Structured "Academic Talk" for English Learners: A Key to Narrowing the Verbal Gap in K-12 Classrooms," presentation at OELA Fifth Annual Celebrate Our Rising Stars Summit (Washington, D.C.: Office of English Language Acquisition, October 2006).

Kinsella, K. *Reading and the Need for Strategic Lexical Development for Secondary ESL Students* (California Social Studies Review, 2000).

McLaughlin, M., and D.J. McGrath, M.A. Burian-Fitzgerald, L. Lanahan, M. Scotchmer, C. Enyeart, L. Salganik. *Student Content Engagement as a Construct for the Measurement of Effective Classroom Instruction and Teacher Knowledge* (Washington, D.C.: American Institutes for Research, 2005).

Peitzman, F., and G. Gadda (Eds.). *With Different Eyes: Insights into Teaching Language Minority Students Across the Disciplines* (White Plains, N.Y.: Longman Publishers Group, 1994).

University of Northern Iowa. *Technology as a Facilitator of Quality Education Model* (A Component of Integrating New Technologies into the Methods of Education (Cedar Falls, Iowa: University of Northern Iowa, College of Education, 1999).

Voke, H. "Student Engagement: Motivating Students to Learn," *Infobrief* (Alexandria, Va.: Association for Supervision and Curriculum Development, February, 2002) No. 28.

Walqui, A. *Access and Engagement: Program Design and Instructional Approaches for Immigrant Students in Secondary School*, chapter 4. (McHentry, Il.: Delta Systems, 2000).

Originally published in the *IDRA Newsletter*, March 2007

Mentoring New Teachers for First-Day, First-Year Success

by Adela Solís, Ph.D.

A word commonly associated with the beginning teacher is *struggle*. That's because many teachers begin their careers struggling. The optimism and excitement typical of new professionals also is there, of course, but these feelings seem to dissipate faster in new teachers.

What is more common to see in the first day and first year of teaching is much anxiety and confusion (Wong & Wong, 2009) with little help in learning the ropes of teaching, which causes many to change schools or leave within the first four years (Baldacci & Moore Johnson, 2006). The mentoring and coaching provided to novice teachers in the early stages of their careers is critical to promoting teacher excellence, retention and student success.

Being a new teacher means being concerned, from day one, with testing and accountability, with teaching a learner-centered curriculum and, most importantly, with getting to know children and parents who in most parts of the country come from diverse culture and language backgrounds.

Throughout the year, many new teachers ask these questions: How do I build relationships with my students and my colleagues? If I teach to the test can I really reach all of my students? What if they don't speak English?

Being a mentor teacher, then, requires that the specific needs of new teachers be addressed thoroughly through strategies informed by national research, state guidelines and insights from fellow mentors. The mentoring suggestions in this article come precisely from these sources. They are incorporated into the mentoring for success training strategies employed by the IDRA professional development team that trains mentor teachers via its Coaching and Mentoring for Novice Teacher Model.

Mentoring for Success Principles

Research on what works in schools informs the professional practice of mentoring and teaching. Several principles derived from the literature guide our work in preparing mentors to help beginning teachers succeed:

- Peer mentoring and coaching by experienced teachers is a powerful way to support beginning teachers (New Teacher Center, 2008; Kortman & Honaker, 2004).

- An experienced teacher does not necessarily make a good mentor (Daresh, 2003; New Teacher Center, 2008).
- The heart of mentoring is providing instructional support in the classroom (ASSIST Beginning Teachers, 2006a).
- The culture and belief system of the classroom and the school as a whole play an important role on the level of teacher success with diverse children (Villarreal, 2009).
- Highly qualified teachers teach all students to high standards (TEA, 2002).
- Teachers in diverse classrooms can teach for student success when they are empowered to become highly qualified culturally proficient teachers (Lindsey, et al., 2007; Michigan State University, 2007).

Principles in Practice

Putting mentoring principles into practice involves taking strategic steps to ensure that mentors satisfy the new teacher's needs and as well as state expectations and pedagogical requirements. A mentor asking, *How can I be there for the new teacher on his or her first day and first year?*, can follow these selected important suggestions to put into practice strategies for mentoring success.

1. Be the Right Mentor

Mentoring for success must include a set of procedures for mentor selection (by the school), but it is even more essential that prospective mentors reflect on why they want to be mentors. Questions a teacher should ask before agreeing to be a mentor include: Should I be a mentor? What can I offer a beginning teacher? How can I be responsive to a beginning teacher's needs? How can I work with beginning teachers to foster their professional growth?

An important next step for new mentors is to assess the mentoring expectations set by the school or school district. Some desired characteristics for mentors in Texas classrooms are described in the Texas Beginning Educator Support System (TxBESS) for example and include the following: (a) having a wide repertoire of experiences and skills; (b) having the ability to provide different types of mentoring and support activities that are based on what new teachers want and need; and (c) being willing to participate in appropriate and rigorous training (Texas SBEC, 2005). A good source for more ideas on being the right mentor can be found at http://www.assist.educ.msu.edu/ASSIST.

2. Address the Beginning Teacher Teaching Standards

A well-designed mentoring program promotes teaching excellence and in turn meets local and state teaching standards. To provide on-target mentoring and support, a mentor should be familiar with and use the teaching standards or expectations for new teachers.

In Texas, the standards are called the TxBESS Framework (Texas SBEC, 2005). This framework provides parameters for mentors to guide new teachers to plan and deliver instruction that is learner-centered in an environment that promotes excellence and equity.

3. Focus on What Beginning Teachers Need, Want and Value

When new teachers feel valued and fulfilled and their students are successful, teachers will excel and want to stay. An important role of the mentor teacher is to assess the needs of the new teacher in a timely and responsive manner. This initial assessment should keep in mind an important rule of thumb: if the new teacher says something is a need, then it is a need. For the sake of first-day survival, it is important for the mentor to listen and honor the requests of the new teacher. Later, the mentor may use his or her own expertise and insight to discern needs (Moir, 2004). For example, at mid-year, the new teacher may say that he's still struggling with discipline, when in reality creativity in lesson delivery is the underlying issue.

Discovering what new teachers need requires more than listening though. To build success throughout the first year, assessment must be systematic and integrated as much as possible with mentoring and coaching activities. The mentor can begin with a framework that organizes mentoring into three types: emotional, technical and instructional (ASSIST Beginning Teachers, 2006b; Wong & Wong 2009).

Integrated mentoring and assessment may look like this: A mentor visits to help with classroom management and concurrently gives technical support in record-keeping and showing how the technology works. During a meeting to discuss a lesson, emotional support is provided by assuring the new teacher that students do like her and that she will be an important member of the grade level team. As the survival phases passes, the mentor can move into mentoring for instruction because instruction is a heart of mentoring and coaching. Many suggestions for addressing what diverse new teachers, need, want and value can be accessed online at http://teachers.net and http://teachers.net/gazette/wordpress/october-2009/.

Some tools that yield accurate assessments include: (a) interviewing the new teacher during the first mentor-mentee session; (b) observing teaching during an unplanned classroom visit; (c) analyzing videos or audio recordings of teaching; (d) examining the classroom setting to see how it is organized; and (e) taking notes of student feedback and reaction during lessons (Solís, 2007a).

4. Adopt a Valuing Perspective to Mentoring

Mentors who acknowledge the principle that new teachers will excel and want to stay teaching when they feel valued and fulfilled can and should easily adopt a valuing perspective to mentoring. What does valuing mean? IDRA's work, whether with students, families or teachers, is grounded in a set of valuing assumptions. The intent is to champion and speak for the inclusive and nondiscriminatory idea that all students are inherently good and worthy of being treated with respect, dignity and value (Montemayor

& Romero, 2000). IDRA's Aurelio Montemayor describes the IDRA Valuing Assumptions further in Episode 11 of the Classnotes podcast (http://www.idra.org/Podcasts).

IDRA's professional development, including the mentoring and coaching conducted in many schools, is guided by this valuing philosophy. It is expressed like this: During professional development, trainers and mentors: (a) respect the knowledge and skills of all teachers; (b) treat teachers as partners and adult learners; and (c) identify teachers' assets and build on their strengths. Mentors of new teachers committed to a valuing perspective to mentoring can write and post in their room a statement like this: "I commit to Maggie (new teacher) that I will be a critical friend and will listen as much as I talk, and, further, that my advice will always be prefaced with statements of the great things I see her do."

5. Follow a Culturally Responsive Mentoring and Coaching Plan

An effective mentor knows that the path to student success for the new teacher is through a rigorous and relevant instructional approach. Rigor is promoted when the mentor uses coaching. Coaching is a collegial act. It is about having an advocate and a partner who can stimulate curiosity, facilitate learning and support specific needs (Peddy, 1998).

Relevance is accomplished when instruction embraces the diverse characteristics (needs, interests and values) of all students (Solís, 2009a; Villarreal, 2009). One particular coaching approach, Culturally Proficient Coaching (Lindsey, et al., 2007), provides a framework for mentoring that can accomplish the goal of rigorous-relevant instruction. It brings together a set of strategies from two models (see Solís, 2009b). One is *Cultural Proficiency for School Leaders* (described in Lindsey, et al., 2007), which incorporates strategies for valuing, respecting and honoring diverse backgrounds while looking deeply at one's own beliefs. The other is *Cognitive Coaching* (Costa & Garmston, 2009), which involves the use of self-directed learning and mediated thinking strategies to build the new teachers' critical thinking and teaching skills. The desired end result of cultural proficiency in this model is for the mentor and new teacher alike to move in a positive direction along a cultural proficiency continuum that includes these levels: destructiveness, incapacity, blindness, pre-competence, competence and proficiency (Lindsey, et al., 2007).

A mentor's cultural proficiency coaching action plan to help a new teacher deal with sensitive diversity situations (as expressed in this statement: "I can't stand the sound of Spanish in my classroom") may do the following: (1) Use the basic structure of cognitive coaching: reflecting, planning and problem-solving; and (2) During conference or classroom observations, the mentor looks through a cultural proficiency lens using five steps of the cultural proficiency action plan. (For a complete description of the action plan, see Lindsey, et al., 2007.)

Five Steps of the Action Plan for Cultural Proficiency

- Anticipate and be conscious of own emotional state and that of person being coached.
- Listen and look for verbal and nonverbal responses that elucidate cultural issues or content important to the person being coached.
- Respond thoughtfully using coaching skills, such as: pausing to allow thinking time, paraphrasing what is being said and inviting thinking through probing to get specifics of the situation.
- Monitor conversation for zone of opportunity (to shift thinking toward equity) by listening for level of awareness of culturally competent behavior and posing questions to prompt flexibility and new perspectives, and assessing your level of cultural competence.
- Determine your intention and choose appropriate actions: continuing the conversation as a coach, or offer support and resources as a consultant.

Source: Culturally Proficient Coaching: Supporting Educators to Create Equitable Schools by Lindsey, Martinez and Lindsey (2007) pp 151-152.

Conclusion

The desired outcome for sharing the mentoring for success strategies in this article is to empower mentor teachers to transform the struggling new teacher into a competent, highly qualified, culturally proficient teacher. By putting the key principle-driven practices into action, it becomes possible to materialize the optimism and excitement that new teachers bring to school on the first day and during the critical first year. By eliminating uncertainty and anxiety and giving new teachers the right tools to succeed, it will be more likely that they will feel valued, fulfilled and willing to make teaching a life-long career, even in the most challenging classrooms.

The mentoring for success strategies described in this article are part of a larger repertoire of tools and techniques for training mentor of beginning teachers. IDRA's Coaching and Mentoring for Novice Teachers model is the framework for mentor training tailored to district needs. The Mentor as a Culturally Proficient Coach and Summer Institutes for First Year Mentors are two focused (long-term) training programs available for school districts upon request.

Resources

ASSIST Beginning Teachers. Organizing Induction: Teacher Mentors, web page (Michigan State University, 2006). http://assist.educ.msu.edu/ASSIST/school/mentor/indexmentor.htm

ASSIST Beginning Teachers. What Can I Offer the Beginning Teacher, web page (Michigan State University, 2006). http://assist.educ.msu.edu/ASSIST/school/mentor/educmentoring/indexducment.htm

Baldacci, L., and S. Moore Johnson. "Why New Teachers Leave… Why New Teachers Stay," *American Educator* (Washington D.C.: American Federation of Teachers, February 2006).

Costa, A., and R.J. Garmston. Overview of Cognitive Coaching Center for Cognitive Coaching, web page (Highlands Ranch, N.J.: Center for Cognitive Coaching, 2009). http://www.cognitivecoaching.com/overview.htm

Daresh, J.C. *Teachers Mentoring Teachers: A Practical Approach to Helping New and Experienced Staff* (Thousand Oaks, Calif.: Corwin Press, 2003).

Davis, B. "A Menu for Mentor Growth," *Reflections* (Santa Cruz, Calif.: New Teacher Center, Winter 2007) Vol. 9, No. 1, pp. 2-3, 19.

Kortman, S., and C. Honaker. *The Mentor Teacher: Guiding You Through the Mentoring Process* (Dubuque, Iowa: Kendall/Hunt, 2004).

Lindsey, D.B., and R. Martinez, R.B. Lindsey. *Culturally Proficient Coaching: Supporting Educators to Create Equitable Schools* (Thousand Oaks, Calif.: Corwin Press, 2007).

Michigan State University. "What is Culturally Responsive Teaching," *ASSIST Beginning Teachers Newsletter* (February 2007).

Moir, E. "On the Move with Formative Assessment," *Reflections* (Santa Cruz, Calif.: New Teacher Center, Fall 2004) Vol. 7, No. 2.

Montemayor, A. "Valuing Families in Children's Education," IDRA Classnotes Podcast, Episode 11 (San Antonio, Texas: Intercultural Development Research Association, April 20, 2007).

Montemayor, A., and A.A. Romero. "Valued Parent Leadership," *IDRA Newsletter* (San Antonio, Texas: Intercultural Development Research Association, June-July 2000).

New Teacher Center. "High Quality Mentoring and Induction Practices," *Reflections* (Santa Cruz, Calif.: New Teacher Center, Winter 2008) Vol. 10, No. 1, pp 14-15.

Peddy, S. *The Art of Mentoring: Lead, Follow or Get Out of the Way* (Corpus Christi, Texas: Bullion Books, 1998).

Solís, A. "The Teacher as a Culturally Proficient Coach," IDRA Classnotes Podcast, Episode 58 (San Antonio, Texas: Intercultural Development Research Association, September 18, 2009).

Solís, A. "Culturally Responsive Mentoring and Coaching: An Overview," *Mentors as Culturally Proficient Training Handbook* (San Antonio, Texas: Intercultural Development Research Association, 2009).

Solís, A. "Discovering New Teacher Needs" (handout), in *Coaching and Mentoring Novice Teachers Regional Training Handbook* (San Antonio, Texas: Intercultural Development Research Association, 2007).

Solís, A. "IDRA Valuing Approach to Professional Development" (reading), in *Coaching and Mentoring Novice Teachers Regional Training Handbook* (San Antonio, Texas: Intercultural Development Research Association, 2007).

Texas Education Agency. *Professional Development and Appraisal System: Teacher Manual* (Austin, Texas: Texas Education Agency, 2005).

Texas Education Agency. No Child Left Behind Public Law 110-107: Goal 1, brochure (Austin, Texas: Texas Education Agency, Fall 2002).

Texas State Board of Educator Certification. Texas Beginning Educator Support System, Tx-BESS Framework (Austin, Texas: Texas Education Agency, 2005).

Villarreal, A. "Ten Principles that Guide the Development of an Effective Educational Plan for English Language Learners at the Secondary Level – Part II," *IDRA Newsletter* (San Antonio, Texas: Intercultural Development Research Association, February 2009).

Wong, H., and R. Wong. *The First Days of School: How to Be An Effective Teacher* (Mountain View, Calif.: Wong Publications, 2009).

Originally published in the *IDRA Newsletter*, November-December 2009

Curriculum Quality and Access

IDRA's Community of Learners Approach to Instructional Quality

Three Critical Questions that are Rarely Asked in a Curriculum Audit

by Abelardo Villarreal, Ph.D., and Bradley Scott, Ph.D.

If you are not satisfied with the success that your campus is having with traditionally underserved students – primarily English language learners, low-income students and minority students – or if you have been cited for the poor academic performance of any or all of these groups of underserved students, you may be wondering if this is the year when you will be on the list of schools that did not meet adequate yearly progress (AYP) requirements and face the scrutiny of students, parents and the community as a whole.

Or perhaps your campus is on its second year of warned status because of failure to show improvement in meeting the performance needs of underserved students.

Or maybe you are simply seeking ways to increase your school's responsiveness to ensure that *all* students have the opportunity to an education that reflects quality and excellence. Improvement plans have been developed and implemented, and still the desired academic improvement is not obtained.

Sometimes there are flaws in the questions we ask ourselves when planning school improvement. This article provides school administrators and communities with a brief description of the three most critical questions that are rarely asked in a curriculum audit and suggests a community of learners approach to appraising curriculum and instructional quality of programs and practices and incorporating these questions.

First Rare Question

Are administrators, teachers and other school personnel articulating and showing evidence of high academic expectations for traditionally underserved students?

Recently, in a student-focused group activity, students were asked to name one major reason that students fail in their classes. The response given by many students was that they know some teachers do not care for them. The students felt that teachers do not think highly of them as learners.

Research correlates low expectations held by teachers to low achievement and performance of students. How he or she is treated, respected and valued by important others, including administrators, teachers and other education personnel, has a domino effect on a student's self concept, self-efficacy and persistence that immensely contributes to the level of success that he or she will attain in school.

For many students, attending a school with a teacher who already has a preconceived disparaging concept of who they are, what their educational aspirations are and how much they will be able to accomplish is a negative reality that cannot be ignored if we, education planners and change agents, are to effectively guide a curriculum audit effort.

Unfortunately, many students are victims of the "low expectations vicious cycle" whereby teachers will change their expectations of students only after seeing them progress. Yet students feel confined and will never show that required progress because they recognize the teachers' low expectations of them.

Tragically, in this negative scenario, the opportunity to show progress is never an option. And the self-fulfilling stereotype that these student groups cannot learn prevails. Communicating low expectations has a great propensity to truncate achievement.

As educators, we must always remember the words of Peter Senge: "All human beings are born with unique gifts. The healthy functioning of our community depends on its [schools'] capacity to develop each gift" (Morris & Hammonds, 2004).

Ways to address this issue in a curriculum audit include conducting a self-survey of teachers; conducting a self-survey of students, particularly middle and high school students; and conducting "reflection and action" sessions to describe what school practices should be implemented.

Second Rare Question

Does the school's vision specifically speak to the academic performance and college preparation of traditionally underserved student groups, and if so, is the school showing evidence that adequate and timely progress is being achieved?

As part of an improvement planning process, schools are asked to collaborate with the community in establishing a vision for the school. This vision should guide the school in setting the right direction or course to follow.

When working on the school vision, it is common to address all students in the vision, but the planned action often tends to shortchange the spirit and intent of the vision and, in particular, minority, low-income and English language learners. For all practical purposes, in some cases, the school vision has benefited *some* students but not those students who have been traditionally underserved.

The question becomes: What needs to happen in developing a vision that ensures that all student groups are covered in that school vision?

A working definition of the vision is one way to address this issue. The working definition describes how the school will be accountable for its own success and impact on the various student subgroups and how it plans to eliminate any achievement gaps among groups, if any exist.

How he or she is treated, respected and valued by important others, including administrators, teachers and other education personnel, has a domino effect on a student's self concept, self-efficacy and persistence that immensely contributes to the level of success that he or she will attain in school.

Presently, the most prevalent way we measure a school's success and positive impact on students' lives is through the state-mandated tests of academic performance. While disaggregated student achievement data are critical to school accountability, we have seen an overemphasis on a curriculum that is test-driven and restricted to specific, pre-selected competencies, rather than focusing on creating more widely-focused world-class learning environments.

Therefore, a good vision should include other measures of success that are not captured through academic achievement tests. Some of these measures include evidence of self-efficacy, self-directed learners, resourcefulness and creative power within a school.

Third Rare Question

Do teachers demonstrate a level of confidence, self-efficacy and expertise necessary to successfully address the challenges of traditionally underserved students?

DuFour states: "Humans have a fundamental longing to believe we are successful in what we do – our need to achieve. Educators are typically denied this sense of success. Bombarded with too many state, national and district standards for students to master, teachers are often unclear as to what they are supposed to accomplish" (2004).

Administrators and teachers in schools with traditionally underserved students are not only bombarded with standards, but they also have to demonstrate knowledge and a sense of self-efficacy in working with traditionally underserved students if they are to be successful.

For the most part, school districts provide workshops and work sessions designed to increase the knowledge base on how to effectively teach these student groups.

Research appears to support the belief that self-efficacy is closely associated with good teaching and student outcomes. A high level of self-efficacy is correlated to higher teacher achievement in reaching these students. Developing a level of confidence or self-efficacy is a much more complicated matter that requires: (a) a positive attitude and beliefs about these students as learners, (b) a high level of knowledge and expertise on engaging and teaching them, (c) strong support and beliefs from campus leaders that teachers can make a difference, (d) a feeling of empowerment to become a risk taker, and (e) a strong commitment to make a positive difference in the lives of these students.

Unfortunately, teachers' self-efficacy and confidence are rarely factored into any campus improvement plan. The Teacher Efficacy Scale by Gibson and Dembo developed at Ohio State University is one instrument that could be used for this purpose (1984). However, adaptation to factor in the educational needs of traditionally underserved students would be required for teachers of these students.

Building a Community of Learners

A *community of learners* approach to re-look at existing and non-successful school improvement plans and particularly to help answer these key questions given the context of your school and community is a useful strategy.

The focus of the community of learners approach is on bringing together crucial stakeholders in the educational process across grade levels, in a campus and/or across campuses within a school district. They create a forum to reflect and act upon best practices that lead to increased academic opportunities for *all* students that ultimately lead to achievement in the basic disciplines of literacy, mathematics, social studies and science.

In appraising the quality of instruction provided to traditionally underserved students in a school district or campus, it is critical that the community of learners include stakeholders who represent various perspectives of the educational change process. At a minimum, this should include parents and teachers of traditionally underserved students, educators with expertise in effective instruction of these students, district and campus administrators, community leaders representing the private sector, activists, district and campus support personnel, and students who represent these underserved student groups.

> A comprehensive approach to designing school reform requires a more intense look at factors that affect the quality of teaching provided to traditionally underserved students.

This type of shared leadership is described by Schlechy as being "less like an orchestra, where the conductor is always in charge, and more like a jazz band, where leadership is passed around… depending on what the music demands at the moment and who feels most moved by the spirit to express the music" (Morris & Hammonds, 2004).

The decision to change must come from within an educational institution and cannot be relegated to consultants or external organizations.

Campus improvement plans that fail to pro-actively address the above three questions have failed to address the full spectrum of instructional needs of traditionally underserved students. A comprehensive approach to designing school reform requires a more intense look at factors that affect the quality of teaching provided to traditionally underserved students, and a commitment to create a school vision of success that will ensure and be accountable for equity and access to an excellent education for *all* students. The community of learners must be respected for its objectivity, fairness, optimism and resolve to make a difference.

Resources

DuFour, R. "Leading Edge: Leadership is an Affair of the Heart," *Journal of Staff Development* (2004) Vol. 25, No. 1.

Gibson, S., and M. Dembo. "Teacher Efficacy: A Construct Validation," *Journal of Educational Psychology* (1984) 76, 569-582.

Morris W., and B. Hammonds (Eds). *Leading and Learning for the 21st Century* (No. 19 - August 2004).

Originally published in the *IDRA Newsletter*, March 2008

Successful Bilingual Education Programs

Criteria for Exemplary Practices in Bilingual Education

by María "Cuca" Robledo Montecel, Ph.D., and Josie Danini Cortez, M.A.

Twenty-five common characteristics contribute to the high academic performance of students served by bilingual education programs. IDRA identified these characteristics through funding by the U.S. Department of Education, Office of Bilingual Education and Minority Languages Affairs (OBEMLA). IDRA rigorously and methodically studied exemplary bilingual education programs in schools across the nation as determined by limited-English-proficient (LEP) students' academic achievement. IDRA now is helping others identify successful programs or raise the bar with their own bilingual education programs.

The 25 indicators that emerged from the research were clustered around five domains:

- School Indicators,
- Student Outcomes,
- Leadership,
- Support, and
- Programmatic and Instructional Practices.

This study comes at a critical time. There are an estimated 3.7 million LEP students in the United States, a persistent achievement gap between LEP and non-LEP students, and a critical shortage of bilingual education teachers with the preparation, skills and tools to ensure that *all* of their students succeed.

Over the next six months, the *IDRA Newsletter* will feature a series of articles on our research study's significant findings. The series will provide information on each of the five indicators and outcome standards with first-hand accounts from teachers, administrators, parents and researchers across the country. (The full series is online at: http://www.idra.org/images/stories/Successful_BE_Series.pdf.)

We begin the series this month with an overview of the research study. The primary purpose of this study was not to prove that bilingual education works – there are years of rigorous research that prove it does work when implemented with integrity. Instead, the purpose of this research study was to identify those characteristics that are contributing to the high academic performance of students served by bilingual education programs. First, we will present some background information.

Condition of Education for LEP Students

Bilingual Education Act

The *Bilingual Education Act* (BEA) was first enacted in 1968 as a response to the 80 percent dropout rate of language-minority (Hispanic and Native American) students. California offers an excellent example of the condition of education for language-minority students prior to the *Bilingual Education Act*.

In 1872, California legislators passed an English-only classroom mandate that lasted 95 years. In 1967, then Governor Ronald Reagan signed Senate Bill 53, repealing the English-only mandate and authorizing bilingual education in California schools.

> English language learners should not have to give up their language, their culture, or their diversity as the price for learning English.

In his 1999 testimony to the Senate Committee on Health, Education, Labor and Pensions, Dr. Joel Gomez, director of the Institute for Education Policy at the Graduate School of Education and Human Development at George Washington University, cites the reasons for the English-only repeal: "It [the English-only mandate] kept students from learning their academic subjects in a timely fashion; it caused language-minority students to be retained in grade because they were behind in their academic studies; it caused students to become frustrated, to give up and drop out of school. And most ironic of all, English-only instruction did not lead to mastery of the English language."

Prior to the repeal of the English-only mandate in California, only half of the California Mexican American youth between the ages of 18 and 24 had even completed the eighth grade.

The intent of the 1967 California *Bilingual Education Act* and the federal version in 1968 was to help states and school districts develop and implement quality education programs for LEP students.

The word *quality* must be underscored for it was the intent that LEP students be afforded an equitable and excellent education, using programs and approaches that would accelerate their academic achievement and performance and hold all students, including LEP students, to high standards.

LEP Enrollment

There were an estimated 3.5 million LEP students in the United States in 1996-97 – a conservative estimate of LEP student enrollment as reported by the nation's state education agencies that receive Title VII funds. This represents a 6.9 percent increase from the previous year. This is considered a conservative estimate also due to the incomplete response rate of state education agencies to OBEMLA's annual *Survey of States' Limited English*

Proficient Students and Available Educational Programs and Services, which is one of the primary methods used to collect data on the number of LEP students in the various states and outlying territories and jurisdictions. For the 1996-97 school year, 54 states or jurisdictions responded to the survey – Pennsylvania, Virginia and West Virginia did not participate nor did American Samoa, Northern Marianas, and Wake Islands.

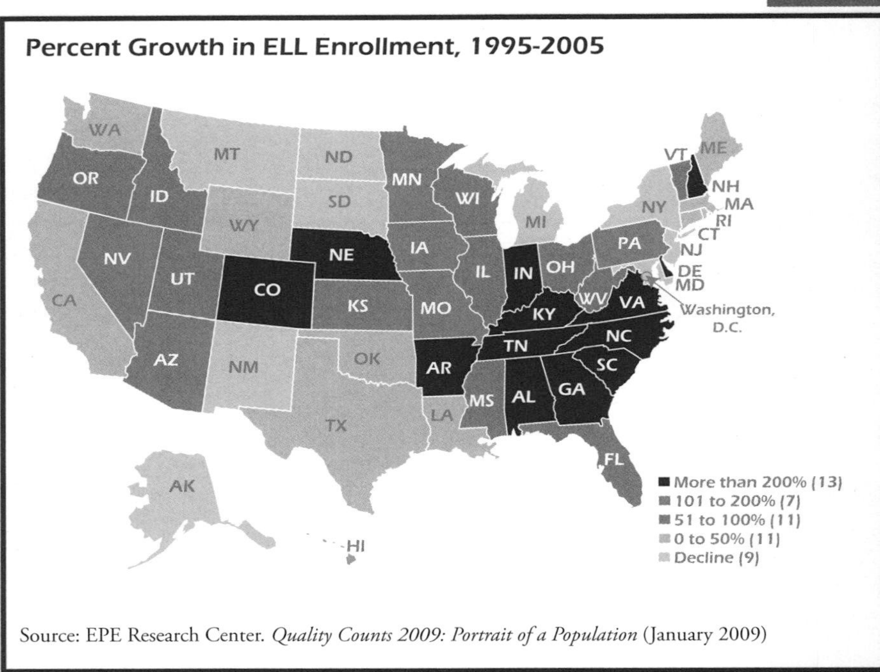

Source: EPE Research Center. *Quality Counts 2009: Portrait of a Population* (January 2009)

Confounding the data collection and analyses is the fact that there is no federally mandated definition of limited English proficiency. While the *Bilingual Education Act* does include an operational definition of "limited English proficiency," LEP status depends largely on state and local agencies. In the 1996-97 survey, most of the state education agencies based their definitions of limited English proficiency on a combination of a non-English language background and/or difficulties with speaking, reading, writing and understanding English.

LEP Student Assessment

State education agencies use various assessment methods to identify LEP students, including home language surveys (which may be used to identify language backgrounds or determine limited English proficiency), teacher observations, parent information, achievement tests and/or referrals, student records, and teacher interviews. A few states report using between the 30th and 50th percentile cutoff on standardized tests as a criterion for determining limited English proficiency.

Language proficiency tests also are used by states to determine limited English proficiency, including Language Assessment Scales, Idea Oral Language Proficiency Test and the Language Assessment Battery.

The primary reasons that the survey results are incomplete in determining the educational condition of LEP students are the variations in assessment instruments across states and the exemption of LEP students from testing or data not reported by the category of "LEP student."

Educational Status of LEP Students

With these caveats in mind, the national snapshot of the educational status of LEP students as reported in the survey is dismal:

- Thirty-three states reported that 5.1 percent (37,837) of their LEP students were retained one or more grades the previous year (1995-96). These states reported a total of 740,516 LEP students collectively. This is only 21 percent of the 3.5 million LEP students at the time.
- Thirty-three states reported that 1.7 percent (14,032) of their LEP students dropped out of school the entire year before the survey. Few states even reported any information regarding academic achievement as measured in performance on standardized tests.
- Thirty states reported 19.3 percent (253,763) of LEP students scored below state norms in English reading.
- Thirty states reported 16 percent (211,433) of LEP students scored below state norms in mathematics.
- Eighteen states reported 6.9 percent (52,880) of LEP students scored below state norms in science.
- Seventeen states reported 6.6 percent (51,388) of LEP students scored below state norms in social studies.

LEP Student Services

Forty percent of U.S. teachers reported having LEP students in their classrooms in 1994, but only 29 percent of these teachers had received any training at all in how to serve them. Diaz-Rico and Smith report that between 100,000 to 200,000 bilingual teachers are needed in U.S. classrooms (1994). The critical shortage forces schools to rely on uncertified aides. Haselkorn reports that in California, two out of five adults providing bilingual instruction are bilingual aides (1996). In fact, California, the state with the most LEP students, was unable to serve 23 percent of their LEP students in 1995.

This is an important statistic to factor in any assessment of student achievement. The achievement gap between LEP and non-LEP students is indicative that many teachers lack the preparation, skills and tools to ensure that *all* of their students succeed.

In the year 2000, the numbers of LEP students in California served by bilingual education programs has been dramatically affected by the passage of Proposition 227. In June 1998, California voters passed Proposition 227 that officially mandated an end to bilingual education in that state (with few exceptions). Now, less than 12 percent of LEP students are enrolled in bilingual education programs (California Department of Education). Thus, most LEP students are not receiving the services and programs they need for an equitable and excellent education.

Despite the political and educational realities of California, the country's leadership is still calling for *all* students to receive equitable and excellent educational opportunities, including equitable and excellent bilingual education programs.

The importance of this call to action is the underlying premise that native languages and cultures are assets, not deficiencies. English language learners should not have to give up their language, their culture, or their diversity as the price for learning English. The inherent value of all students and their characteristics must be recognized, acknowledged and celebrated. When LEP students walk into a classroom in this country, they should not be limited in their access to an equitable and excellent education. For that to occur, teachers must be prepared to serve them.

Methodology Used for This Study

IDRA had one primary research question: *What contributed to the success of a bilingual education classroom as evidenced by LEP student academic achievement?*

"Success" was operationally defined as evidence of academic achievement (compared to district and/or state standards) for LEP students in bilingual education. Additional indicators and research questions that guided the IDRA study included the following.

School Indicators

- What are the school indicators, including retention rate, dropout rate, enrollment rate in gifted and talented programs and in advanced placement programs, enrollment in special education or remedial programs, test exemption rates, and program exiting standards (by LEP and non-LEP percentages)?

Student Outcome Indicators

- What are the student outcomes for oral and written language proficiency (by LEP and non-LEP percentages)?
- What are the student outcomes for content area mastery in English and the native language (by LEP and non-LEP percentages)?

School Level Indicators

- How evident is leadership at the school level, and what are the characteristics?
- How evident are the vision and goals at the school level, and what are the characteristics?
- What are the characteristics of the school's climate?

Indicators of Success for Bilingual Programs

School Indicators	Student Outcomes	At the School Level: Leadership	At the School Level: Support	At the Classroom Level: Programmatic and Instructional Practices
✓ Retention Rate	✓ Written Language Proficiency	✓ School Climate	✓ Parent Involvement	✓ Curriculum and Instruction
✓ Dropout Rate	✓ Content Area Mastery in English	✓ Linkages	✓ Teacher Accountability and Student Assessment	✓ Teacher Expectations
✓ Enrollment in Gifted and Talented/ Advanced Placement Programs	✓ Content Area Mastery in Native Language	✓ School Organization and Accountability	✓ Staff Selection and Recognition	✓ Program Articulation
✓ Enrollment in Special Education or Remedial Programs	✓ Leadership	✓ Professional Development	✓ Community Involvement	
✓ Test Exemption Rates	✓ Vision and Goals		✓ Program Model	
✓ Program Exiting Standard			✓ Classroom Climate	
✓ Oral Language Proficiency				

Intercultural Development Research Association, 2001

- What linkages exist between central office and school level staff? How are they characterized?
- How is the school organized?
- What are the demographic characteristics of professional staff, and what opportunities for professional development are provided?
- What is the type, level and quality of parent involvement in the school and the bilingual education program?
- How do staff hold themselves accountable for student success, and how are students assessed?
- How are the staff selected and recognized?
- What is the type, level and quality of community involvement in the school and the bilingual education program?

Classroom Level: Programmatic and Instructional Practices

- What are the characteristics of the bilingual education program model?
- What are the characteristics of the classroom climate?
- What are the teacher expectations regarding student success?

- How is the program articulated across grade levels?

IDRA ensured that programs selected for site visits reflected the diversity of U.S. schools and included elementary and secondary schools, different language groups, LEP concentrations, and Title I targeted assistance and schoolwide programs as well as Title VII grantees (current and former).

In addition to the review of quantitative student and school outcome data, school demographic data, surveys of principals, teachers and administrators, and structured formal classroom observations were other sources of quantitative data. Qualitative data included structured interviews with the school principals and the administrators and focus group interviews with teachers, parents and students (whenever possible). Additional qualitative data were elicited from school profiles.

A framework was provided for describing each site visit thus providing a context and background for the visit. IDRA gathered, analyzed and synthesized all of these data. Results were then triangulated to provide a rich and accurate picture of each program. Patterns and trends across programs were also identified, providing the empirical basis for the resulting criteria.

It is important to note that this research study was *not* an evaluation of bilingual education programs, that is, we did not evaluate programs using a set of characteristics and criteria already established. Instead, we developed the criteria by observing and learning from programs that had evidence of achievement for all of its students. These criteria can now be used by practitioners and researchers to assess programs and recognize areas that are strong and others that may need improvement.

It is also important to note that if each of the programs in this study were to conduct a self-assessment by these criteria, there would be no perfect program – one that meets 100 percent of the criteria. They would, however, meet most of the criteria with room for improvement for a few. Perhaps one of the most important lessons these programs teach is the need for constant assessment in a context of school accountability for student success, and/or focus on improvement and celebration of achievements. It is in this spirit that we present the major findings of this study. Next month, we will feature the school indicators, including school profiles and organizing similarities.

Note: Additional information about this research and the related guide, Good Schools and Classrooms for Children Learning English, visit http://www.idra.org/Research/Good_School_and_Classrooms/.

Resources

Diaz-Rico, L.T. and J. Smith. "Recruiting and Retaining Bilingual Teachers: A Cooperative School Community-University Model," *Journal of Educational Issues of Language Minority Students* (Winter 1994) v. 14 p. 255-268.

Haselkorn, D. "Breaking the Class Ceiling," *Education Week on the Web* (August 7, 1996).

Originally published in the *IDRA Newsletter*, August 2001

Integrating Technology for Quality Curriculum

Moving from a WIBCI (Wouldn't It Be Cool If) Mentality to a SAWr (Students Are World-ready) Reality – Widening the Lens of Student Engagement

by Kathryn Brown

Wouldn't it be cool if… you walked into a science class where students were co-designing a natural habitat using three-dimensional virtual tools for a multitude of marine species, collaborating via web cams with experts from the Monterey Bay Aquarium, New England Aquarium, and the Georgia Aquarium. And what if they were communicating their innovative and progressive thinking via the web to other students across the world about a habitat that supported the education and research of marine-life?

Wouldn't it be cool if… you walked into the math classroom next door and students were contributing to Google Earth's "Cities in Development" galleries, creating realistic and well-constructed three-dimensional, textured models to build a futuristic city or one of hundreds of cities and locations around the world that anyone could "visit" at anytime? And during their learning experiences, what if they kept in touch with their parents by telling them what they were doing through Twitter or sending an e-mail through their cell phones using Jott? Parents wouldn't need to ask their children what they learned that day. Conversations at the dinner table would be kicked up to the next level to how they applied what they learned and how they created intricate and innovative solutions to awesome problems.

Students in both of these classrooms would understand the content in the deepest, truest sense. The students in the mathematics classroom would have a complete understanding of "three-dimensional geometric figures and related two-dimensional representations and use these representations to solve problems" (Texas Education Agency, Texas Essential Knowledge and Skills in Geometry, 2006) as well as environmental science and geography.

Students in the science classroom would have a complete understanding of habitats, ecosystems and their interrelationships. This type of interaction would enable students to make justifiable recommendations that restore life in a natural habitat.

What if we merged these two content areas – math and science – that are often taught in isolation, where students could define problems in our environment and use mathematics, science and technology to engineer innovative solutions and make *visual predictions* through animation and video. These *visual predictions* could show what would happen to our world's resources and ecosystems if we continue using them up at the rate we are. Students could then use another animation to simulate what would happen if we actually went with their recommendations.

In this type of curriculum, the world becomes students' laboratory and their reason for learning is more real.

And wouldn't it be cool if… the curriculum we taught prepared students for their today, their now, where walking into any classroom in any school one would witness technology being infused in meaningful ways that engage students in real, non-superficial learning experiences?

What we are up to in educating our students though is not preparing them for their now or a *future* of possibilities where proficiency in math, science and technology are essential for success in pursuing a college education or immediately joining a workforce that requires 21st Century skills (Partnership for 21st Century Skills, 2007a; see box on Page 168 for more data).

Texas ranks 41 out of 51 in its total score on the *Chance-for-Success Index*. For example, and the Governor's Competitiveness Council calls for finding a solution to workforce deficits that exist in key industries (including energy, computer technology, advanced technologies in manufacturing, and aerospace and defense). With this and the cutting off of students to possibilities for themselves and their families, we must move forward with a focused urgency in creating quality curriculum that integrates technology. (Education Research Center, 2008; Stutz, 2008)

For many decades, we have been on a path to technology integration into the curriculum. But, we have yet to realize the dream that the pioneers of technology integration in teaching and learning envisioned. Technology integration at its best has been sporadic even in "technology rich" schools. And because of many factors, it is often viewed as optional and is used at a superficial level.

This is evident in a recent report by the Education Research Center where Texas earned an overall C+ on the State Technology Report Card 2008 and its technology standards (Technology Applications – Texas Essential Knowledge and Skills) are written as a discrete, stand-alone document instead of being embedded in the state content standards.

Traditional thinking about technology has made it more of an "add-on" instead of integral to learning. We need to take the *WIBCI* (pronounced "wib-key") *Wouldn't it be cool if* mentality and embrace a new even more powerful way of thinking where our *students are world-ready (*SAWr).

There are challenges and barriers when integrating technology into curriculum. These challenges encompass teacher stress experienced when there is a lack of fit between the technology demands and teacher knowledge or between availability of supplies and teacher needs, leadership and instructional support, technical support, and resources in terms of hardware and software, and resources in terms of curriculum that specifically details how to create technology-infused, meaningful learning experiences (Al-Fudail & Mellar, 2008; Eteokleous, 2008).

How do we meet these challenges? How do we create a quality curriculum that ensures that our students are world-ready when they leave high school and are prepared for a knowledge-based economy? The pathway to creating technology-enriched, quality curriculum is for new thinking to emerge by paralleling experiences of teachers and students and expanding on our idea of what curriculum is and how it is developed.

Lateral Thinking and Parallel Experiences

We have tried a linear "pile it on top of everything we are already doing" approach when "integrating" technology into content curriculum. So, in addition to teaching math, now a teacher has to teach technology.

We need to think laterally instead of linearly. There is great promise that can be achieved through lateral thinking.

Integrating technology is sometimes overwhelming because we think this means that the teacher must know every technology tool that is out there. But it is more about knowing the types of technologies, their uses and relationships to creating a world-ready student. It is about orchestrating the learning experiences and tools that result in building knowledge.

With the emergence of new technologies coming into play every day and the Internet transforming how we communicate and collaborate via Web 2.0 social media tools, it becomes imperative that we adopt a new way of thinking that encourages *lateral thinking* at its core.

Lateral thinking is a term that describes a "set of approaches and techniques designed to find radically new approaches to problems – to come at them from the side rather than the front" (Sloane, 2003). To be innovative, one has to implement a creative idea that is focused on the goals. This means taking a risk and having the creative space and the leadership support to take these risks in a classroom. It is in this state of innovation that we learn and refine continuously and look for new ways of achieving the goal of preparing students who are world-ready.

We need new approaches to integrating technology into the curriculum. Bringing together creative and lateral thinking techniques will result in transformations in how we integrate technology, teach and learn.

Parallel experiences for teachers and leaders will provide a pathway to these lateral approaches. If one has never experienced a technology-infused learning experience that is required for a 21st Century learner as outlined

Demands for Knowledge in Math, Science and Technology are Increasing

In its 2006 report, Are They Really Ready to Work?, The Conference Board, Corporate Voices for Working Families, The Partnership for 21st Century Skills, and the Society for Human Resource Management brought forward the reality that "the future competitiveness of the U.S. business community will be dependent on America's ability to produce a highly skilled workforce."

- Only 24 percent of new entrants with four-year college degrees have "excellent" basic knowledge and applied skills and deficiencies exist at every level in important areas of knowledge
- Alarmingly, 42 percent of surveyed employers reported an overall deficiency in the preparation of high school graduates
- Of the 400 employers surveyed, 81 percent reported deficiencies in written communications, 70 percent cited deficiencies in professionalism, and 70 percent reported deficiencies in critical thinking.
- Educators were identified by the business community as being the most influential and crucial sector in creating a competitive workforce.

The 10 fastest growing occupations for college graduates by the year 2014 as reported by the College Board and the U.S. Bureau of Labor Statistics (http://www.bls.gov) all require proficient knowledge in math, science and technology. Five out of the 10 occupations are jobs directly in technology fields.

Compiled by Kathy Brown, Intercultural Development Research Association, 2008.

in the National Educational Standards (ISTE, 2007 and 2008) and the Framework for 21st Century Skills (Partnership for 21st Century Skills, 2007b), then how can one create these learning experiences? It would be like expecting someone to teach a child how to ride a bike and all of the skills necessary to ride an 18-speed (fitting the bike, balancing, shifting gears, pedaling, thinking and looking ahead, etc.) when the "teacher" has never ridden or even seen a fully assembled bike. The teacher may have learned about some parts of the bike and may have used one or two pieces but has never ridden one.

Teachers' parallel experiences play a critical role in the development of quality curriculum. Teachers are the implementers of curriculum and should participate in the process to realize the full potential of technology in learning and building knowledge (Eteokleous, 2008). A strong, quality curriculum stems from a community of learners and practice, reducing stress associated with technology integration and bringing together examples of student work and lessons (Al-Fudail & Mellar, 2008; Boss, 2008).

Equitable Access to Quality Curriculum and Instruction

The development and implementation process also must be such that *all* students gain access to quality curriculum and instruction to ensure equity. One concern is the digital divide that is present *within* schools, where some students have access to technology and technology-enriched lessons and others do not, depending on whose class they are enrolled in and if that teacher integrates technology as an "add-on" or on a daily basis (O'Neal, 2007). This also is true if the student is a "good student" and gets the assignment done early or is seen as a tech-savvy student who gets to connect the cables and run the computer.

> To be innovative, one has to implement a creative idea that is focused on the goals. This means taking a risk and having the creative space and the leadership support to take these risks in a classroom.

This is not to say that lessons should be scripted; technology allows for dynamic solutions and dynamic instruction. However, it is imperative that all students have access to curriculum and instruction that does the following (The Partnership for 21st Century Skills, 2007; Sloane, 2003; Marshall, 2006).

- Provides pathways to innovative, creative and lateral thinking.
- Connects across content areas, interdisciplinary studies, 21st Century skills and real-world contexts with a focus on teaching for understanding.
- Blends various types of technologies in non-prescribed ways.
- Integrates research-based teaching strategies that foster 21st Century skills (project-based learning, problem-based learning, cooperative learning, problem-solving, inquiry-based learning, etc.).
- Is a dynamic guide on what to teach and how to teach it in a way that teachers contribute through online collaborative tools that model collective knowledge building and where they reflect on teaching practice and creating curriculum units.
- Connects to experts around the world, especially in the new technologies, sciences and areas that are being developed (i.e., nanotechnology).

Include Student Voice

Technology is a tool that our students use with such ease and finesse; it is imperative that we include student voice in the development of quality curriculum. This helps meet the goals of preparing world-ready students and of overcoming challenges in creating relevant and engaging learning experiences. Students blend technologies very naturally. It is innate and at the same time complex thinking that our students do with such elegance and efficiency.

Students as "contributors and co-creators of quality curriculum" shifts the concept of learning from one that is top-down to one that is collaborative with the teacher as facilitator. It makes the curriculum organic and alive. By learning and implementing the curriculum alongside students, teacher stress is reduced, but more importantly, teachers are modeling for students a crucial skill: the skill of "life-long" learning. It would be most awesome to see teachers, students and experts as co-creators and co-learners.

There are many implications when moving toward a quality curriculum that integrates technology in ways where the WIBCIs (*Wouldn't it be cool ifs*) that have been sporadic move to a continuous stream of meaningful learning experiences where students are world-ready (SAWr) to pursue a college education or join the workforce. Through a process that integrates creative and lateral thinking approaches, parallels learning experiences of teachers and students, ensures equitable access and includes student voice, we have the tools necessary to create new possibilities and realities for all our students.

Wouldn't it be cool if… we all took these suggestions and followed through with this call for urgency right now?

Resources

Al-Fudail, M., and H. Mellar. "Investigating teacher stress when using technology," *Computers & Education* (Oxford, UK: Elsevier Science Ltd., 2008) 51, 1103-1110.

Boss, S. "Overcoming Technology Barriers: How to Innovate Without Extra Money or Support," *Edutopia* (August 6, 2008).

The College Board. "Hottest Careers for College Graduates," web posting (2008).

Education Week Editors. "The Push to Improve STEM Education," *Technology Counts* (March 27, 2008).

Education Research Center. "State Highlights Reports," *Quality Counts 2008* (Bethesda, Md., Education Research Center, 2008).

Eteokleous, N. "Evaluating computer technology integration in a centralized school system," *Computers & Education* (Oxford, UK: Elsevier Science Ltd., 2008) 51, 669-686.

Google 3D Warehouse. *Modeling a City: A Guide for Creating Your Google Earth Environment* (2008).

International Society for Technology in Education. "National Educational Technology Standards for Students," web posting (Eugene, Ore.: ISTE, 2007). https://www.iste.org/AM/Template.cfm?Section=NETS

International Society for Technology in Education. "National Educational Technology Standards for Teachers," web posting (Eugene, Ore.: ISTE, 2008). https://www.iste.org/AM/Template.cfm?Section=NETS

Marshall, J. "Math Wars 2: It's the Teaching, Stupid!" *Phi Delta Kappan* (January, 2006) 356-363.

O'Neal, C. "The Digital Divide Within: Creating a Level Playing Field for All Students," *Edutopia* (June 7, 2007).

Partnership for 21st Century Skills. "21st Century Curriculum and Instruction," web posting (2007). http://www.vtsbdc.org/21st_century_skills_curriculum_and_instruction.pdf

Partnership for 21st Century Skills. "Framework for 21st Century Learning," web posting (July 23, 2007). http://www.p21.org/index.php?option=com_content&task=view&id=254&Itemid=120

Sloane, P. *The Leader's Guide to Lateral Thinking Skills* (Philadelphia, Penn.: Kogan Page Publishers, 2003).

Stutz, T. "Texas must improve math, science education, task force says," *Dallas Morning News* (August 7, 2008).

Texas Education Agency. Chapter 111. Texas Essential Knowledge and Skills for Mathematics Subchapter C. High School §111.34. The provisions of this §111.31 adopted to be effective September 1, 1996, 21 TexReg 7371; amended to be effective August 1, 2006, 30 TexReg 4479.

The Conference Board, Corporate Voices for Working Families, The Partnership for 21st Century Skills, and The Society for Human Resource Management. Are They Really Ready to Work? Employers' Perspectives on the Basic Knowledge and Applied Skills of New Entrants to the 21st Century U.S. Workforce (New York, NY: The Conference Board, et al., 2006).

Zhu, J. "Application of computer technology in public school classrooms: Usage dimensions and influencing factors," Unpublished doctoral dissertation (Pennsylvania State University, Penn.: 2003).

Originally published in the *IDRA Newsletter*, September 2008

Chapter Six – Outcome Indicators

Jettison the Jargon ~ Keep the Goals!

Aurelio M. Montemayor, M.Ed.

'Outcomes' and 'indicators' cold jargon
(School people's shorthand sometimes useful)
'Results from schooling' that's fruitful.
Students' disappeared, unlearnt, not a bargain.

Our sieve-like schools aren't holding on
To many school-age youth: that's truth!
Harsh facts bother, but can't stop to soothe
Bruised egos with masses of students gone.

Keeping kids in school is a necessary condition,
But not enough of an outcome – proof of learning
Needs be visible. Their success and yearning
For more must include college ambition.

School holding power gives institutional onus:
Most desired is student growth shown to us.

Chapter Preface

The Quality Schools Action Framework points to two powerful outcome indicators: school holding power and student success. These two concepts represent a leadership paradigm for how we view students and value their indispensable contribution to our society and our future. They are an invitation to begin an inside-out process of organizational change that has no short cuts and requires that we first recognize our own assumptions as educators about the children and families we serve, and second to examine and change the school policies and practices that impede the overall goal of supporting success in terms of high school completion and college readiness for every student. Educators who commit to these outcome indicators are leaders who hold a transformational view of their role and who understand the moral imperative of ensuring that all students have access to quality schooling within our democratic society.

We are poised to have rare power in shaping the educational destiny of our children. Will we seize this moment in history to maintain, or even increase, our decision making power in education that will affect our children? Or will we succumb to a lesser role and lose the privilege and responsibility to chose quality education for all? Will we find our individual and collective voice to make a difference in the future of public education?

Our decision is certain to affect our next generation of leaders. Public schools markedly affect the fabric of the communities they serve with educational, economic and cultural consequences. We cannot afford any casualties in this process, meaning we cannot to lose the spiritual, intellectual and economic capital and leadership potential represented in our youth that is so desperately needed for the future.

- We learn more about the need and use of sophisticated indicators to improve the preparation of students for college and careers through an article by Roy L. Johnson, M.S., "School Holding Power – A Quality Schools Indicator," that highlights three interconnected and interdependent change strategies of community capacity building, coalition building and school capacity building.
- María "Cuca" Robledo Montecel, Ph.D., in "Time to Make High School Graduation the New Minimum," underscores the heightened attention and historic opportunity to engage citizens for truly accountable schools that prepare children for life and college readiness through competent teachers, parent and community engagement, and high quality accessible curriculum.

- In "Defying Conventions for Policies and Programs Intending to Strengthen School Dropout Prevention," Abelardo Villarreal, Ph.D., and Rosana G. Rodríguez, Ph.D., provide specific research-based practices on promoting high student self-efficacy and strong educator-student relationships necessary for an authentic, relevant and engaging curriculum, and effectively creating a "circle of supporters" through family engagement that leads to college readiness and student success.
- In the article, "Defining Student Success in the Context of College Readiness," Rosana G. Rodríguez, Ph.D., issues a call for dialogue and action to create schools as centers of college readiness as an investment in future leadership for our nation. The article encourages pro-active, collective steps to recruit, train and select quality teachers who can ensure equity, access and excellence.
- In "'InterAction' Needed from All Sectors to Support College Access and Success," Dr. Robledo Montecel illustrates how breaking down barriers among schools and communities and across levels from K-12 to college is essential to opening paths to post-secondary education.
- In a keynote presentation entitled, "Musical Chairs and Unkept Promises," before the National Dropout Prevention Network conference, Dr. Robledo Montecel calls for changing the rules of the game so that all students stay in and all students succeed.
- And finally, Dr. Robledo Montecel offers lessons from working with the issue of dropouts in Texas for so many years in "From 'Dropping Out' to 'Holding On' – Seven Lessons from Texas."

School Holding Power – A Quality Schools Indicator

by Roy L. Johnson, M.S.

Texas public high schools lose about one-third of their students before they graduate with a high school diploma. In its latest annual attrition study, IDRA found that for every 100 ninth grade students in 2005-06, 31 students were lost from the high school graduation pipeline by 2008-09. This translates to a loss of about 125,508 students from the class of 2009.

Cumulatively, between 1985-86 to 2008-09, a total of 2.9 million students have been lost from Texas public schools without receiving a high school diploma. Graduation from high school with a diploma and being fully prepared for college, a career and citizenry, are the ultimate outcomes for high school students. Yet for these outcomes to be attained, students must be provided a quality education through high quality teaching, high quality school leadership, high quality curriculum, high quality learning environment, high quality student engagement, and high quality parent and community engagement.

The education system has been plagued with many issues that impact the quality of teaching and learning in our schools. Schools and communities are having difficulty keeping students in school, engaged in learning, and meeting high academic standards. Effective schools know that graduating students with a diploma, backed by an excellent education, must be the focal point of systems change in education (Robledo Montecel, 2005).

Framework for Action

Through its Quality Schools Action Framework, IDRA has presented a process for achieving systems change in education. The framework is based on experience and empirical evidence emerging from existing theories of change that assert that lasting systems change depends on sustained action within and outside of those systems (Robledo Montecel, 2005).

Several components make up this comprehensive approach to school transformation – levers of change, change strategies, school system fundamentals and indicators, and outcome indicators. Within the framework, there are three interconnected and interdependent change strategies: (1) community capacity building, (2) coalition building, and (3) school capacity building.

The framework examines the links among key education indicators: teaching quality, effective governance, curriculum quality and access, student engagement, parent and community engagement, and fair and equitable funding. In the framework, the final outcomes are that students are kept in school, that students succeed academically, and that students are prepared for college and career.

Increasing School Holding Power

School holding power is defined as the ability of schools to keep students enrolled in school and learning until they graduate. High quality schools have good school holding power and prepare all students to succeed in college and career.

Research suggests that quality schools possess the following characteristics: (1) high expectations for every student; (2) strong school leadership; (3) qualified teachers in every classroom; (4) rigorous curriculum and fair assessments; (5) sufficient resources that help all students achieve; (6) safe, healthy and supportive learning environments; (7) schools and classrooms equipped for teaching and learning; and (8) parent and community support (Give Kids Good Schools, nd). All of these elements are contained in strategic components of IDRA's Quality Schools Action Framework.

IDRA's push for increasing school holding power is rooted in the notion that high quality schools must establish goals to graduate all students with a high school diploma. In its recently-released policy brief, "Moving Beyond AYP: High School Performance Indicators," the Alliance for Excellent Education calls for the use of sophisticated indicators to stem the tide of the high school dropout crisis and to improve the preparation of all students for college and career (2009). The alliance supports aligning proficiency and graduation rates with the goal of every student graduating ready for college and career.

The lack of school holding power impacts everyone socially and economically. The magnitude of the school dropout problem in Texas and in the nation is related to a number of negative outcomes – higher unemployment rates, lower pay, smaller tax base, higher rates of incarceration for dropouts, etc. According to IDRA President and CEO, Dr. María "Cuca" Robledo Montecel, the magnitude of the dropout problem calls for a *seismic shift from "dropout prevention" to "graduation for all."*

Conclusions

In order to increase school holding power, schools and communities must not only set new goals pertaining to graduation rates, they also must examine schools as systems and pro-actively address issues that fail to keep students in school.

Working together, schools and communities must align educational goals with quality school indicators. IDRA's Quality Schools Action Framework provides specific recommendations on building community capacity, building coalitions, and strengthening school capacity to produce high quality schools and stem the leaks in the secondary school pipeline.

High School Attrition in Texas in 2008-09

Much has changed in 23 years…
but the dropout rate hasn't.

IDRA's annual attrition study finds that in 2008-09, Texas schools lost 31 percent of their students. In IDRA's 1985-86 inaugural study, 33 percent of students were lost.

42 percent of Hispanic students, 35 percent of Black students, and 17 percent of White students were lost from public school enrollment.

The attrition rate gaps between White students and Black students and between White students and Hispanic students persist. The gap today is higher than 24 years ago.

Since IDRA's first study, more than 2.9 million students have been lost from public schools.

Texas schools are losing a student every four minutes.

At current pace, the state will lose an additional 2.3 million to 6 million students before reaching an attrition rate of zero in 2042.

Source: Johnson, R.L. "Texas Public School Attrition Study, 2008-09 – Overall Attrition Rate Declines, But Gaps Persist Among Racial and Ethnic Groups," *IDRA Newsletter* (San Antonio, Texas: Intercultural Development Research Association, October 2009).

Resources

Robledo Montecel, M. "A Quality Schools Action Framework: Framing Systems Change for Student Success," *IDRA Newsletter* (San Antonio, Texas: Intercultural Development Research Association, November-December 2005).

Give Kids Good Schools. "What Makes a Quality Public School?" web site and fliers (Washington, D.C.: Public Education Network, no date).

Pinkus, L.M. "Moving Beyond AYP: High School Performance Indicators," *Policy Brief* (Washington, D.C.: Alliance for Excellent in Education, June 2009).

Originally published in the *IDRA Newsletter,* October 2009

Time to Make High School Graduation the New Minimum

by María "Cuca" Robledo Montecel, Ph.D.

On October 31, 1986, IDRA completed and published the Texas School Dropout Survey Project. The seven-volume work, commissioned by the State of Texas, was the first statewide study of dropouts and was released in Austin at a gathering of educators, policymakers and community members.

As principal investigator for the study, I provided the gathering with key findings: many, many young people were dropping out of Texas schools, most schools reported no plans to address the fact that one out of three students were leaving school before obtaining a high school diploma, and the costs of undereducation to dropouts, their families and the state were enormous.

The cost analyses conducted as part of that study indicated that education is a good investment: every dollar invested in education resulted in a nine-dollar return. (Cárdenas, Robledo & Supik, 1986; see also the Appendix)

The 1986 study had an immediate effect on policy and practice. State policy requiring dropout data collection and reporting was passed in April 1987. As a result, data collection systems were put into place at the Texas Education Agency. The first report by TEA (1988) pointed to a statewide longitudinal dropout rate of 34 percent. Also, as a result of new state policy and regulation following the IDRA study, most school districts identified dropout prevention coordinators and developed dropout plans.

However, focused resources and productive actions attendant to assuring that schools in Texas increase their ability to hold students through to high school graduation were short-lived. Instead, resources and actions went to explaining away the problem by blaming students or families and by lowering the dropout counts through changes in dropout definitions. The results are evident.

Our latest attrition study indicates that 137,000 Texas students, or 35 percent of the freshman class of 2002-03, left school before graduating in the 2005-06 school year. In the last 20 years, the racial-ethnic school holding power gap has widened with attrition rates increasing for Hispanic students and Black students while decreasing for White students. At the same time that the gap in schools' ability to hold on to minority versus White students has widened, minority youngsters have become the majority of the school-aged population in Texas schools. (For more information on IDRA's October 1986 Texas School Dropout Survey Project, the latest attrition study results, and trends in yearly attrition data over the last 20 years, see http://www.idra.org/Research/Attrition/.)

These statistics are not new to the many educators and community members who are committed to equity and excellence for all students. What is new is a palpable sense of public awareness of the dropout problem in Texas and the nation, and a growing political will to address it.

In recent months, we have seen new national-level attention to the issue, such as President Bush's High School Initiative, a bipartisan attempt to promote national graduation-for-all policy, and the National Governors Association's compact to develop consistent state-level data.

It is now time that we make high school graduation and college readiness the new minimum. The economics of undereducation demand it. Our children deserve no less.

We have seen new foundation investment in combining school reform with citizen awareness campaigns, such as StandUp!, a public will campaign funded by the Bill and Melinda Gates Foundation. Media coverage, including the coordinated release in April 2006 of a two-part segment aired on the Oprah Winfrey Show and a cover story in *Time* magazine, have brought new attention to what has been called "the high school dropout crisis in America."

And we have seen a sharpened focus on the problem by a wide array of research institutes, non-profit organizations, coalitions and networks. Reports from the National Center for Education Statistics, the U.S. Bureau of the Census, the Harvard Civil Rights Project, the American Diploma Project Network, and the Alliance for Excellent Education are underscoring the magnitude of the problem and strengthening a knowledge base.

This level of dramatically heightened attention presents a historic opportunity for a sea change in Texas and in the nation's recognition of the problem and willingness to address it. But that moment can fade or make little difference for schools and for students.

To seize the moment and produce results, it is important to learn from the past as we engage citizens, develop public policy and promote truly accountable schooling (see "From 'Dropping Out' to 'Holding On' – Seven Lessons from Texas," by Robledo Montecel on Page 207).

It is also important to work from what we know about schools. To graduate students who are prepared for later life, IDRA research indicates that schools must have: (1) competent caring teachers who are paid well and are supported in their work, (2) consistent ways to partner with parents and engage the local communities to whom they account, (3) ways to really know students and have students know that they belong, and (4) high quality, enriched and accessible curriculum (Robledo Montecel, 2005).

Schools and the communities to which they belong need consistent, credible data sets that assess graduation data in relationship to quality teaching, parent-community engagement, student engagement and high quality curriculum.

To respond to this need for actionable knowledge at the local level, IDRA's Graduation Guaranteed/*Graduación Garantizada* initiative is piloting a web-based portal that can be used by community-school partners as they craft a shared vision; assess local needs and assets; identify proven practices that strengthen school holding power; develop ways to implement, monitor and evaluate local actions plans; and build inclusive enduring partnerships to sustain momentum and action.

Losing children, particularly poor and minority children, from our school systems before high school graduation has been and is today a defining feature of education in the United States. The feature and its assumption that fewer students will graduate than started in the ninth grade and even fewer children will graduate than started in kindergarten is built into teacher hiring practices, into ways in which schools deal with parents and communities, into whether and how schools connect with kids, and into curriculum decisions about which courses will be offered and to whom. Student attrition is built into facilities planning and funding decisions. It is time to change.

Not too long ago, it seemed unreasonable to think that this country would have universal education through elementary school. It is now time that we make high school graduation and college readiness the new minimum. The economics of undereducation demand it. Our children deserve no less.

Note: IDRA's School Holding Power portal is online at: http://www.idra.org/portal. *See Page 229 for more information.*

Resources

Cárdenas, J.A., and M. del Refugio Robledo, J.D. Supik. *Texas School Dropout Survey Project* (San Antonio, Texas: Intercultural Development Research Association, 1986).

Robledo Montecel. M. "From 'Dropping Out' to 'Holding On' – Seven Lessons from Texas," *IDRA Newsletter* (San Antonio, Texas: Intercultural Development Research Association, April 2004).

Robledo Montecel, M. "A Quality Schools Action Framework: Framing Systems Change for Student Success," *IDRA Newsletter* (San Antonio, Texas: Intercultural Development Research Association, November-December 2005).

Originally published in the *IDRA Newsletter,* October 2006

Defying Conventions for Policies and Programs Intending to Strengthen School Dropout Prevention

by Abelardo Villarreal, Ph.D., and Rosana G. Rodríguez, Ph.D.

Some call it an epidemic, others an educational dilemma, and others a national disgrace with significant economic, social and personal consequences for the future of this country. Students are not graduating from high school in shocking proportions (30 to 50 percent). The problem is the worst for our growing populations of minority and low-income students.

Despite renewed national interest, many communities and policymakers continue to ignore this problem and operate as if it was transitory and will automatically resolve itself through existing school reform efforts. The fact is that policy and school reform efforts typically focus entirely on "overhauling" perceived student deficits and have not seriously delved into the contextual factors and their collective impact on students leaving school.

Such school reform efforts shortchange minority and low-income students who, since their enrollment in school, became the prey of inappropriate learning assessments, low expectations, inappropriate instruction and misguided parent involvement programs. This article provides some thoughts about present day conventions and assumptions and describes some solutions that defy these conventions.

Debunking the Myth: Student Deficit vs. School Deficit

Students who are most at risk of dropping out go through a gradual process of disengagement, isolationism and indifference. This leads to a loss of self efficacy, self esteem and resiliency. For these students, there is often a long history of academic underachievement, dysfunctional behaviors and eventual physical exiting from the school environment. This gradual process starts manifesting itself through behavioral, emotional and learning difficulties.

Early research of the 1980s by IDRA (1989) and more recent research by Battin-Pearson, et al., (2000) reveal the major manifestations expressed by students who are at risk of dropping out. These are: chronic cycle of tardiness and absence, failing classes, suspensions, transitions between schools, student disrespect toward self and others, isolationism, and disrespect for law and order. These tend to gradually accumulate creating a problem with serious implications to the individual student, the teacher, the school, the family and the community.

Unfortunately, existing policies and school programs typically do not address the problem of school dropouts from a structural or systemic perspective. Instead, they target students' dysfunctional behaviors and low academic achievement as the key factors. They neglect school contextual factors that lead to student disengagement and isolation.

The two-pronged challenge for schools is to: (1) tend to the severe damage that has already impaired many of our youth; and (2) ensure that school practices that caused this damage for many of our youth immediately change so that more students and their families feel welcomed in school, experience academic success, and eventually graduate and go on to college.

Our attention must shift from student and parent blame to a shared school responsibility. We must adhere to a philosophy of shared responsibility ingrained in the term, *school holding power*.

As educators, we must take a step back, reflect and act in ways that defy conventions that contribute to a school's lackadaisical attitude. Our attention must shift from student and parent blame to a shared school responsibility. We must adhere to a philosophy of shared responsibility ingrained in the term, *school holding power*.

School holding power is the capacity of a school to keep and graduate students who have reached a threshold where dropping out becomes a serious alternative, and the ability of the school to self-renew and change paradigms toward valuing all students and feeling responsible for the success of every student.

Building Strong School Holding Power

What can schools do? Many school leaders will need to undertake a serious endeavor to change their attitudes and low expectations of students and take greater responsibility for the success or failure of their students. By doing so, their schools will become successful by virtue of their strong school holding power.

Schools with a strong student holding power embody the following practices.

Provide High Self Efficacy

- Promote skill-building, responsibility, supportive relationships and belonging throughout the school's curriculum.
- Implement special programs that promote skill-building, responsibility, supportive relationships and belonging to students who need additional help.
- Acknowledge achievement.

- Ensure students' participation in extracurricular activities so that all students are supported and have multiple opportunities to excel.
- Support extracurricular activities that build positive youth development and social skills to promote self worth.
- Make special efforts to provide opportunities for students deemed at risk to being viewed instead as "at promise."
- Monitor students' progress in self-esteem and self efficacy through observations and standardized measures.

Promote Strong Educator-Student Relationships

- Promote school board support for programs that strengthen relationships and create school structures to personalize instruction.
- Offer quality instructional programs that create opportunities for graduation and preparation for college and the workplace.
- Use teacher "looping" practices (where students have the same teacher for multiple years) to ensure that continuity and relationship strengthening offer the potential for academic and social benefits.
- Demonstrate strong and committed leadership that *will not allow* for any student to stay behind.
- Ensure that all students have at least one caring adult in their school lives.
- Teach a core set of social and emotional competencies (self-awareness, self-management, relationship skills and responsible decision-making).
- Create a schoolwide environment in which everyone participates in setting rules and follows the same rules of conduct, recognizing that students do not feel connected in environments that are chaotic and where adults are punitive.
- Support learning approaches, such as service-learning, cooperative learning and noncompetitive games that increase connectedness to school.
- Implement early interventions and intensive interventions that are aimed at children who are having difficulty feeling connected. Samples of these interventions include the Coca-Cola Valued Youth Program and the AVID program.
- Promote a school climate that ensures school connectedness by creating "communities of learners," including students, teachers, administrators and parents, that meet periodically to set goals, collaboratively develop projects and share accomplishments.

Provide for an Authentic, Relevant and Engaging Curriculum

- Engage students cognitively, physically and emotionally.
- Provide extensive professional development on implementing authentic assessments, curriculum, pedagogy and instruction.

- Use authentic pedagogy that challenges students to understand concepts deeply, find and integrate information, assemble evidence, weigh ideas and develop skills of analysis and expression.
- Use authentic instruction that focuses on active learning in real-world contexts calling for higher-order thinking, consideration of alternatives, extended writing and an audience for student work.
- Implement intensive interventions that supplement and give extensive practice to students who are having difficulty keeping up with the class.
- Promote intellectually challenging work that demands rigorous intellectual work and mirrors that of professionals, e.g., mathematics and science instruction that produces what mathematicians and scientists do.
- Link instruction to student and community experiences that make sense to students.
- Honor students' home language, history and culture.
- Focus more time on core curriculum, streamline course offerings and allow time for personalized instruction and attention.
- Use project-based instruction that is multidisciplinary, relevant and challenging.
- Provide for internships with professionals.

Effective Family Engagement vs. Neglect and Disregard for Parents

Engaging parents and extended family members who constitute the student's "circle of supporters" (parents, grandparents, aunts and uncles, close friends) is key to a successful partnership that leads to student success academically, socially and emotionally. Many schools are not seizing the opportunity to engage this most valuable educational resource that can enrich the teaching and learning experience.

This "circle of support" is a treasure of information and can serve as a powerful team that shares responsibility for the academic progress of each student. Schools with a strong student holding power do the following for home-school connections.

- Create a family engagement program where parents and educators discuss implications of a challenging program and the different and mutually supportive roles that educators and parents both play in creating a successful learning environment for the student.
- Provide periodic assessment data on students and school performance in implementing a challenging instructional program.
- Provide assessment data in a manner (and language) that parents can understand, interpret and take action.
- Be a clearinghouse for parents to access educational, social and psychological services for the family and students.

- Provide training and assistance to parents on topics related to strengthening relationships among students, school staff and other families.
- Provide ongoing training for teachers and staff on positive family engagement practices aimed at student academic success.

Summary

Most young people can bounce back from adversity, stress, trauma, crises and other debilitating issues and can experience success when facilitated by significant others, such as teachers, administrators, parents and friends who have gained their respect and admiration. School personnel can have a direct positive impact on reversing a process that leads to a student's total disassociation with schools.

Understanding how the problem begins to manifest itself, the factors that contribute to these manifestations, and those research-based practices that schools have used to successfully address these factors is critical to strengthening school holding power. While these lists of practices are by no means exhaustive, they provide a schema of some critical practices, based on research, that are associated with schools with a strong student holding power.

Resources

Battin-Pearson, S., and M.D. Newcomb, R.D. Abbott, K.G. Hill, R.F. Catalano, J.D. Hawkins. "Predictors of Early High School Dropout: A Test of Five Theories," *Journal of Educational Psychology* (2000) 92, 568–582.

IDRA. *The Answer: Valuing Youth in Schools and Families – A Report on Hispanic Dropouts in the Dallas Independent School District* (San Antonio, Texas: Intercultural Development Research Association, 1989).

Originally published in the *IDRA Newsletter*, September 2007

Defining Student Success in the Context of College Readiness

by Rosana G. Rodríguez, Ph.D.

There is little question that student success for the 21st Century must be viewed in light of college readiness and that it is linked to the type of leaders this nation will produce. We are uniquely poised at this moment in history to consider education as the civil rights issue of our century, which has been aptly identified by President Barack Obama and U.S. Secretary of Education, Arnie Duncan (2009).

Public schools are the bedrock of our democracy. For K-12 schools and colleges to be relevant and responsive in the future, teachers must be excellent in their content fields, culturally competent, and pedagogically equipped to serve a diverse student population. School leaders must have a strong vision of college readiness for all students.

In fact, our collaborative vision and commitment will need to evolve to create excellent public schools that are "centers of college readiness" for *all* children.

We can achieve this by fostering new forms of collaboration and alliances among schools, colleges and communities. Through these alliances, we can create the positive changes needed in teacher preparation, school leadership programs and professional development that focus on college readiness. We cannot continue to recruit, select, place, support and reward teachers and principals the ways we have in the past if we don't want the same results that perpetuate gaps in support to minority and English language learner students.

Current teacher preparation and educational leadership programs also typically fail to adequately prepare teachers and school leaders to value or engage parents and communities as meaningful partners in the teaching and learning process.

Action dialogues focused on college readiness, quality teaching and community engagement are needed among communities, higher education, schools and policymakers to implement actions that are relevant and sustainable in addressing college access, enrollment and persistence. This requires greater articulation between schools, community colleges and universities, with a comprehensive review of policies and practices along the K-20 continuum, particularly at key transition points – middle to high school and high school to college.

Information linked to action must be readily accessible to families, communities and all stakeholders for making good decisions aimed at college preparedness (Posner & Bojorquez, 2008). Student voices also are indispensable in planning effective action. Schools need to continue to create avenues for student voices to be heard in the planning process.

What follows are several premises upon which to draw as a basis for action and reform as we consider the implications for creating centers of college readiness.

1. College readiness both expands and changes the goal of high school graduation from obtaining just minimum requirements to creating a supportive college prep context upon which all students emerge with the social, emotional, intellectual and instructional background and experiences to ensure college success. To do so mandates collaboration between high schools and colleges for shared planning, articulation agreements, and access to greatly expanded advanced placement courses and early college credit courses.

This also requires commitment to teach students requisite study skills and provide access to high level courses. Beyond the coursework, college prep requires problem solving skills, decision-making, time management, interpersonal and social competency, and cross cultural skills.

2. College readiness for minority students and English language learners implies looking at structures, policies and practices within schools through an equity lens. In order to ensure that all students graduate fully prepared for college success, we must diligently eliminate all disproportionality in policies and practices within schools as they relate to gender, race, ethnicity, national origin, language and disability. Ongoing and rigorous monitoring and implementation of the goals of equity outlined by the IDRA South Central Collaborative for Equity (see Page 82) and by key principles for English language learner education (Villarreal, 2009a&b) can help guide schools in organizing for college readiness.

3. College readiness requires a deep examination of the curricular and instructional practices that engage and surround students in the continuum from preschool through high school graduation and into higher education. IDRA's Quality Schools Action Framework provides a change model through informed family-school-community partnerships and enlightened policymaking. It offers a strong foundation upon which to conduct a comprehensive evaluation of the critical structures and the curricular and instructional practices that comprise excellence and equity in education. The framework identifies three strategies for changing schools: building capacity of the community to influence schools, building coalitions, and building the capacity of the schools themselves. The evidence-based collaboration that is called for in the model is a holistic guide to view benchmarked standards in creating centers of college readiness.

4. College readiness has implications for effective community engagement and parent involvement programs. Ensuring that every student is fully prepared for high school graduation and beyond requires informed engagement and purposeful action of home-school-community strategies aimed at developing a shared vision for college readiness through collaborative planning and shared accountability for the success of all students. This includes school boards, superintendents, teachers and school leaders working together to set this expectation, creating a culture of engagement with parents that acknowledges the funds of knowledge represented in families and communities to achieve this goal. From the earliest grades, effective partnerships between home and school must pro-actively foster the expectation of college readiness and establish clear pathways, with all necessary and appropriate supports for the transition from high school into higher education.

Where will our future leaders come from? Our future leaders will emerge from schools that are centers of college readiness, representing the sum of what they have been taught from preschool through higher education, reflecting the context of the families and communities from which they came.

5. College readiness implies we create a school culture that focuses on valuing the giftedness of every student. While our focus, appropriately so, continues to be on reducing the achievement gap and improving the quality of educational opportunities for students who are culturally or linguistically diverse, we also should be concerned about the under-representation of these students in gifted and talented programs. Ford, Grantham and Whiting (2008) note that Black students, Hispanic students and Native American students have always been significantly under-represented in gifted education programs. King, Kozleski and Lansdowne (2009) underscore the need to focus on giftedness, finding student strengths as a powerful strategy for discovering and encouraging the development of the multicultural assets of students.

To create a culture of college readiness we may need to deliberately redirect our thoughts toward that expectation, dramatically shifting the paradigm from one that sees some children and their families as "problems to be solved" to one that recognizes all children are gifted and can graduate college ready. Latino and other minority families have high expectations for their children to go to college and see them as gifted; schools must catch up to this vision.

6. College readiness is linked to the type of leaders this nation will produce and to its competitive standing in the world. The future will certainly require more participatory and inclusive leadership that is shared and focuses on the group rather than just the capacity of one individual (Robledo Montecel, 2005b).

A new frontier of leadership research and practice is emerging that reflects leadership of the many vs. leadership of only a few chosen ones. This fundamental shift assumes a process that acknowledges the strengths to be found within diverse communities and cultures, one that honors and celebrates the gifts of history, language and culture as valuable resources upon which we all benefit (Louque, 2002). Responding to this call will mean that schools draw fully upon the social, intellectual and spiritual capital represented in their diverse students, families and communities.

In 2005, IDRA hosted a dialogue with emerging and existing leaders to explore dimensions of leadership linked to community, history, language, culture, spirituality and institutional transformation, the *Ohtli Encuentro*. While focusing on women of color, the lessons learned are relevant to college readiness. Women leaders from across the nation cited the importance of maintaining their roots, language and cultural ties, as well as their individual forms of spirituality inextricably linked to their leadership journeys. The *Ohtli* dialogue underscored the importance of hearing the voices of existing and emerging leaders to add to and expand upon our present constructs of leadership (Robledo Montecel, 2005b).

In looking at Latino leadership, one comprehensive study shows that some groups, such as Latinos, place a much higher priority on leadership traits associated with compassion and community service (Ramirez, 2001), while other research finds similarities between Latinos and African Americans (Walters & Smith, 1999; Kilson, 2000).

Where will our future leaders come from? Our future leaders will emerge from schools that are centers of college readiness, representing the sum of what they have been taught from preschool through higher education, reflecting the context of the families and communities from which they came. One hopes they will be guided by a profound desire to live a life of service, embracing a world perspective, where one's purpose is to work for the benefit of our communities: leaders who are culturally competent, who act from a place where concern for "me" and "mine" is laid aside and consciously replaced with commitment and action that contribute to the greater good, through awareness, compassion, dignity, grace, generosity, integrity, openness, warmth and wisdom.

That will require a new view of what constitutes student success. It is an urgent call for schools to become centers of college readiness, preparing all students to exercise fully all their options in higher education and beyond to become knowledgeable, politically engaged and responsive adults. For as one civil rights leader, Cesar Chavez, has said, the end of all education must surely be service to community, not for their sake but for our own (Olmos, et al., 1999).

Resources

Duncan, A. "Partners in Reform," remarks before the National Education Association recognizing the 45th anniversary of the enactment of Title VI of the Civil Rights Act of 1964 (Washington, D.C.: U.S. Department of Education, July 2, 2009).

Ford, D.Y., and T.C. Grantham, G.W. Whiting. "Culturally and Linguistically Diverse Students in Gifted Education: Recruitment and Retention Issues," *Exceptional Children* (March 22, 2008).

Kilson, M. "The Washington and DuBois Leadership Paradigms Reconsidered," *The Annual of the American Academy of Political and Social Science* (2000).

King, K., and E. Kozleski, K Lansdowne. "Where Are All the Students of Color in Gifted Education?" *Principal* (May-June, 2009).

Louque, A. "Spicing it Up: Blending Perspectives of Leadership and Cultural Values from Hispanic and African American Scholars," *Educational Leadership Review* (2002).

Olmos, E.J., and C. Fuentes, L. Ybarra. *Americanos-Latino Life in the United States* (Boston, New York: Little, Brown and Company, 1999) pg. 38 translated.

Posner, L., and H. Bojorquez. "Knowledge for Action – Organizing School-Community Partnerships Around Quality Data," *IDRA Newsletter* (San Antonio, Texas: Intercultural Development Research Association, January 2008).

Ramirez, A. "Reflecting an American Vista: The Character and Impact of Latino Leadership," *Latino Leadership Perspectives* (January 2001).

Robledo Montecel, M. "A Quality Schools Action Framework, "*IDRA Newsletter* (San Antonio, Texas: Intercultural Development Research Association, November-December 2005).

Robledo Montecel, M. *Foreword to The Ohtli Encuentro – Women of Color Share Pathways to Leadership, an initiative of the Intercultural Development Research Association* (San Antonio, Texas: Sor Juana Press, 2005).

Scott, B. "Teaching Must be Culturally Relevant to be Quality," *IDRA Newsletter* (San Antonio, Texas: Intercultural Development Research Association, May 2009).

Villarreal, A. "Ten Principles that Guide the Development of an Effective Educational Plan for English Language Learners at the Secondary Level – Part I," *IDRA Newsletter* (San Antonio, Texas: Intercultural Development Research Association, January 2009).

Villarreal, A. "Ten Principles that Guide the Development of an Effective Educational Plan for English Language Learners at the Secondary Level – Part II," *IDRA Newsletter* (San Antonio, Texas: Intercultural Development Research Association, February 2009).

Walters, R.W., and R.C. Smith. *African American Leadership* (Albany, N.Y.: State University of New York Press, 1999).

Originally published in the *IDRA Newsletter*, November-December 2009

"InterAction" Needed from All Sectors to Support College Access and Success

by María "Cuca" Robledo Montecel, Ph.D.

Editor's Note: IDRA convened a series of policy action forums to create reform solutions that address disparities in higher education access and success of Latino students. The InterAction forums, supported by the Houston Endowment Inc., brought together K-12 educators, college and university leaders, and community and business advocates from urban, rural and border communities in Texas. Thirty-one policy solutions generated from InterAction were presented at a statewide seminar in February 2005 and are available online at http://www.idra.org. Below is a portion of the keynote presented by Dr. María "Cuca" Robledo Montecel at the opening forum.

InterAction is an initiative that we intend to be a vehicle for increasing Latino college access and success in the state of Texas. Let us look a little bit at this word "InterAction." *Inter-* implies, of course, interconnectedness, interdependence and interrelatedness of purposes, of people and of systems. Each of you brings to this forum a set of particulars that come from what you do, be it at a university or a community college, in schools or in the community or a business entity, and those particulars that you bring are very important. The perspective and the insights from those three sectors – higher education, elementary and secondary education, and community – are very essential to this gathering.

At the same time, there is an opportunity to look at the challenge of Latino college access and success from a broad and big platform. One that creates not only common ground but common cause. One that examines not only state level policies, but also institutional and system policies. One that assumes that the future is neither in someone else's hands nor in our individual hands, but in our connected hands.

Let's look at the second part of this word "InterAction," *-action*. It is not enough to deplore the facts. Most of us are painfully aware of the loud drumbeat of statistics that paint a dismal picture of education opportunity for Latinos in Texas. Many of us in fact, myself included, are convinced that hard hitting, valid, credible statistics are necessary in order to create the public will, the accountability mechanisms and the fair funding that is going to produce lasting results. There are indeed a lot of facts to explore.

Facts are Telling

Here is a little bit of what we do know from the facts: IDRA's research shows that the Texas high schools lose one-third of their students before graduation. Of the total who graduate with a high school diploma, one of two is White, one of three is Hispanic and one of six is Black. And of those students, only one of five enrolls in a Texas public university the following fall.

Close to one of four enrolls in a two-year college, but more than half of high school graduates will not enroll at all. We know that students have the best chance of returning for a second year if they continue as full-time students. This seems to be a more important factor than the type of diploma they earn in high school. But full-time college status is difficult given that one of four high school students is economically disadvantaged and that there is a dearth of needs-based financial aid.

It is especially difficult for Latinos given that one of two Latino students in the state of Texas is poor, compared to one in 10 White students. We also know that Texas colleges and universities are being priced out of the market for most Texas families. Texas earned a "D" in affordability in a recent study state report card. The study called "Measuring Up," and I know many of you are familiar with it, indicates that the cost of a public four-year education for low- and middle-income students is equivalent to 40 percent of the family's income, 40 percent (NCPPHE, 2004). For a community college education, it is at 30 percent of the annual family income.

Regrettably, the steepest increases in public college tuition have been imposed during times of the greatest economic hardship for the state and for the country. Over the past 10 years, tuition in Texas public two-year institutions increased 29 percent, and tuition in Texas public four-year institutions increased 63 percent. During this same period, the median Texas family income increased only 8 percent.

But tuition isn't the only problem. On Page X is a graphic of the vanishing future for Texas education. In Texas, the feigned kindergarten-through-20 pipeline is not only clogged at various transition points, it is, in fact, nonexistent. There is no pipeline for Texans. There is no pipeline that moves students from quality early childhood education to college graduation and beyond.

So, there are many facts to deplore; but clearly we must act. We must act now; and we must act with what is so, today. But take action around what? Well, obviously around a vision.

Survival Requires Interconnectedness

"Every Texan educated to the level necessary to achieve his or her dreams. No one is left behind. Each can pursue higher education. Colleges and universities focus on the recruitment and the success of students and in all levels of education. The business community and the public are constant partners in recruiting and preparing students and faculty who will meet the state workforce and research needs." (THECB, 2000)

Higher education, elementary and secondary education, community, Latino, African American, White, the government sector, the for-profit sector, nonprofit sector, rich to middle class and poor, we are all caught in an inescapable network of mutuality. And so the name "InterAction."

You may have recognized this statement as the vision statement of the Texas Higher Education Coordinating Board in the "Closing the Gaps" effort. Dr. Ed Apodaca said that this statement is not a vision statement; that it is, in fact, for the state of Texas, a *survival* statement.

Many would agree that in order to survive, the state of Texas must increase the current 5 percent participation rate in higher education and that the current 3.7 participation rate for Hispanic students in higher education affects not only themselves but everyone.

So, what do we do? How do we interact? IDRA has developed a particular framework that may begin to create common cause and to frame common cause. Those areas are:

- preparing students,
- college access,
- institutional persistence,
- affordability,
- institutional resources,
- graduation, and
- graduate and professional studies.

I invite you to remember as we move forward that in the words of Martin Luther King, "We are all caught up in an inescapable network of mutuality." I believe that the long-term progress in Latino access and success requires acknowledging and building on that mutuality. Higher education, elementary and secondary education, community, Latino, African American, White, the government sector, the for-profit sector, nonprofit sector, rich to middle class and poor, we are all caught in an inescapable network of mutuality. And so the name "InterAction."

Shopping List for the Future

There's an interesting fact in the "Measuring Up" report as well that I want to share with you. It concludes that if all ethnic groups in Texas had the same educational attainment and earnings as Whites, total personal income in Texas would be about $31.4 billion higher, and the state would realize an estimated $11 billion in additional Texas revenue (NCPPHE, 2004).

And what could Texas do with an additional $11 billion in tax revenue? Those of you of who are superintendents, who are presidents of universities, who are involved with policy at many levels, know that with $11 billion a lot could be done.

So, here's my shopping list. We could invest $3.4 billion in kindergarten through grade 12 public education in Texas and reach at least the U.S. average of spending per student. Textbook costs for students next year will total $560 million. With double that amount, we can provide for enough materials for the growing number of English language learners, more library books in the low wealth schools and better equipped computer and science labs. We could provide additional dollars for student financial aid.

The Texas Be On Time Program, which currently costs $388 million to serve a few students based on financial need and contingent on completing four years at a four-year institution or two years at a community college, could create other ways to find means-based assistance. So, let's say that we allocate double the amount that has been allocated so far to the Texas Be On Time Program. That would be $776 million.

And then we could fund technology for teachers and students. A Hewlett Packard Pavilion laptop computer costs $1,229. For Texas' 288,386 teachers, that would amount to $354,426,395. Then we could get a laptop for 2 million of Texas' 4.2 million students, for about half of them, and that would cost $2,458 million.

We could invest $31 million in what is needed for Texas to reach the average level of national spending for public transit, and we could spend an additional $983 million to reach the national average for spending on highways and streets.

And then we could do a little bit about health care. We would have the $1.3 billion that is needed for Texas to be on par with the nation's average spending for public health. And then we could restore the health care aid for children and the elderly that was cut in 2003. In Bexar County that would be $21.8 million; in Dallas County, $26.5 million; in Harris County, $43 million; in Travis County, $7 million; about $100 million, rounded out to take care of children and the elderly in the state of Texas.

And then I totaled my list and ended up with $10.5 billion, which leaves us about $500 million for good measure. So, that is what $11 billion could buy the students of Texas; but in order to do that, we have to create educational parity for all Texans.

I say that we owe it to ourselves, to our children and to our children's children to find out what educational parity would look like. How might we, you and I here today, and the InterAction initiative as we move forward, interact and interconnect? What might we be able to do? That is what today is about. I look forward to hearing your thoughts and your vision for the future.

Resources

National Center for Public Policy and Higher Education. *Measuring Up – The State Report Card on Higher Education* (San Jose, California: NCPPHE, 2004).

Texas Higher Education Coordinating Board. *Closing the Gaps: The Texas Higher Education Plan* (Austin, Texas: THECB, 2000).

Originally published in the *IDRA Newsletter*, November-December 2005

Musical Chairs and Unkept Promises

by María "Cuca" Robledo Montecel, Ph.D.

Editor's Note: The following is adapted from a keynote presentation made by Dr. María "Cuca" Robledo Montecel at the National Dropout Prevention Network conference.

The year 2000 is a good time to take stock of where we are, why we are here, and what is needed. Really, we already know what is needed. You may recall a book by Robert Fulghum, entitled *All I Really Need to Know I Learned in Kindergarten.*

In another of his books, Fulghum tells a story of a philosophy class he taught (1993). On the first day of class, he announced that they were going to play musical chairs. The students enthusiastically arranged their chairs in a line with the seats in alternating directions. No one asked how to play. They already knew the rules.

He started the tape recorder playing "Stars and Stripes," and the students marched around the chairs. Mind you, these were seniors in high school. They had not played musical chairs since second grade. But they still knew how and jumped into the game without hesitation. Musical chairs! All right!

He removed a few chairs and stopped the music. The students scrambled to find seats. Those without chairs were stunned. They knew how this game worked: the music stops, you get a chair. How could they not have a chair so soon? Written across their faces was, "How dumb can I be?"

Oh well, too bad. They were losers. You are out. Go stand against the wall – over there.

The music continued as the remaining students marched around. Chairs were removed. The music stopped. Students went crazy trying to get a chair.

As the game went on, the quest for chairs became serious. Then it became rough. The girls were not going to fight jocks for chairs. Losers to the wall.

Now they were down to two members of the wrestling team. They were willing to push, knee, kick, or bite to get that last chair. This is war! When the music stopped, one guy jerked the chair out from under his opponent and slammed down into it. He had a look of triumph on his face. He raised his hands high with his forefingers signaling Number One, Number One!

He acted as if the class admired him and his accomplishment. He got the chair. "I'm the winner!"

Wrong. The losers, lined up against the back wall, thought he was a jerk.

This is not a game. Games are supposed to be fun. This got too serious too fast – like high school life, like real life.

Did they want to play again? A few of the jocks did. But not the rest of the class. It all came back to them now. Big deal.

Traditional Education Game

That is how we traditionally play the game of musical chairs. It is similar to the way we traditionally deal with schooling.

For example, if you are watching the game being played, you can usually tell who is not going to make it. In musical chairs, it is easy to see who is moving slower than the others. You can tell by the way a particular girl behaves that she may be embarrassed to run too fast or to fight too hard to get a chair. You can tell who seems confused when the music is stopped, who lets others grab chairs from under him. It is easy to see who will fail.

This problem of playing the traditional education game that blames the students and families is perhaps the main reason we have failed to reduce dropout rates.

Sometimes, when the person leading the game, and playing the music, watches the marching students, there is even some choosing when to stop the music to help favorite students win.

We do the same with school children. It is usually easy to see who is moving slower than the others. We can tell who is easily distracted. We think less of those we believe do not want to run or do not fight very hard.

Judgements are made about students' potential. We stop and start praise, encouragement, and resources based on our judgements of who can win. Often, those judgements follow students all the way through school – and through life. How many times have you heard people say they can look at a class of first graders and identify who will not make it to graduation?

In the game of musical chairs, there are certain characteristics you have to have to do well. It helps to be of a certain size. You really need to be able to take stock quickly of what is happening around you. You must be fast and you have to keep an ear out for the music. If you do not have those characteristics, too bad. You are out.

Schools have traditionally been designed to serve students with certain characteristics too. It has often made sense to many people to prescribe teaching methods and programs to serve the most students with the least amount of effort or expense.

So, grand school reform schemes have been designed based on the characteristics of White, middle-class, mostly male children who speak English. And then, almost as an afterthought, they are adopted or slightly adapted for children of color, for girls, for those who speak another language, and for poor kids.

Such "trickle down" efforts usually end up reforming schools to benefit those who are already doing well and say "life's tough" to those who are not.

What happens when a student who was out tries to get back into the game? In musical chairs, no one is allowed back. It would not be fair to the other players. You can watch, but you cannot be a part of the action. You do not have the skill, you do not have the speed. If someone tries to get back in, there is an uproar. You should be satisfied with how far you made it. The game is for someone else now. Be quiet.

In a school setting, if a young person has been labeled at risk, what happens? Students labeled at risk immediately become problems. And what do people do with problems? They either ignore the problems, get rid of them, or try to fix them.

Ignore the problems: Put the problem kids in special education classes or in classrooms with watered-down, connect-the-dot curriculum or give them the least-experienced, least powerful teachers, babysit them – be not concerned about whether or not they are learning – and they will not interfere with the real students.

Get rid of the problems: Send the students who do not fit the mold to alternative settings or encourage them to leave school.

Try to "fix" the problems: If only they were not poor, or they spoke English better or their parents cared, then they could learn. Fix them by providing remedial instruction and compensatory programs and slow things down in order for the students to get it. Try to train parents on how to raise their kids, and we tell poor parents to think like middle-class ones. Ignore, get rid of, fix…

But, if we are just re-arranging the same number of chairs, can more students find a seat when the music stops?

Obviously, re-arranging the chairs in the game does not accommodate more winners. We can do the math: 10 chairs in a line is the same as 10 chairs in a circle. Yet in schools, we often re-arrange personnel and programs but keep the same barriers in place.

Winners and Losers

There are certain things we get as a result of the way we play this education game. We get low achievement. We get caring teachers who burn out. And we get students dropping out.

Many reports show that despite the success of some dropout initiatives in some areas, the dropout picture remains strikingly troublesome. The National Center for Education Statistics (NCES) released a report indicating that the dropout rate has climbed since 1982, and it is currently even higher than it was in 1967 (1997).

The NCES findings are consistent with IDRA's attrition analyses in Texas and an IDRA dropout study released earlier this year entitled, *Missing: Texas Youth – Dropout and Attrition Rates in Texas Public High Schools* (Supik & Johnson, 1999).

Thirteen years ago at IDRA, we conducted the first comprehensive statewide study of school dropouts in Texas. Using a high school attrition formula, IDRA estimated that 86,000 students had not graduated from Texas public schools that year, costing the state $17.12 billion dollars in foregone income, lost tax revenues and increased criminal justice, welfare, unemployment and job training costs.

By 1998 – 12 years later – the estimated cumulative number of Texas school dropouts has grown to more than 1.2 million. Because these students were unable to complete high school, the state of Texas loses $319 billion.

Schools often assume that the target population – whether the target population is defined by race, by gender or by language – is to blame for educational failure. Deficit-models always try to change the characteristics of the student and the family, so that the student will fit into the school program.

A close look at national data dispels some myths about the reasons for the high dropout rates among Hispanic students.

Poverty is often cited as the reason so many Hispanic students dropout. But according to the data, poverty does not explain it. Within each income level, Hispanic students are substantially more likely to drop out.

Immigration status does not explain it either. The dropout rate of Hispanic students born in the United States is 17.9 percent.

Language proficiency is another reason that is often given. (We will ignore for the moment that English is the first language for many Hispanic students.) But speaking Spanish does not explain the high dropout rates among Hispanic students.

Hispanic students who speak Spanish at home and also speak English "well" or "very well" are as likely to remain in school as are their peers who speak only English.

IDRA studies have found that Hispanic students whose first language is Spanish and those whose parents encouraged bilingualism are more likely to remain in school.

Sometimes, the deficit view is more narrow: "Parents, or minority parents, don't care." Let me tell you about a friend of mine and her bright son. Like his sisters before him – and like most young children – Mark cried when his mother took him to his pre-kindergarten class. The teacher assured his mother that she would take care of him. Instead, when his mother left, the teacher locked Mark in a storage room all morning. He finally managed to climb out and tried to walk home. He got lost, and it took two hours for his mother to find him.

When he was in the first grade, he was struggling with his work. His parents worked with him, and his mother even visited the classroom to observe. But she never heard from the teacher and at the end of the school year, Mark had failing grades.

The teacher recommended retaining him. His parents knew that was not the best thing for Mark. The principal agreed since Mark had excellent test scores. The next year, Mark's second grade teacher constantly compared him to his older sister, "You're nothing like your sister." By this time, Mark was already internalizing what was happening. He thought there was something wrong with him.

In the third grade, he was placed in a special education class where he was challenged even less. His parents continued to plead with the school officials. A school psychologist told them, "You Mexican people, you're so close to him that you've damaged him." Mark comforted his parents while still feeling guilty inside.

Throughout the following years, Mark continued to move through school, unchallenged, struggling, alone. His parents did everything they could. They got support from an outside agency, they remained active in school leadership. His mom was even PTA president by the time he reached high school.

It was then that a teacher told Mark, "You will never amount to anything, you should just drop out and get a GED." That is what Mark did early in high school. With the GED he could have attended a graduation ceremony, but he refused knowing he had not earned a real diploma. He also had the daily reminder of three sisters who were succeeding in college.

Today, he is 24 years old and works night shifts at a grocery store. He appears well-adjusted, funny, religious. But his mother recognizes that he still has a low self-esteem. He tells her not to give up on him. He attended a community college for a semester and wants to try again someday.

He has no desire to get married until he can support his wife. And, as he says, if he is blessed with children, he wants to make sure he can support them like his father supported him.

Our families contribute much. The day-to-day activities that families do with their children – story-telling, singing, playing games, reading, talking and listening – all these have intellectual, emotional and physical benefits that enhance the child's development and are strengths that the school can use.

This problem of playing the traditional education game that blames the students and families is perhaps the main reason we have failed to reduce dropout rates. You cannot really expect to solve a problem unless you diagnose it correctly.

In musical chairs, the promise is that the game will be fun – the music, the anticipation, being part of things. In education, the promise is that schooling is for everyone and is good for your future, that adults in school care about you, and that you will succeed if you do your best.

Mark did his best. The promise was broken for him. The promise is broken for the 1,370 young people who drop out of our nation's schools every day.

A New Way to Play the Game

Back in Robert Fulghum's philosophy class, the students had no desire to play musical chairs again. It was not fun after all.

But, he insisted that they play one more time, with one rule change. This time, if the students do not have a chair, they will sit in someone's lap. Everybody stays in the game, it's only a matter of where you sit. The students had to think about it for a minute. Well, OK.

They reset the chairs as before. Fulghum started the "Stars and Stripes." They marched. He removed some chairs and stopped the music. There was a pause in the action. (Do I want a chair to myself? Do I want to sit on someone's lap or have someone sit in mine? And who?) The class got seated, but the mood had changed. There was laughter, giggling. When the game began again, there was a change of pace. What is the hurry?

When the number of chairs dwindled to force two to a chair, a dimension of grace entered in, as the role of sittee and sitter was clarified: Oh no, please, after you. Some advance planning was evident.

As the game continued and more and more people had to share one chair, a kind of gymnastic dance form developed. It became a group accomplishment to get everyone branched out on knees. Students with organizational skills came to the fore – it is a people puzzle to solve now. "Big people on the bottom first, put your arms around him, sit back, easy, easy."

When there was one chair left, the class laughed and delightfully managed to make sure their weight was evenly distributed. If they tumbled, they would get up and try again until everyone was sitting down. Everyone was triumphant.

The only one who had trouble with this paradigm shift was the guy who won the first time, under the old rules. He did not know what winning was now.

Fulghum then told the class that they would play one more round. He would remove the last chair. When the music stopped, they would all sit down in a lap.

"How on earth can we do that?" they said. "You can find a way," he replied.

One more time, they marched to the music and stopped. They looked at each other and started giving each other direction to stand in a perfect circle. "Step toward the middle to make a tighter circle." "Place your hands on the hips of the person in front of you." "On the count of three, slowly sit and guide the person in front of you onto your knees." "Ready. One. Two. Three. Sit." They all sat. No chair.

Fulghum presents this true story of how people face the problem of diminishing resources. Is it always to be a winners-losers world, or can we keep everyone in the game?

IDRA's research on strategies for reducing the dropout rate, stemming from research-based effective strategies and IDRA's experience in schools over the last 26 years, shows five components are vital to successful dropout prevention.

First, *all* students must be valued. Success will require that we value *every single* child. In fact, success will be *measured by how* we value every single child.

Second, there must be a support network in smaller schools with smaller class sizes where students are well known and where at least one educator in a student's life is totally – and for the long haul – committed to the success of that student.

Third, families must be valued as partners with the school.

Fourth, schools must change and innovate, providing challenging curriculum to match the characteristics of their students and embracing the strengths and contributions that students and their families bring.

Fifth, school staff – especially teachers – must be highly qualified and equipped with the tools needed to ensure their students' success, including the use of technology, different learning styles and mentoring programs. Effective professional development can help provide these tools.

We must also get rid of one important myth: the myth that equal opportunity exists. The truth, as researcher Linda Darling-Hammond has stated, is that "the U.S. educational system is one of the most unequal in the industrialized world, and students routinely receive dramatically different learning opportunities based on their social status" (1998). The wealthiest 10 percent of U.S. school districts spend nearly 10 times more than the poorest 10 percent. Yet despite differences in funding, teacher quality, curriculum, and class sizes, the prevailing view is that if students do not achieve, it is their own fault.

By understanding how the school environment contributes to a student's failure, we can change what blocks success. What works are sound, effective and efficient educational strategies that encourage students to remain in school. There are many such strategies. Upward Bound, Communities In Schools, and the IDRA Coca-Cola Valued Youth Program use such strategies.

The IDRA Coca-Cola Valued Youth Program is dear to my heart. It is based on the creed that all students are valuable, none is expendable. This philosophy, that all students are valuable, is helping more than 200 schools keep 98 percent of Valued Youths in school, keeping these young people in the classroom and learning.

The idea is simple and may seem unusual at first glance. We work with schools to identify students who are considered to be in at-risk situations and place them as tutors of younger students.

Participating tutors have been the ones who traditionally *receive* help; never had they been asked to *provide* help. These were the "throwaways," students who were not expected ever to graduate from high school. Yet, when given the appropriate structure, they can and do succeed.

In addition to the changes this program produces in young people, the Coca-Cola Valued Youth Program succeeds because it subtly but powerfully challenges and ultimately changes people's beliefs and behaviors.

One administrator recounted her first experience with the program. She knew Paul Hayes by his reputation as a student who "sent teachers into early retirement."

She watched him get off the bus at the elementary school where he would be tutoring that day. She kept a vigilant eye on him as he entered the classroom and watched in amazement as he put on a hand puppet and began teaching three little ones.

What she saw in that classroom was "Mr. Hayes." She saw Mr. Hayes' students following his every word and learning. And she heard the elementary teacher tell how she would be lost without Mr. Hayes in her classroom.

As she watched him get back on the bus that would take him to his middle school, she wondered if his middle school teachers would see the Mr. Hayes that was in him or would they only see Paul, the at-risk student?

The greatest "at-risk" circumstance students face may be the school's low, and self-fulfilling, expectations.

A philosopher once said, "The actual proves the possible." The Coca-Cola Valued Youth Program works, as do other programs across the country. All students can and are succeeding in some schools. It can happen in every school.

Everyone Wins

After the launch of Apollo 13, NASA is faced with a dreadful problem. You may remember the movie telling of the story. Three astronauts are in space with a malfunctioning shuttle. It has been struck by something floating in space. There is not enough oxygen for them to breath. They do not have the tools they need to make the repairs for a problem they cannot even examine closely. It seems hopeless.

On the ground, hundreds of scientists are scratching their heads. They have been up for hours and cannot think of a workable solution. Everything they come up with brings with it a new set of problems. They start pointing fingers.

They are overwhelmed, sitting back wringing their hands. We cannot fix this. They are about to give up.

The mission director listened to the group's list of difficulties. If only this, we could have done that. It's hopeless. Then he emphatically reminded them, "Failure is *not* an option!"

Failure was not an option because it would mean losing the lives of the three men in the shuttle. It would mean breaking promises made to their families. Failure was not an option because the brain power was there to create a new solution by thinking about the problem differently. Failure was not an option.

The scientists were a little bruised at first. But seeing the situation in a new light they pulled together.

They relooked at the resources before them. Once discarded as useless for their traditional purposes, the resources were now seen as possibilities. The scientists became very creative. And they succeeded. The shuttle and the astronauts were brought home safely.

What we are here today to face is a problem with even more powerful implications. Many more than three people are affected. We have tried different things, some more successful than others. Yet the dropout rate continues to climb. Many people are overwhelmed, wringing their hands. There is a lot of finger-pointing. We cannot fix this. We cannot fix them.

Robert Fulghum changed only one rule in musical chairs: to keep all the kids in the game.

The only thing we have to change is our belief that some students deserve success and others do not. The new rule is: All students stay in. The new promise is: All students succeed. Failure is not an option.

Resources

Darling-Hammond, L. "Unequal Opportunity: Race and Education," *Brookings Review* (March 22, 1998).

Fulghum, R. *Maybe (Maybe Not): Second Thoughts from a Secret Life* (New York: Ballantine Books, 1993).

National Center for Education Statistics. *Dropout Rates in the United States, 1995* (Washington, D.C.: U.S. Department of Education, July 1997).

Supik, J.D., and R.L. Johnson. *Missing: Texas Youth – Dropout and Attrition Rates in Texas Public High Schools* (San Antonio, Texas: Intercultural Development Research Association, 1999).

Supik, J.D. "The Coca-Cola Valued Youth Program: An Idea that Works," *IDRA Newsletter* (San Antonio, Texas: Intercultural Development Research Association, October 1994).

Originally published in the *IDRA Newsletter*, January 2000

From "Dropping Out" to "Holding On" – Seven Lessons from Texas

by María "Cuca" Robledo Montecel, Ph.D.

Editor's Note: The following is expanded from the presentation to the Education Writers Association's Regional Seminar, "Left Behind? Dropouts and High School Reform," February 27, 2004, by Dr. María "Cuca" Robledo Montecel.

Eighteen years ago, no one knew how many students in Texas were leaving school without a high school diploma. Then, IDRA was commissioned to conduct the first comprehensive statewide study of high school dropouts in Texas. That pioneering study, conducted for the Texas Department of Community Affairs, answered three questions.

The first question was: How many students are dropping out? The answer was: Many. More than 86,000 students did not graduate that year from Texas high schools.

The second question was: Why are students leaving? The answer was: Students are not connected to the school. Students left for many reasons, but a lack of connection was an underlying theme.

The third question was: What is it costing us? The answer was: $17.2 billion over the lifetime of those students in foregone income, lost tax base, increased unemployment costs, increased criminal justice costs, and increased welfare costs. In fact, IDRA's cost benefit analysis indicated that for every dollar invested in keeping kids in school, nine would be returned (Ramírez & Robledo Montecel, 1987; see Appendix).

That was 1986. At the time, individual student records were not collected. To conduct the study in the absence of student-level numbers, IDRA pioneered an attrition methodology that utilized enrollment data from the Texas Education Agency to develop dropout count estimates. The IDRA study pushed the development of official dropout identification, counting, and reporting policies and procedures.

Now it is 2004. IDRA has conducted a dropout study every year using the same methodology based on enrollments. But progress on accurate counting by the state has been slow and halting. Dropouts in Texas have been systematically under-reported. This has created a false sense of security. By minimizing the problem, the state has promoted inaction.

At the national level, the *No Child Left Behind Act* federal education requirements around graduation rates are casting a national spotlight on the issue of dropouts. Several organizations have created dropout count methodologies that parallel the enrollment methodology that IDRA pioneered. In Texas, as in the rest of the country, many students drop out, many students are disconnected from schools, and the costs are high.

Fortunately, many educators, parents and students have not waited for the official counts to change. They know there is a problem. They know there are solutions. Around the country, schools and communities, in partnership with IDRA and in a range of other initiatives, have pioneered new ways to turn the tide. Class by class, they have found ways to transform schools from *places that misplace children into settings that hold on to them*.

Having dealt with this issue so closely for so many years, IDRA offers the following seven lessons from Texas in the hope that many more will take up the call to action.

Lesson One: Losing Children from Our School Systems ("Dropout") Is a Persistent, Unacknowledged Problem

Since 1986, when IDRA conducted Texas' first comprehensive statewide study of high school dropouts, Texas schools have lost close to 2 million students with a net loss to the state of nearly $500 billion. This is like losing Austin or Dallas over the course of a decade and a half.

And this first lesson can be seen across the country. The Civil Rights Project at Harvard University reported earlier this year: "Every year, across the country, a dangerously high percentage of students – disproportionately poor and minority – disappear from the educational pipeline. Nationally, only about 68 percent of all students who enter the ninth grade will graduate 'on time' with regular diplomas in the 12th grade" (Orfield, 2004).

The Civil Rights Project also reported that "dropout data mislead the public into thinking that most students are earning diplomas" (Orfield, 2004).

The National Board on Educational Testing and Public Policy reported: "Despite setting a national goal of a high school graduation rate of 90 percent in 1994, only two states, New Jersey and Wisconsin, met that goal in the academic year 2000-01. Shockingly, there were 24 states with graduation rates of 75 percent or less" (Haney, 2004).

Since every student counts, we simply must count every student.

Lesson Two: Fraud Is a Red Herring – Distracting Us from the Real Problem That Is Before Us. Undercounting Is the Result of Institutional Intransigence, Not Massive Fraud

As compelling as stories of fraud can be, by and large, undercounts have nothing to do with fraud. Even if all Texas school districts reported data within the letter of the law, as the system currently stands, they would seriously undercount lost students.

Texas uses *29 leaver codes.* This results in a gross undercounting and underreporting of students who have never received a high school diploma. In the past – as recently as 2000-01 – the state has used as many as *43 leaver codes.* While a reduction in ways to obscure the dropout count is a step in the right direction, it still skirts the issue.

To be credible, the dropout definition should be simple and clear: *Count as a dropout any student who does not hold a high school diploma.* A GED is never equivalent to a high school diploma – ask any employer, college or university.

More than 150,000 students lacking documented and official transfer status are excluded from Texas' dropout counts every year.

As long as knowing the real status of our students is not a policy reform priority, thousands of students will continue to be lost – not only from schools – but also reflected in losses in tax revenue and income that comes from decreased levels of education among residents.

Lesson Three: Accountability Systems Did Not Create Dropouts

Accountability systems did not *create* dropouts. Losing children from our school systems has long been a problem. Unacceptably high dropout rates pre-date the accountability systems developed over the last several years in response to the concern about the effect of under-education on the current information-based economy. In fact, dropout rates for Hispanic students in the 1940s have been estimated around 80 percent (Cárdenas, 1995).

Accountability systems that do not hurt children will not create dropouts. High-stakes testing does hurt children and will increase the dropout rate (see Lesson Four).

Diagnostic student assessments are useful to guide instruction. And the use of state assessment measures is one of several necessary factors in assessing school effectiveness and for holding schools accountable for educating all of our students. Tests can play an important role in this kind of school accountability – one that accepts the responsibility that schools have toward children and communities.

Lesson Four: High-stakes Testing and Accountability Systems Must Be Uncoupled

Testing of students to promote school accountability is not a new idea. Students have been tested for decades using both locally-developed and standardized tests. But a new dimension has emerged in using a single test to make decisions concerning whether a student gets promoted to the next grade or whether a graduating student will receive a diploma.

The push for using state test scores as the primary basis for promotion, retention and graduation decisions is based on the incorrect assumption that a single test score tells you all you need to know about student achievement.

Recent research on the Texas testing program reveals that improvement in state test scores did not simultaneously result in higher test scores on national tests, and that despite rising state test scores, Texas students were not graduating in higher numbers or increasing their enrollment in college. On the other hand, research has shown that students who are retained in grade do no better the next year. In many cases, retention leads students to drop out before they graduate.

School accountability should not mean: (1) that high-stakes decisions in children's lives (e.g., high school graduation) are made on the basis of tests, or (2) that tests dictate what children learn. Texas and other states should continue to measure schools' performance. This can be done more efficiently and at less expense by moving to an assessment system that tests a sample of students from each school to get a picture of how each school is performing. Current federal policy does not allow sample testing for accountability.

Lesson Five: We Cannot Afford to Decide that Some Kids Do Not Count

Between the 1985-86 and 2002-03 school years, the estimated cumulative costs of public school dropouts in the state of Texas were in excess of $500 billion in foregone income, lost tax revenues, and increased job training, welfare, unemployment and criminal justice costs.

On average, dropouts are more likely to be unemployed than high school graduates and earn less money when they eventually secure work. Two-thirds of inmates in the Texas prison system are high school dropouts. The social and economic costs of the dropout problem have increased by 26 times the initial estimates of $17 billion in 1986.

Lack of school holding power disproportionately affects minority students. Following a 17-year trend, in 2002-03, Texas Hispanic students had the highest attrition rate at 50 percent, followed by African American students at 45 percent and Native American students at 39 percent. White students had an attrition rate of 24 percent.

Lesson Six: Dropout Data Is Not a Legitimate Reason to Give Up On Public Education

Giving up on public education does not solve the dropout problem. Private schools do not have the capacity or capability to absorb large numbers of poor students. Private schools are not accountable to the public for actions or results. Further, distributing public money for private schools would take away money from our communities resulting in higher taxes for homeowners and businesses in the community.

Excellent neighborhood public schools are the foundation of strong communities. The best way to strengthen public schools is to *strengthen* public schools – schools that are accountable to us all.

Lesson Seven: It Is Time to Move From "Dropping Out" to "Holding On"

We know what is needed to address the problem of dropouts in our schools. What we need is the public will and commitment to carry it out.

IDRA's Coca-Cola Valued Youth Program was begun in Texas and is making a difference in schools across the United States and in Brazil. Programs like this demonstrate how schools can change from giving up on certain students to transforming their schools to hang on to them.

While programs alone are not a magic bullet, they demonstrate which elements must be in place to create schools that promote the success of all our children from kindergarten to graduation.

Research demonstrates that to move from *dropping out* to *holding on*:

- *All* students must be valued.
- There must be at least one educator in a student's life who is totally committed to the success of that student.
- Families must be valued as partners with the school, all committed to ensuring that equity and excellence is present in a student's life.
- Schools must change and innovate to match the characteristics of their students and embrace the strengths and contributions that students and their families bring.
- School staff, especially teachers, must be equipped with the tools needed to ensure their students' success, including the use of technology, different learning styles and mentoring programs. *Effective* professional development can help provide these tools.

We know, without a doubt, that the nation faces a huge, untenable problem. But we also know that the problem is *not intractable*. Today, if we re-commit ourselves to schools that work for all children, we can ensure that all children have the opportunity for an excellent education.

Quality education is the key to opportunity, the foundation of democracy, and the heart of a good life. Many have long recognized that all of our children deserve no less.

Resources

Cárdenas, J.A. *Multicultural Education: A Generation of Advocacy* (Needham Heights, Mass.: Simmon and Schuster Custom Publishing, 1995).

Haney, W., et al. *The Education Pipeline in the United States, 1970-2000* (Chestnut Hill, Mass.: Center for the Study of Testing, Evaluation, and Educational Policy, Lynch School of Education, Boston College, 2004).

Intercultural Development Research Association. *Fair Funding for Texas School Children*, Texas education policy digest series (San Antonio, Texas: IDRA, 2002).

Johnson, R.L. "Schools Continue to Lose Students: Texas Public School Attrition Study, 2002-03," *IDRA Newsletter* (San Antonio, Texas: Intercultural Development Research Association, October 2003).

Orfield, G., and D. Losen, J. Wald, C. Swanson. *Losing Our Future: How Minority Youth are Being Left Behind by the Graduation Rate Crisis* (Cambridge, Mass.: The Civil Rights Project at Harvard University. Contributors: Advocates for Children of New York, The Civil Society Institute, 2004).

Ramírez, D., and M. Robledo Montecel. "The Economic Impact of the Dropout Problem," *IDRA Newsletter* (San Antonio, Texas: Intercultural Development Research Association, April 1987).

Robledo Montecel, M. "Texas Needs Diplomas, Not Delusions," *IDRA Newsletter* (San Antonio, Texas: Intercultural Development Research Association, September 2002).

Texas Department of Criminal Justice, 1998.

U.S. Department of Education, National Center for Education Statistics, 1999.

Originally published in the *IDRA Newsletter*, April 2004

Chapter Seven – Closing

A Wise Investment (Epilogue)

Aurelio M. Montemayor, M.Ed.

How you spend your money and your time
Reveals deep values more sharply than a vow.
Dreams aren't wrong, but acts are now:
Peace pretty words, it's the deeds not the rhyme.

Regardless of promises to students we make,
Or displays of posters lining the hall,
Proof of values aren't advertized on a wall,
But nurtured love of learning for learning's sake.

Telling children they're intelligent and great
Motivates not an iota compared to their success
As students, with support and challenge, no less,
Experiencing the ability to solve, invent and create.

Not spending time and money on children is a crime.
Providing excellent schools for all is virtue sublime.

Claiming the Courage to Connect

by María "Cuca" Robledo Montecel, Ph.D.

IDRA's Quality Schools Action Framework gives us a way to set children and ourselves up for success. It presents a way of thinking about all of the important pieces. If we are to make sure that children are able to fully develop themselves, to contribute to their families and to their communities by virtue of having a good education, then here's a place to start. We must be able to look at our schools, at our school districts, at our states to see if we are doing the right things.

The Quality Schools Action Framework calls on us to make connections in several ways. It calls for meaningful connections among people in the school setting: students connecting with teachers, teachers connecting with parents, parents connecting with students, school leadership connecting with teachers.

Our framework also shows how we must connect school outcomes – graduation and college readiness – with what produces those outcomes: connecting actionable knowledge to equip coalitions and the community to work in partnership with their neighborhood public schools, ensuring the presence of fair funding and governance efficacy, and connecting the four school system indicators (student engagement, teaching quality, curriculum quality and access, parent and community engagement) to focus school change.

And importantly, the Quality Schools Action Framework emphasizes the importance of connections between K-12 schools, local community organizations, institutions of higher education, the business community and local policymakers. Neighborhood public schools belong to their communities. Cross-sector relationships facilitate powerful problem solving and innovation that just cannot be done in isolation.

What we need is to draw on our courage to connect so that every student graduates prepared for college and beyond.

In 2009, IDRA celebrated the 25th anniversary of our Coca-Cola Valued Youth Program, an empirically-tested dropout prevention program implemented in 550 schools in the continental United States, Puerto Rico, Brazil and the United Kingdom. The program works by engaging youth at risk of dropping out as tutors of younger students. Valuing youth of all backgrounds transforms perceptions and outcomes: since 1984, the program has kept more than 29,000 students in school and positively impacted more than half a million children, families and educators.

Anchored in this transnational experience and on the occasion of its milestone anniversary, IDRA reflected on lessons we have learned that can guide future action. We were thrilled to present the voices of youth, teachers, family members and program leaders who demonstrate why valuing youth is at the heart of school transformation.

1. Valuing Youth Works. If you provide young people with an opportunity to contribute – to themselves, their families, their communities – they will.

When we began the program in 1984 as a little pilot in San Antonio, we asserted this based on what we felt might be true. We now know, not only in the Coca-Cola Valued Youth Program but in every single educational program that we have worked with, in every school we have worked with, that valuing youth works. And that if you provide young people with an opportunity to contribute, they will.

And so in the case of the tutors who are in the Coca-Cola Valued Youth Program, the students who are considered the at-risk students become tutors of younger children. And what happens when they are put in a position to contribute to others? They do so. They are encouraged by the fact that their young tutees need them in order to learn. They are encouraged by the fact that the adults in their school trust them to be leaders. They rise to the occasion, just like you and I would rise to an occasion when people thought well of us and put us in a position to contribute and then supported us.

> "Research and classroom experience make clear that student engagement – a student's intellectual, social and emotional connection to school – is a prerequisite to learning. Without substantive student engagement, researchers find, 'there is no learning.'
>
> "When students lack a sense of connection to teachers, school and what they are learning, there is little reason to remain. This is especially true at key transition points or when students are struggling to stay on track. But all too often, when students are struggling, we give up on them. Valuing youth, without exception, turns this tendency on its head."
>
> *– Continuities – Lessons for the Future of Education from the IDRA Coca-Cola Valued Youth Program*

In contrast, strategies that attempt to "save" some children at the expense of others do harm. Strategies that purport to have all the answers and that shut out the opinions and contributions of students and their families do harm. Strategies that treat teachers or parents as the enemy do harm. Any strategy that does not value every single child, any strategy that blames a culture for school failure does harm.

So, the first thing we must do is to make a fundamental shift in the assumptions that guide our efforts. The core assumption should be one that values young people – all young people. We cannot afford to value some children and not others, some schools and not others, some neighborhoods and not others, some ethnic or racial group and not others.

All children are valuable; none is expendable.

2. Local Ownership is Key. To scale up and replicate success requires holding fast to essentials while adapting to local contexts.

The question becomes how do you scale up, sustain and replicate success. What we have found to be a transformative practice is to hold fast to the essentials of the change while adapting to the local context. There is no silver bullet that will work in the same way and all places. One can and one must adopt and adapt to local contexts and then create the local ownership that is so very key to fundamental and transformative to change.

3. School Leadership Sets the Tone. To squarely take on attrition, school leaders must inspire innovation, embody engagement, and incorporate actionable knowledge.

If we are going to achieve graduation for all, then leaders at the school level must inspire innovation. They must themselves embody the kind of engagement that we want for our students with school, embody that engagement for themselves with the teachers, for themselves with the students, and for themselves as leaders with the community. Leaders then must incorporate what we know into what we do.

There is a large body of knowledge about what works, and it is important to incorporate that actionable knowledge into what is done. For example, IDRA has developed a School Holding Power online portal that helps community and school partners in Texas examine their school data and plan joint action to improve school holding power. It places accurate, high quality information in the hands of people at the leading edge of systems change. Through the portal, educators and community members find out how well their high school campus is preparing and graduating students, what factors may be weakening school holding power, and what they can do to address them.

4. Realizing the Power of One + One + One. All students must have at least one caring adult in their lives at school and a reason to care.

All students must have at least one caring adult in their lives at school and have a reason to care at school. That adult may be a teacher, an administrator, a counselor, a staff, or maybe someone in the community who on the student's behalf is in the school to assure that the student is supported. The important part of what we know is that there must be one adult who cares for and stands with every young person asserting that they in fact are valuable. And this can't be merely conceptual – "Oh you are so wonderful"

– but it must be: "I am going to stand with you, I am going to support you, I am going to give you all the tools necessary so that you are able to achieve success in a school setting."

> "It is estimated that in the United States, 40 to 60 percent of students feel chronically disengaged from school. That's the bad news. The good news is that stronger ties with at least one caring adult not only fortify students' connections to school but also help to improve their academic achievement."
>
> *– Continuities – Lessons for the Future of Education from the IDRA Coca-Cola Valued Youth Program*

That adult is an advocate for that child. He or she gives that child a reason to care, a reason to hope, a reason to know that he or she can do what is sometimes quite challenging. Importantly, a part of that caring has to be to challenge that student, including setting high expectations.

5. Family and Community Engagement is Essential. *The school-family-community triad is at the heart of holding on to students and ensuring their success.*

Parent and family engagement cannot be just window dressing; it must be real engagement. It must give parents and community real information about how schools are doing and give them an opportunity to support transformation at the local level – where their voices are included and their points of view are integrated into the decisions that are made, and where the strengths that our families and communities bring are incorporated and used in the school setting. To do that, we have to go past the stereotypic notions that society has about minority parents not caring and about poor communities not having anything to offer. We must really build on the strengths and on the vitality of communities that with very little in resources are able to support young people when given the opportunity and the tools to do so.

> When schools, families, and community members work together to support student learning, 'children tend to do better in school, stay in school longer, and like school more.' Family engagement in public education is associated with higher grades and test scores, enrollment in higher level programs, passing classes and earning course credits, better school attendance and social skills, graduation, and advancement to postsecondary education. And these findings hold true for students across diverse cultural, socioeconomic, and educational backgrounds."
>
> *– Continuities – Lessons for the Future of Education from the IDRA Coca-Cola Valued Youth Program*

6. Success Demands Well-Defined Partnerships. *When roles are clear and each partner contributes from its unique strengths, a multi-sector collaboration can reap dramatic results.*

Like most things, partnerships are required in order to achieve success. The partnerships must have roles that are clear. Each partner must contribute its unique strengths. The kind of collaboration that can really reap the dramatic results that we are looking at is multi-sector where we bring

"Whether their role is to design and develop a pedagogical framework; to put the framework into practice; or to test, evaluate or underwrite innovation, each partner must both be aligned with the goals for youth and contribute from its distinctive strengths."

– Continuities – Lessons for the Future of Education from the IDRA Coca-Cola Valued Youth Program

the school, the community, the business folk, the higher education people and others together. There are many examples of multi-sector collaboration that is informed, that builds on the strengths of each if the partners and that is fundamentally based on the value and importance of young people. Working in partnership, parents, educators, students, policymakers, businesspeople can create schools that hold on to all students until graduation and prepare them to succeed.

7. Structure and Innovation Sustain Impact. Transformative impact demands sustained structures, resources and a commitment to valuing all youth.

In order to sustain impact, you must have structure and you must have innovation. Transformation demands structures and resources and commitments. Schools must change and innovate to match the characteristics of their students and embrace the strengths and contributions that students and their families bring.

Parents and communities, working in connection with people inside and outside of schools, have played vital roles in every school reform effort – from fighting for fair funding to making sure that students are not ignored because of the language they speak. In the last few years, scarcity of resources, resegregation, concerns about security, political polarization, and an overall sense of taking care only of our own has pushed against us and pulled us apart.

But that can change.

We invite you to connect: to take these seven lessons and see what they mean in relationship to your own work and your community to use the Quality Schools Action Framework to identify the areas where your school needs to focus, to utilize actionable knowledge available through IDRA's School Holding Power Portal (http://www.idra.org/portal) for Texas and other sources.

If we reclaim our sense of fairness and of opportunity, build on our desire to succeed and have the courage to connect, we can assure today the future of our children, our communities and our country.

Resources

Alliance for Excellent Education and College Board. *Facts for Education Advocates: Demographics and the Racial Divide* (Washington, D.C.: Alliance for Excellent Education, copublished with College Board, 2009).

Robledo Montecel, M. *Continuities – Lessons for the Future of Education from the IDRA Coca-Cola Valued Youth Program* (San Antonio, Texas: Intercultural Development Research Association, 2009).

Appendix

About the Editors

María "Cuca" Robledo Montecel, Ph.D., is president and CEO of IDRA. A nationally-recognized expert on the prevention and recovery of dropouts, her doctorate is in research and evaluation. Her lifetime concern with youth – especially youth who are minority, poor or limited-English-proficient – has provided inspiration and vision for many communities across the country. (formerly María del Refugio Robledo, Ph.D.)

Christie L. Goodman, APR, coordinates IDRA's print and online communications. Accredited in public relations, she has a bachelor's degree in advertising with minors in sociology and art.

About the Contributors

Veronica Betancourt, M.A., was lead developer of IDRA's Science Smart! professional development model. A former classroom teacher, her master's degree is in bicultural/bilingual studies.

Hector Bojorquez, a former teacher himself, guides schools in technology integration. He led development of the IDRA School Holding Power portal.

Kathryn Brown created IDRA's Math Smart! professional development model. She now is an instructional designer with Edvance Research.

José A. Cárdenas, Ed.D., is the founder and director emeritus of IDRA. Now retired, he is nationally recognized as a school finance expert and civil rights advocate for equitable educational opportunity.

Albert Cortez, Ph.D., an expert on minority education policy and education research. His doctorate is in cultural foundations of education with a support area in educational administration.

Josie Danini Cortez, M.A., creates research-based and scientifically-based programs and products. A medical anthropologist by training, she also researches and advises on cross-cultural medical ethics. (formerly Josie D. Supik, M.A.)

Kristin Grayson, M.Ed., researched and developed the IDRA engagement model of sheltered instruction for English language learners. A former school teacher and administrator, she has a master's degree in bilingual, ESL, and multicultural education and is a doctoral student in leadership studies.

Roy L. Johnson, M.S., directs IDRA's research and evaluation and coordinates IDRA's annual attrition studies, which monitor the number of students lost from public school secondary enrollment in Texas. His master's degree is in urban studies.

Aurelio M. Montemayor, M.Ed., leads IDRA's innovative parent engagement work and developed its trainer of trainers model. A former public school teacher at all levels, his master's degree in bilingual education.

Laurie Posner, M.P.A., focuses on community-based strategies and partnerships to strengthen neighborhood public schools. A National Urban Fellow, her master's degree is in public administration.

David G. Ramirez, Ph.D., is president of The Inova Center, Ltd., working with school districts in the areas of evaluative research and the development of solutions to accountability. A Ford Foundation Fellow, his doctorate is in psychology.

Rosana G. Rodríguez, Ph.D., designs and leads projects to strengthen school-family-community partnerships and to build cross-sector, multicultural alliances to improve education. A former teacher and assistant superintendent and trained in clinical psychology, her doctorate is in education with emphasis in evaluation.

Bradley Scott, Ph.D., leads training and technical assistance to schools in race and human relations and equitable schooling. An expert in early childhood and elementary education, he holds a doctor of philosophy with a concentration in educational administration.

Adela Solís, Ph.D., a former bilingual teacher, has extensive expertise in bilingual education and ESL instructional methods. She designs mentoring programs for beginning teachers and holds a doctorate in education with a specialization in applied linguistics.

Abelardo Villarreal, Ph.D., directs IDRA's training and technical assistance to school districts. He has unparalleled expertise in program management, effective technical assistance delivery, curriculum development, and implementing and facilitating innovative models for school change. His doctorate is in curriculum and instruction.

IDRA Resources

Print Resources

Continuities – Lessons for the Future of Education from the IDRA Coca-Cola Valued Youth Program

by María Robledo Montecel, Ph.D.

This publication vividly captures seven key lessons for improving the quality of education for all students. It presents the voices of youth, teachers, family members and program leaders and the reasons valuing youth is at the heart of school transformation. It was released on the occasion of the 25th anniversary of the Coca-Cola Valued Youth Program in 2009 and in celebration of its success in keeping tens of thousands of students in school and positively impacting more than half a million children, families and educators on three continents. (No ISBN; 25 pages; 2009) Available from IDRA for $7, plus shipping, or free online at http://www.idra.org.

Disciplinary Alternative Education Programs in Texas – An Update

by Albert Cortez, Ph.D., & Josie D. Cortez, M.A.

Almost 10 years ago, IDRA gave voice to the thousands of Texas public school students who were being criminalized, ostracized and stigmatized for "offenses" that were formerly managed by a simple timeout or even a visit to the principal's office with its seminal assessment of Texas DAEPs. IDRA's latest policy update released March 2009, shows that in the last decade, more than three quarters of a million students have been sent to DAEPs. Four out of five of them are not there because of serious offenses. Put simply, DAEPs are a mess. They don't work for kids, and they don't work for schools. (No ISBN; 16 pages; 2009) Available from IDRA for $7 plus shipping, or free online at http://www.idra.org.

Education of English Language Learners in U.S. and Texas Schools – Where We Are, What We Have Learned and Where We Need to Go from Here – A 2009 Update

Albert Cortez, Ph.D., & Abelardo Villarreal, Ph.D.

This policy update shows that huge achievement gaps at the middle and high school level in particular show need for changes in policy, teacher training and evaluation. Models can be found in those schools that are demonstrating how English language learners can be more effectively served. This update gives an overview of increasing numbers of ELL students, distribution of ELL students, increasing diversity and varying languages, instructional programs provided, and funding provided to ELL programs along with recommendations. (No ISBN; 16 pages; 2009) Available from IDRA for $7 plus shipping, or free online at http://www.idra.org.

Good Schools and Classrooms for Children Learning English – A Guide

María Robledo Montecel, Ph.D., Josie Danini Cortez, M.A., Albert Cortez, Ph.D., & Abelardo Villarreal, Ph.D.

Thirty years of research have proven that when implemented well, bilingual education is the best way to learn English. Research by IDRA has identified the 25 common characteristics of successful schools that contribute to high academic performance of students learning English. This guide is a rubric, designed for people in schools and communities to evaluate five dimensions that are necessary for success: school indicators, student outcomes, leadership, support, and programmatic and instructional practices. (ISBN: 1-878550-69-1; 64 pages; 2002) Available from IDRA for $15 plus shipping.

The Ohtli Encuentro – Women of Color Share Pathways to Leadership

Elise D. García

This beautiful book presents the voices of 30 African American, Latina and Native American women who share their leadership journeys. IDRA brought together these women leaders to capture, honor and share their inspiring stories of leadership. This book highlights their moving stories. Four dimensions, or pathways, of leadership were shared by the women as they told their personal stories: (1) history, language and culture; (2) community engagement; (3) vision, spirit and values; and (4) social change and institutional transformation. The book is accompanied with analytic reflections that present a brief review of the literature on women's leadership and discusses common themes that arose from the women's interactions in a multicultural, multigenerational gathering designed to explore leadership in women of color. The word ohtli means "pathway" in the Nahuatl (Mexican indigenous) language. (ISBN# 0-9740243-8-4; 112 pages; 2005) Available from IDRA for $15 plus shipping.

The Status of School Finance Equity in Texas – A 2009 Update

by Albert Cortez, Ph.D.

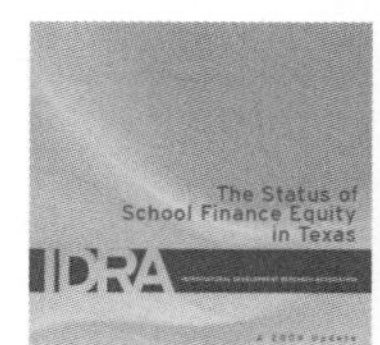

Disparities in per student funding have doubled in Texas, leaving millions of children in schools with severely limited resources for qualified teachers, up-to-date curriculum and basic supplies. This policy update on the status of education funding equity shows that Texas was headed in the right direction until the last two legislative sessions when revisions made to the school funding plan eroded equity among Texas schools. *The Status of School Finance Equity in Texas – A 2009 Update* summarizes where things are and identifies changes that are needed. (No ISBN; 20 pages; 2009) Available from IDRA for $7 plus shipping, or free online at http://www.idra.org.

Texas School Finance Reform: An IDRA Perspective

José A. Cárdenas, Ed.D.

A master story-teller, Dr. José A. Cárdenas offers an insider's view of the 28-year history of school finance in Texas. More than a history, this book provides a blueprint for persons interested in bringing about future reform in schools and other social institutions. Beginning with a description of the Texas system in 1950, the account covers court cases, legislation, and advocacy efforts and concludes with the status and future of school finance reform. Personal vignettes sprinkled throughout offer glimpses of those special untold moments that impacted history. Much of this volume – including the myths of school finance and lessons learned – relate to reform efforts in other states as well. Officially released on April 29, 1997 – the 10th anniversary of the *Edgewood* decision by State Superior Judge of Travis County Harley Clark that struck down Texas' school finance system as unconstitutional. (ISBN: 1-878550-63-2; 387 pages; 1997) Available from IDRA for $30 plus shipping.

For a full list of IDRA resources and to see the *IDRA Newsletter* latest issue and archives, go to http://www.idra.org.

Electronic Resources

IDRA Classnotes Podcast

Classnotes is a twice monthly, award-winning podcast that gives insight and strategies for serving today's diverse student population in order to provide them an excellent and equitable education through to graduation.

This free podcast is designed for public school teachers and administrators. Each episode focuses on a topic specific to improving public education in the United States. Listeners can sign up to receive free e-mail notices when a new episode is available. (English, occasional Spanish)

Visit http://www.idra.org/Podcasts

IDRA Graduation for All e-Letter

Graduation for All is a monthly e-letter for people who are concerned about our nation's dropout problem and are poised to take action to turn the tide. Through Graduation for All, IDRA will bring you up-to-date

information to make a difference in your school and community. (English or Spanish)

http://www.idra.org/School_Holding_Power/Graduation_for_All_e-Letter/

IDRA e-News

Each occasional edition gives you updates, alerts, resources and education news you can use to help create schools that work for all children. IDRA e-news is published online on state and national issues. (English, occasional Spanish)

http://www.idra.org/Press_Room/IDRA_e-News/

Fulfilling the Promise of Brown and Mendez web site

Designed for communities working across sector and race to transform their neighborhood schools.

http://www.idra.org/mendezbrown/index.html

Online Equity Guide for Schools

The South Central Collaborative for Equity web site provides resources for schools. Topics include: race equity, national origin equity, sex equity, IDRA's Six Goals of Educational Equity and School Reform, Response to Intervention, dropout prevention and recovery, education of English language learners and other diverse students, overrepresentation of ELLs and other diverse students in special education, quality teaching for diverse populations, and public school options for parents.

http://www.idra.org/South_Central_Collaborative_for_Equity/

Online Tools for Parents

The IDRA Texas Parent Information and Resource Center is helping to increase parent involvement in education through strong parent-educator partnerships to improve schools and raise students' academic achievement. Online resources include the topics of how the school should treat you (English and Spanish), connecting with other parents, and how to create a family friendly school.

http://www.idra.org/Texas_IDRA_PIRC.htm/

IDRA's School Holding Power Portal

Designed to help educators and community members find out how well their high school campus is preparing and graduating students, what factors may be weakening school holding power, and what they can do together to address them. The portal includes key data to help you determine whether high dropout rates and weak school holding power are a problem for your school; links to attrition rates for every county in Texas, based on IDRA's annual attrition research and the disappearance rates for every campus; easy-to-use tables and comparison graphs on student outcomes and the core features (e.g., teaching quality, curriculum quality and access) that make up strong schools; and e-mail feature you can use to share data with others and attach charts or graphs, keep track of your own notes, or call a community-school meeting to work on a specific issue.

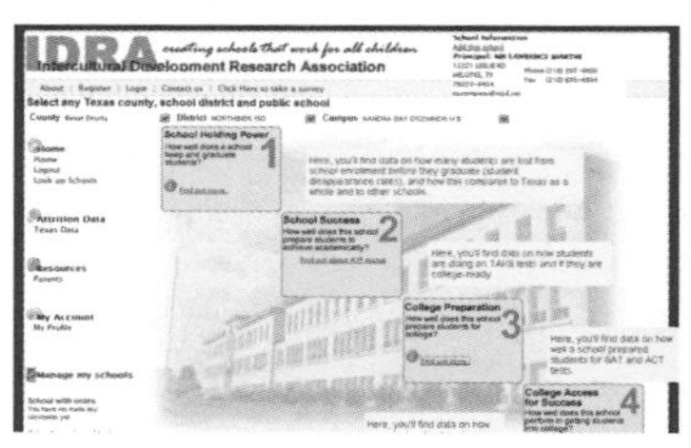

http://www.idra.org/portal

The Texas School Dropout Survey Project – A Summary of Findings

by José A. Cárdenas, Ed.D., María del Refugio Robledo, Ph.D., and Josie D. Supik, M.A.

Editor's note: The following is an excerpt from the Texas School Dropout Survey Project: A Summary of Findings report. The research was conducted by the Intercultural Development Research Association (IDRA) through a contract with the Texas Department of Community Affairs. Then director of the IDRA Center for the Prevention and Recovery of Dropouts, Dr. Robledo served as principal investigator of the Texas dropout study.

The Texas School Dropout Survey Project was the first comprehensive study of the dropout problem in Texas. It led to passage of House Bill 1010 in 1986 mandating increased involvement of school districts and their accountability for reducing the dropout rate and improving student academic achievement. It also required that the Texas Education Agency collect and report dropout data. (For a related timeline of Texas policy regarding dropouts, see "The Texas Dropout Saga – 23 Years and Counting…" by Cortez, J.D., and A. Cortez, in the IDRA Newsletter, November-December 2006.)

The problem of school dropouts has achieved unprecedented urgency at national, state and local levels. The importance given to the issue may reflect not a dramatic increase in the number or rate of students dropping out of school before completing the 12th grade but the increasing educational needs of our society. Whereas, only a few years ago, a low skilled labor pool formed the basis of the economy, recent years have seen a trend toward technology and services as the most important labor need for business and industry. Today, the typical blue collar job requires skills for reading and interpreting instructions, tables, graphs and manuals.

The state of Texas has experienced a similar change in the composition of its labor force. The oil, minerals and agriculture sectors of the economy have relinquished their demand on labor in favor of technology and a service economy. A recent analysis of the Texas labor market projects that, while the state economy will grow by 21.8 percent between 1982 and 1990, technology intensive occupations will grow by 32.0 percent over the same time frame (Texas Department of Community Affairs, 1986). The ability of the state to absorb an illiterate and unschooled labor force has become so limited that there is a state imperative to keep students in school long enough for them to acquire the extensive basic skills, knowledge and competencies necessary to function in our new society.

To address this imperative, the Texas School Dropout Survey Project was initiated in order to establish an information base for analyzing the dropout problem in Texas and to formulate recommendations to the 69th legislature based upon research findings. The project was mandated by House Bill 72 and was funded in the spring of 1986 by the Texas Department of Community Affairs (TDCA) in collaboration with the Texas Education Agency (TEA). The Intercultural Development Research Association (IDRA) was contracted to conduct three of the project's four research tasks:

1 – Measure the extent of school dropouts in Texas through valid and reliable dropout indices (Research Task 1).

2 – Collect and analyze benefit-cost data on the impact of dropouts on the criminal justice and human service systems in Texas (Research Task 3).

3 – Identify and evaluate in-school and alternative training programs for dropouts in Texas (Research Task 4).

In addition to these three major research areas, the measurement of the extent of school dropouts was supplemented by three tasks in response to requests made by TDCA and TEA. These additional research tasks included the following:

1 – Conduct meta-analysis of existing school district dropout documentation.

2 – Design and implement procedures for tracking of student withdrawals in a sample of districts.

3 – Generate estimates of macrocommunity dropout rates in the state.

The research that examined the principal causes for school dropouts (Research Task 2) was conducted by Texas A&M – Prairie View under a separate contract. No causal data are included in this IDRA report.

This report summarizes only the studies conducted by IDRA as part of the Texas School Dropout Survey Project. Comprehensive reports for each area of study are available in seven volumes.

Volume 1: Magnitude of the Problem – Census Analysis
Volume 2: Magnitude of the Problem – Attrition Analysis
Volume 3: Magnitude of the Problem – Tracking Study
Volume 4: Magnitude of the Problem – School District Research and Procedures
Volume 5: Benefit-Cost Impact of the Dropout Problem
Volume 6: Program Responses – Their Nature and Effectiveness
Volume 7: Study Methods and Procedures

In conducting the research, several methodological concerns were addressed. The variability and general unavailability of dropout data required multiple methods of analysis in order to generate valid and reliable dropout estimates. Both microtechniques and macrotechniques were used to examine the magnitude of the problem. Microtechniques included: (a) collecting data on district dropout identification procedures, (b) examining available district research on dropouts, and (c) conducting a student tracking survey. Through these techniques, intradistrict and interdistrict issues of measurement and definition were identified. Macrotechniques were used to estimate dropout rates. Estimates were generated by developing attrition indices using 1982-83 and 1985-86 Fall Survey data provided TEA. Estimates also were generated by analyzing the 1980 Census 5 Percent Public Use Microdata Sample.

The assessment of the economic impact of the dropout problem to the state was derived from data from state agencies, including the Texas Department of Human Resources (TDHR), the Texas Department of Corrections (TEC), TDCA and TEA.

In-school and out-of-school alternative training programs for dropout prevention and recovery were identified through surveys sent to school districts, community colleges, service delivery areas, colleges and universities, and private industry councils. Information on the types of programs and services provided was collected and organized into a statewide directory. A meta-analysis of evaluative programs data was deemed inappropriate due to the small number of programs with evaluation data.

Executive Summary

This report presents the results of the dropout studies conducted IDRA. The major research tasks were designed to examine three primary questions:

What is the magnitude of the dropout problem in the state of Texas?

What is the economic impact of the dropout problem for the state?

What is the nature and effectiveness of in-school and alternative out-of-school programs for dropouts in the state?

The research was conducted during the period of May to October, 1986. Given the paucity of reliable data on dropouts, research methods included primary analyses of data collected by IDRA and secondary analyses of available databases, including Fall Survey and Annual Performance Report information collected by TEA and census data collected by the U.S. Bureau of the Census. Major findings are listed below.

Major Findings

Magnitude of the Problem

1. The 1985-86 attrition rate for Texas high schools was 33 percent.
2. One in five Texas young people (nearly half a million) age 16 to 24 were not enrolled in school and had not completed the 12th grade in 1980.
3. Three out of 10 Texas dropouts – 152,000 young people – had completed fewer than nine years of schooling when they left school.

4. Approximately 85 percent of Texas dropouts were born in the United States; less than 15 percent were born in another country.
5. Of the nearly half a million Texas dropouts age 16 to 24, more than half (52 percent) were male.
6. Among females, attrition rates ranged from a low of 26 percent for White females to 43 percent for Hispanic females.
7. Attrition rates differed markedly for three racial ethnic groups in the state: 27 percent for White students, 34 percent for Black students and 45 percent for Hispanic students.
8. Hispanic youth age 16 to 19 were twice as likely, and youth age 20 to 24 nearly three times as likely to have left school prior to the completion of the 12th grade as their White counterparts.
9. Nearly half of Hispanic dropouts had completed less than ninth grade when they discontinued schooling compared to 18 percent of White and Black dropouts who discontinued schooling before the ninth grade.
10. Black male dropouts were less likely to be employed than either Hispanic or White male dropouts; two in five Black male dropouts, age 16 to 19, in contrast to one in five of Whites and 26 percent of Hispanics in that age group, were not in the labor force.

Dropout Accounting Procedures

11. Thirty-nine percent of Texas school districts have a system for identifying dropouts.
12. The majority of school districts follow similar but not identical forms of the TEA dropout definition.
13. Sixty-two percent of school districts do not use a dropout formula for calculating their dropout rate; among districts who have a formula, 9 percent use Average Daily Attendance while 24 percent use Average Daily Membership as the base figure.
14. Only 3.5 percent of school districts have conducted some form of dropout research, with only nine school districts conducting formal research studies on dropouts.
15. Sixteen percent of the students tracked who were presumed dropouts had not dropped out of school.
16. Twenty-eight percent of the students tracked were employed; of these, most worked at labor intensive, minimum wage jobs.
17. The majority of the students tracked left school because of poor grades, marriage/pregnancy, or financial problems.

Available Dropout Programs

18. Approximately 12 percent of Texas school districts reported having a dropout program; the number of programs reported by colleges, service delivery areas and other agencies was not commensurate with the magnitude of the problem.

19. Approximately 89 percent of dropout programs in Texas reported having no evaluation data.

20. The dropout problem is costing the state $17.12 billion in (a) foregone income and lost tax revenues, and (b) increased costs in welfare, crime and incarceration, unemployment insurance and placement, and adult training and education (for each cohort of dropouts). Every dollar invested in educating potential dropouts is estimated to result in a return of nine dollars.

Implications of the Research

1. There is a need to develop and use a standardized dropout definition with explicit identification procedures.

Findings from the school district dropout identification and procedures surveys, the dropout research reviews, and the student tracking surveys point to a need for a standardized, uniformly-applied dropout definition with necessary identification procedures. Only 61 percent of school districts reported having a system for identifying dropouts. Among these school districts, definitions were similar but not uniform. The lack of standard definitions effectively precludes aggregating individual district data across campuses within a particular school system.

Any definition and identification procedure at the state level must accommodate contextual variables at the school district level and also be rigorous enough to result in reliable aggregation across districts. In addition, the definition must be sensitive to such issues as summer versus school-term withdrawals, non-attenders often carried on membership rolls, verifiable transfer procedures and completion of graduation requirements.

State efforts at standardizing dropout identification procedures were initiated in the TEA 1985 Annual Performance Report requirements. Dropout reporting requirements for 1986 focus on a districtwide base figure for grades 7 through 12. Student identification and tracking procedures also are being put in place with the Public Education Information Management System (PEIMS) being developed by TEA. Both of these efforts can serve as a springboard for further standardization.

2. There is a need to develop standard procedures for calculating the dropout rate.

As a corollary to the development of a standard dropout definition, calculation procedures must be standardized and clearly specified. IDRA research findings indicate that 62 percent of school districts do not use a formula for calculating the dropout rate, despite current reporting requirements developed for local use.

Critical manipulable factors involved in the calculation of dropout rates include: (a) the time frame during which the number of students is counted, e.g, annual versus longitudinal; (b) the range of grade levels included in the dropout rate calculation, e.g., the greater the grade span, the lower the dropout rate; and (c) the student accounting procedures used by the district, e.g., average daily attendance versus average daily membership.

While calculations of district dropout rates must remain useful at the local level, state-level rates must be used to guide policy deliberations and monitor the effects of state and local intervention strategies.

3. There is a need to develop a centralized and standardized system for collection of dropout data.

The extensive variability in district dropout definitions and calculations noted above makes comparability across districts difficult at best. Even with standardization, however, it will become important to develop and maintain a centralized means of aggregating and analyzing dropout data across districts. With a centralized data base, the overall effect of intervention strategies as well as the effect of these efforts on particular populations can be monitored.

4. There is a need to develop tracking mechanisms that will increase the reliability of dropout counts and will result in more appropriate program interventions.

Research findings clearly indicate that current communication between and within school districts does not facilitate tracking of students who withdraw from a particular school. Approximately 16 percent of the presumed dropouts tracked across the state by telephone or mail reported having never dropped out of school but either transferred or were still enrolled. Within school districts, procedures for tracking of students are varied and depend, in part, on school district size and resources. Across school districts, standard record-keeping and transfer documentation and follow-up procedures for student withdrawals would greatly facilitate tracking of students as they move from one school district to another.

The Migrant Student Record and Transfer System (MSRTS) is the only national longstanding system for tracking of students. The centralization of achievement and other data at a single location currently required by the MSRTS might be circumvented through the use of a computer bulletin board concept with subsequent transfer of records remaining at the district to district level. Whatever the configuration of a feasible tracking system, it is imperative that tracking mechanisms be identified that will enhance monitoring our progress in addressing the dropout problem.

5. There is a need for early dropout intervention efforts given the large numbers of students who leave before the ninth grade.

IDRA research evidence reveals that three out of 10 Texas dropouts had completed fewer than nine years of schooling. Among Hispanic dropouts, almost half had discontinued schooling before completing the ninth grade. Reviews of existing dropout prevention programs in Texas revealed that few focus on pre-high school students. If dropout prevention efforts are to impact effectively at-risk populations, prevention efforts must begin at earlier levels. In doing so, strategies must be program-focused and avoid merely labeling and stigmatizing students at earlier grades.

6. There is a need for developing and replicating model dropout prevention and recovery programs for particular types of high risk groups.

Reviews of available literature and IDRA findings related to existing state programs indicated that information on "what works" is generally fragmented. While some exemplary or model programs are in operation across the country and in the state, there is little systematic and generalizable information that would permit program replication. It is, therefore, important to develop and replicate prototypic programs which have the components that are known to be successful: teaching of basic skills, survival skills training, work-study programs, individualized instruction, strengthened guidance and counseling, highly committed and caring teachers with high expectations for their students, and community, parent and business liaisons.

7. There is a need to expand the pool of available dropout prevention and recovery programs in order to service the large and diverse dropout population in the state.

Research on existing dropout programs in Texas revealed that the number currently in operation is inadequate when contrasted with the magnitude of the dropout problem in the state. There is a dearth of formal, structured programs specifically targeted at dropout or dropout-prone youth both within and outside the state's public school districts. In addition to developing and replicating model programs, successful models and strategies must be incorporated into a substantially larger number of diverse programs that will service diverse needs within the dropout population.

In order to serve the diverse migrant population, for example, a Graduation Enhancement Model is being developed by TEA and the Texas Migrant Interstate Program. According to data compiled by the coordinator of the program, migrant dropout rates are estimated to be in the 60 percent to 90 percent range. It is obvious, then, that more and varied programs are needed.

8. There is a need to develop systematic approaches to the evaluation of dropout prevention and recovery efforts.

The survey of dropout prevention and recovery programs indicated that 89 percent had no evaluation data. In the absence of such data, conclusions about program effectiveness are not possible. In developing guidelines and standards for evaluation, it is important to ensure that evaluation designs serve to identify programs that work for particular types of participant in particular types of situations. Strategies and results in a prevention program may differ from strategies and results in a recovery effort. Success in a prevention program for non-migrant students may differ from that for migrant students. The enormity of the dropout problem leads to the inevitable conclusion that all students do not leave school for the same or similar reasons or under the same or similar conditions. Neither the reasons nor the solutions can be the same. Evaluation designs must be able to generate information about what works, for what target group and under what conditions.

9. There is a need to develop and link public and private sector initiatives that are proportionate to the massive number of dropouts in the state.

There are ongoing substantive efforts directed at the dropout issue in the state of Texas. State agencies, including TEA and TDCA, have already begun initiatives designed to address the problem from both a prevention and recovery perspective. Private corporations, including Coca Cola USA and Southwestern Bell, are sponsoring efforts designed to raise awareness of the issues and to develop program alternatives. Foundation support also is being directed at the dropout problem. The Ford Foundation, for example, has established a national dropout initiative that involves public and private sector collaboratives. Further development of communications networks and other linkages between private and public sector initiatives is central to effective dropout interventions. Coordination also is crucial to maximizing the return on the investment that must be made.

The linkages and networking that are necessary to producing results in the area of school dropouts will be facilitated by working within the concept of the educational pipeline. A focus on the student, as he or she progresses through the pipeline, i.e., kindergarten through public schooling and on to a college education, provides context and continuity. The Dallas County Community College District, for example, has established Adopt-A-School partnerships with area middle schools. College faculty are given release time in order to provide staff development and technical assistance to schools.

10. There is a need to make an investment in dropout prevention and recovery efforts that is commensurate with the magnitude of the problem and its economic impact in the state of Texas.

The number of dropouts for the graduating class of 1985-86 was estimated to be 86,000. This represents a 33 percent attrition rate for a single group of high school students over a three-year period. Over the course of their lifetime, projected losses in tax revenue averaged $58,930 per cost of keeping each of these students in school was $3,859 per averted dropout. In addition, the state would have realized a savings of $652 million in social expenditures related to crime, welfare, incarceration and unemployment costs. Every dollar invested in educating potential dropouts will result in a return of nine dollars. An investment in human capital yields substantial short- and long-term results.

Resource

Texas Department of Community Affairs. *Governor's Coordination and Special Services Plan: Job Training Partnership Act Program Years 1986 and 1987* (Austin, Texas: Texas Department of Community Affairs, 1986).

Originally published in the *IDRA Newsletter*, November 1986

The Economic Impact of the Dropout Problem

by David Ramirez, Ph.D., and María del Refugio Robledo, Ph.D.

Editor's note: The following is excerpted from the Texas School Survey Dropout Survey Project (October 1986) which was conducted by the Intercultural Development Research Association, Center for the Prevention and Recovery of Dropouts, under contract with the Texas Department of Community Affairs and the Texas Education Agency.

It is implicit in most of the literature related to dropouts that "dropping out" is detrimental to both the individual and society. Popular conceptions abound relating dropouts to increased crime, lower wages, higher unemployment and diminished life satisfaction, to name but a few. Additionally, many argue that as employers focus greater attention on higher levels of educational achievement, the economic penalty paid by dropouts will become even more severe. Society also is said to suffer both directly and indirectly in lost productivity, a diminished tax base, greater vulnerability to foreign competition, and greater general dissatisfaction in the population.

Yet to prevent or remediate such conditions, substantial financial resources must be allocated. The prevention of dropouts would at minimum require two major areas of expenditures: (a) the public education costs required to continue the education of dropouts past the point at which they would have dropped out, and (b) the cost of implementing effective dropout prevention programs. This latter expense is based on the assumption that the current educational system has failed to retain these students and hence an alternative set of programs is required to effect prevention.

The allocation of resources by society to dropout prevention programs is an investment in individual students with an implicit assumption that there will be a positive return to society as a whole. The use of benefit-cost analysis as employed in this study represents an effort to test this assumption. Specifically, will society in general realize a fiscal benefit by providing effective education to those within society who are currently early leavers of the formal education system?

Currently there are costs associated with dropouts. Dropouts do use educational services even though their programs are prematurely aborted. Dropouts also tend to utilize various human services in disproportionate numbers. Further, dropouts are represented in the criminal justice system at a higher percentage than the population as a whole. Dropouts also appear to be unemployed at a higher rate, and of those who are employed, most are found in low-income jobs. Their high rate of unemployment and their overrepresentation in low-income jobs not only diminishes their potential lifetime earnings but also reduces the overall federal, state and local tax bases (Levin, 1972; Catterall, 1985). The preceding litany serves as only a partial list of costs incurred by society due to dropouts.

Phenomena such as poverty and incarceration have some quantifiable societal costs associated with them. However, not all the costs in these or similar areas lend themselves to quantification. Not only is it difficult to quantify costs, it is equally difficult to categorize what the costs and benefits would be.

Many of the costs and benefits to be discussed have implications for both the individual and society. If, for example, an individual has a higher probability of going to prison if he or she is a dropout, this represents a cost to both the individual and to society. The individual pays with time, lost wages, psychological and physical pain; his or her family also loses. Society pays directly through the costs of its judicial and correctional system, and indirectly in the loss of contributions this individual could have made to the overall society. To avoid such a situation is a benefit for both the individual and society. Therefore, the elimination or curtailment of many of the costs to be detailed here can be considered direct benefits.

Psychological literature contains a great many studies demonstrating the positive benefit to the individual of having options in life. Indeed, much of the literature related to hopelessness refers to the psychological experiences of those who consider themselves without such options. The literature related to dropouts indicates that one of the negative impacts of dropping out is the limitations this act may place on the individual. The student who drops out is said to: (a) increase his or her probability of unemployment; (b) decrease the range of jobs for which he or she is qualified; (c) increase his or her probability of earning lower wages if employed (which initiates a number of concurrent negative effects associated with lower socio-economic levels); and (d) increase the chances of ending up in what many term "dead-end jobs." Each of these results has the effect of decreasing the potential options available to the individual and possibly to the family.

Negative impact on the individual is difficult to quantify with any degree of accuracy. However, it may act as a precursor to other negative impacts that are more easily measured. The relationship between crime and dropping out is often based on the notion that many individuals with limited options might turn to crime if he or she is unable to succeed in legal settings. Drug and alcohol abuse have been linked to the sensation of hopelessness in the abuser. Violence is also cited as a possible result of a prolonged sense of hopelessness.

Education is but one means of increasing an individual's options. Therefore we must estimate the subset of cases of avoidable problems as a function of increasing education levels. Even assuming for the moment that this is only a subset of the total number of cases, there is another question: How do we ascribe a value to what was lost or suffered in these cases?

In part, a cost can be ascribed. We can, for example, estimate the costs paid by the judicial, correctional and social welfare systems to serve the subset of individuals who, for want of an adequate education, found themselves with too few options in life. We can estimate the increase in potential positive contributions of these individuals to society had they had an adequate education. While this summary does not permit detailed discussion of all areas examined in the benefit-cost model, key areas are briefly highlighted below.

Lost Wages and Tax Revenues

Over the course of an average lifetime of earnings, differentials in earning power result in substantial losses in wages and tax revenues. In previous studies of the cost associated with inadequate education, estimates of lost wages and tax revenues have played a pivotal role (Levin, 1972; Catterall, 1985). These studies support the conclusion that the costs in lost wages and tax revenues alone can serve as adequate justification for investing in the provision of a more complete education to the pool of would-be dropouts. The present study replicated the work of Levin (1972) and Catterall (1985) to arrive at an estimate of the impact of lost wages and tax revenues to Texas as a function of the dropout problem.

Numerous census reports have documented the lower annual wages earned by dropouts as compared to individuals that complete four years of high school (U.S. Bureau of the Census, 1983; U.S. Bureau of the Census, 1984). In the context of these issues, the central question is: How much less over the course of a lifetime will the average dropout earn in comparison to an individual that graduates from high school?

The *Lifetime Earnings Estimates for Men and Women in the United States: 1979* (U.S. Bureau of the Census, 1979) was used as the primary data source in this area. The report indicates that a man with less than 12 years of education can expect, from age 18 to 65, lifetime earnings of $601,000, while a male high school graduate can anticipate earnings of $861,000. This represents a $260,000 difference. Likewise, a woman with less than 12 years of education is estimated to earn $211,000 as opposed to $381,000 for a woman with a high school diploma. The difference for women is therefore $170,000. Since the current study focuses on Texas, a number of adjustments in the national figures were necessary. After adjusting for regional differences in income and a number of other factors, lifetime earnings losses of $241,630 for men and $146,072 for women were generated.

The Texas attrition rate estimates reported elsewhere in this volume were used to generate the cost figures in the area of lost wages. The attrition rate data indicate, on the basis of the size of the ninth-grade class in 1985-86, a loss of 86,000 students. Assuming, as did Catterall (1985), that 52.72 percent of the dropouts were male and 47.27 percent were female, the resulting estimates are shown in the box on Page 242.

Projected Total Earnings and Tax Losses to Texas Due to Projected Attrition Rates Among 1982-83 Ninth Graders

Sex	Estimated Number of Dropouts	Individual Lost Earnings (Adj.)	Total Lost Earnings
Male	45,000	$24 1,630	$10.955 billion
Female	40,656	$146,072	$5.938 billion

Total gross earnings lost:	$16,893 billion
Approximate loss of tax revenues assuming all taxes represent 30 percent of income:	$5.068 billion
Estimated net lost earnings (less taxes):	$11.825 billion
Total Lost Earnings and Taxes:	**$16.893 billion**

The estimated losses in tax revenues were generated by the same method employed in previous studies. Levin (1972) and Catterall (1985) both developed an estimate of the lost tax revenues that would accompany the lost income using an estimate of 30 percent of income. Based on these estimates, this group of students, allowed to leave school at the rates noted, will over time result in a loss in earnings and resultant taxes of approximately $137,504 per dropout and an average loss in taxes of $58,930 per dropout.

Impact on Social Welfare Services

Virtually all human service programs exist in a climate of capital rationing in that not all those that need services can actually be provided services. The literature on human service organizations contains many pleas for the implementation of primary prevention techniques in hopes of stretching the limited resources available for social problems.

Hence, if a given percentage of potential clients would not require the services of these social agencies through the provision of a more adequate education, the service slots these individuals would have taken would simply be replaced by other clients in the community that needed help but would not have received it. If this is the case, there would be two levels of benefit associated with the prevention of selected cases through the provision of a more adequate education: (a) the savings in the services that would have been provided to these individuals, and (b) the fulfillment of a portion of the "unmet need" in the community that could not have been served had the resources been used on the dropouts.

The present study concentrated on four major human services program areas: (a) welfare costs, (b) unemployment costs, (c) job training programs, and (d) adult basic education costs. In determining welfare costs, for example, the study involved an analysis and estimate of the impact that a lower incident of dropouts might have on the services provided by the Texas Department of Human Services. Before reviewing some of the findings in these areas, this estimation model used will be described in a hypothetical

Cost Estimation Model

	General population		Service population	
Step 1:	1,000 people in the general population	&	100 people in the service population	
Step 2: Estimate % dropouts	20% dropouts	80% non-dropouts	75% dropouts	25% non-dropouts
Step 3: Apply %	200 dropouts	800 non-dropouts	75 dropouts	25 non-dropouts
Step 4: Users to population	75 dropouts used	25 non-dropouts used		
Step 5: Convert to rate	37.5/100	3.1/100		
Step 6: Assume non-drop rate of 3.1/100	6.2 users	25 users	Compare 6.2 to the figure in Step 3 (i.e., users) to the original figure of 75	

Result = 69 less users or *69 percent savings* in expenditures.

Adjustment of inaccuracy of relationship

Step 7: Recalculate with new rate for only half the dropouts

200 dropouts		800 non-dropouts
100 new rate (3.1/100)	100 old rate (37.5/100)	original rate (3.1/100)
3.1 users	37.5 users	25 users

New projected total users = 65.6 vs. 100 or approximately 34% less

Final result of the model is an estimate of *34 percent savings* in expenditures.

sense to give the reader an opportunity to examine its structure. The box above will serve as a reverence point for the discussion to follow.

Let us assume that we have a social program that serves 100 people every year and that a total of 1,000 people live in the community. Our first step will be to examine the percentage of dropouts found in the community as a whole and in the subset of 100 social program users. Let us further assume that upon examination we find in Step Two the percentages to be as follows: 20 percent dropouts in the total population and 75 percent dropouts in the social service user population. Step Three simply applies the percentages to the two groups and determines that 200 of the 1,000 individuals in the overall population are dropouts, and 75 of the users are dropouts.

Since the users are a subset of the total, in Step Four we note that 75 of the 200 dropouts in the overall community showed up as users whereas 25 of the 800 non-dropouts were found to be users of our hypothetical service. In Step Five, we simply convert these proportions to rates per 100 in order to compare the incidence of being a user in the dropout vs. the non-dropout group. We find that the dropouts are using the service at a rate of 37.5 per 100 in contrast to the 3.1 per 100 rate shown for non-dropouts.

In critical Step Six, we conjecture how many of the 200 people in the community who were dropouts would have shown up for service had they had the same rate of usage as their non-dropout counterparts. If the rate of 3.1 per 100 were ascribed to the 200 dropouts, we would expect to still see 6.2 individuals in the service users from the original 200. Note that 6.2 vs. 75 persons would have shown up for service. That is, 69 of the original 100 service users might not have shown up for service. To this point, the model assumes that there is a direct relationship between being a dropout and being a user of the service agency. Clearly, a perfect relationship is not in evidence or we would not have expected the original 800 non-dropouts to yield 25 users. Nonetheless, a level of relationship is in evidence given the disproportionate representation of dropouts in the user group. Assume that in only 50 percent of the cases would converting the 200 dropouts in the community to non-dropouts result in their exhibiting the non-dropout rate of usage. Hence, for 100 of the original dropouts the increase in education would not affect their rate of service use. However, for the remaining 100, the new rate of 3.1 per 100 would be in evidence.

In Step Seven, we note that such an adjustment would cause a decrease of 35 persons rather than the 69 noted in Step Six. In essence, we have cut our original estimate of the service expenditures related to dropouts in half to adjust for our inability to isolate the exact magnitude of the relationship that exists between these two phenomenon. Given the extreme overrepresentation of dropouts in the service users, this adjustment may result in an overly conservative estimate. Nonetheless, this example of the implementation of our estimation model would result in an anticipated savings of 35 percent in the expenditures of our hypothetical service activity.

This estimation model was employed to generic estimates reported for the various service activities. Using this methodology, the cost attributed to inadequate education in the two social welfare programs of AFDC and Food Stamps was $253.7 million ($94.8 million in AFDC and $158.9 million in Food Stamps).

It is important to note that this study is in no way considered the cumulative financial, physical and psychological costs to the children represented in these programs. If a situation of poverty could have been avoided through a more complete education for a group of the parents represented in these programs, what would the benefits have been to their children? Conversely, how many children of social welfare program users will themselves grow up to also need these services? There is evidence to support the contention that these children have a much higher probability of also needing such services when they grow up. These cumulative costs were not included in this study.

Unemployment Costs

The possible costs of unemployment insurance and employment placement services that might be attributed to inadequate education also were considered. The primary question in this area was: What will Texans spend (a) on unemployment benefits for the dropout group that might have been avoided, and (b) helping the dropout group to seek employment through the provision of job placement services?

National data indicate that the unemployment rate for dropouts in 1984 was 27.7 percent, or more than twice the rate for high school graduates not enrolled in college, i.e., 13.4 percent (U.S. Bureau of Labor Statistics, nd). We would, therefore, expect to see an overrepresentation of dropouts in the group receiving unemployment compensation and job placement services.

Using the model described earlier, the cost savings in the area of unemployment compensation costs related to inadequate education is estimated to be $15.7 million per year. This figure represents approximately 2.5 percent of all the money paid out in unemployment insurance claims in 1985. In order to compare the present findings to previous studies, we might note that Levin's (1972) estimate of ascribed costs in relation to unemployment compensation was approximately 20 percent of benefits. Likewise, the resent study's cost estimation model indicates that 2.78 percent of the expenditures related to job placement services, or $1,896,286 might have been avoided had the dropout problem not existed. In total, these two areas sum to an estimated loss of $17,630,000 annually.

Crime and Prison Costs

As already indicated, previous research has attempted to estimate the cost of crime associated with inadequate education. The following three areas were considered in this study: (a) costs associated with incarceration; (b) judicial costs and the costs associated with police protection; and (c) a very rough estimate of the cost of crime to victims in the single area of stolen property. We will briefly discuss the impact on prisons since this area is often cited.

The central premise is that there exists a subset of individuals incarcerated in Texas prisons who for lack of a more complete education have committed crimes, have been convicted, and were sent to an institution within the Texas Department of Corrections (TDC) system. The phrase "convicted and sent to prison" is critical in our discussion of the costs of crime associated with inadequate education. National statistics for 1983 reported by the U.S. Department of Justice indicated that on the average, only 20.6 percent of the 11.4 million offenses reported were cleared by an arrest (U.S. Bureau of Justice, 1985). Only a portion of these arrests ever led to a conviction, and only a subset of these resulted in incarceration in a state prison.

It is also of interest to note that between 1975 and 1985 the inmate population reported by the Texas Department of Corrections virtually doubled (18,151 to 37,320). In addition, the operating costs of TDC in 1985 (about $286 million) were over eight times greater than the operating costs reported in 1975 (about $33 million). A preliminary report of a 10-year facilities study conducted by the Texas Department of Corrections (Henningson, Durham & Richardson, nd) noted: "If no actions were taken to reduce the influx of new admissions or the average length of stay, the population will approach 95,000 inmates in 1995" (p. III).

The study went on to note that such an increase in the population and related costs would cause the annual operating figure in 1990 to reach about $614 million and just over $1 billion in 1995. The projected 1990 costs are approximately double the costs noted in 1985.

That there is some relationship between education and incarceration appears to be supported by the disproportionately high number of inmates with low levels of educational attainment in comparison to the general population. Again it is impossible to establish any unequivocal measure of cause and effect between education and incarceration. We can, however, note that, if the general dropout population in Texas were to have the same incidence of incarceration as the non-dropout population, we would expect to see fewer people in prison. Summing all the costs we identified in relation to incarceration and education we arrived at a total of $131 million that might have been saved.

As stated earlier, the tie between crime and inadequate education is based on the concept that some portion of crime is committed by persons who, due to an inadequate educational preparation, find themselves in life conditions with limited options. National data for 1984 indicated that the unemployment rate for high school graduates not enrolled in college was 13.4 percent (U.S. Bureau of Labor Statistics, nd). In contrast, the unemployment rate in that same year for school dropouts was a staggering 27.7 percent (U.S. Bureau of Labor Statistics, nd).

Not only are more dropouts out of work, they also possess fewer of the educational skills required to get a job. The number of jobs for unskilled labor is decreasing and is expected to continue to decrease. The chronically unemployed dropout might go on welfare as a means of subsistence. For some females (those with children) there is the possibility of AFDC assistance. The average recipient will be provided around $4,000 per year in AFDC and Food Stamp benefits to support themselves and their children. For males, the situation is even more interesting to consider. Outside of the Food Stamp program (which appears to provide a yearly average of less than $700 per participant), what other types of program support are they eligible to receive? We could identify no other public welfare programs that would provide significant financial support to this group.

We are not asserting that being poor and possessing few if any perceptible options constitute a justification for the commission of crime. We are simply asking the reader to consider the possibility that there may be a relationship between inadequate education which often results in a constricted range of life options and crime.

Levin (1972) attributed roughly 33 percent of the costs of crime to the problem of inadequate education. For the present study, we used a proportion of 12.5 percent or a conservative estimate of approximately one third the size of that used by Levin in his 1972 study. Employing our figure of 12.5 percent attributable to inadequate education, we arrive at a cost estimate of $5,881,870 in relation to judicial costs at $116.1 million that might have been saved in the area of police protection through the eradication of the dropout problem.

By surveying the annual reports of a number of urban police departments in Texas, an estimate of $66 per capita in losses due to stolen property was determined. Assuming that there are approximately 14.5 million people in Texas, our cost estimate for the entire state would be nearly $1 billion in losses in stolen property. Again using our estimate of a possible 12.5 percent of crime attributable to inadequate education, the cost in this area is approximately $119.6 million. In summary, the total costs related to crime/incarceration and inadequate education was estimated at approximately $367.77 million.

The Cost of Educating Dropouts

Estimating costs resulting from the dropout problem must be put in perspective in relation to the costs Texans will bear in educating this group. The costs in the following three areas will be considered: (a) the cost of completing a high school education; (b) the cost of college for that percentage that will go beyond high school; and (c) the cost of providing effective dropout prevention programs.

The first area we must consider is how much it would cost to complete the education of a would-be dropout. Clearly, such a cost would span a number of years. Since dropouts leave at different points in the education process, it is difficult to know how many additional years of education they require. The present study used an estimate of 3.5 additional years required.

Based on the September 1986 findings of the Accountable Costs Advisory Committee of the Texas State Board of Education, the yearly cost of educating a student in 1987-88 will be $275. The committee also projected that the 1988-89 costs will increase by slightly over 8.7 percent to $2,952 per student per year. Using these figures, we estimated a total cost of $10,622 for 3.5 years. The attrition study reported in this document estimated the number of dropouts from the graduating class of 1985-86 to be 86,000. Using this figure, we arrive at an education cost of $913.5 million.

Secondly, we must consider that some of these averted dropouts may continue their education beyond the high school level. Additional years of schooling in college would cost roughly double the annual amount for public school education per year (Levin, 1972). In the projection of foregone income discussed earlier, the present study assumed that of the averted dropouts: (a) 15 percent would complete four years of college; and (b) 3 percent would attend college for five or more years. Again using our estimate of 86,000 dropouts that might be averted, the resultant cost estimates for a portion of the group (30 percent) continuing on to college were fixed at $656.3 million.

The final cost that must be estimated is associated with the expenditures required to implement the dropout prevention efforts that would cause the 86,000 dropouts instead to complete their education. There are few models that can be cited and even fewer for which estimates of annual costs per student are available.

Let us assume that school districts would have a difficult time identifying who might or might not drop out and that their dropout prevention efforts would need to be targeted to at least 50 percent of the students in a given graduating class. There were about a quarter of a million students in the ninth grade in 1982-83 who were later to be the graduating class of 1985-86. Hence, half this figure, or 125,000, would be targeted for dropout prevention.

Let us further assume that the prevention efforts must be applied for the entire duration of the estimated average of 3.5 years of additional schooling required by the potential dropouts. Finally, let us estimate that prevention efforts will add as much as 25 percent per targeted student to the overall estimated costs of public school education.

Clearly, these are liberal estimates of the costs. It is doubtful that effective prevention efforts would need to take such a "shotgun approach" in which half of all the students in a graduating class would be targeted and served. Also, effective prevention efforts might deter the potential dropout within a much shorter time period than the estimate of 3.5 years used here.

Nonetheless, using the figures of the annual costs per student in Texas schools, we calculate the costs of an additional 25 percent over a 3.5-year period to be $2,655 per student. If we multiply this cost by the 125,000 students in the overall prevention target group, the resultant cost is $331.9 million. Since we estimate that we are trying to avert approximately 86,000 dropouts, the figures for prevention efforts indicated above represent an average cost of $3,859 per dropout. Hence as shown in the box on Page 22, the total cost in the area of education is approximately $1.90 billion.

Benefit Cost Analysis Conclusions

Having briefly reviewed the estimates on the benefits and costs shown in the box on Page 249, let us take stock of what we have learned. The benefits are expressed in terms of: (a) the savings in expenditures in relation to welfare, crime, incarceration, unemployment insurance payments, employment services, adult education and job training services that might result from the eradication of the dropout problem; and (b) the potential gains in earnings and taxes resulting from dropouts having a higher earning potential if they become high school graduates. The costs relate to the expenditures that would be required to: (a) complete the high school education of averted dropouts; (b) pay for public costs related to the years in college that some might attend after graduation form high school; and

Summary of Costs and Benefits

Benefit Categories		
I. Possible savings related to the following		
Welfare Costs		
AFDC costs	$94.80 million	
Food Stamps	$158.90 million	
Category Total	$253.70 million	
Training and Adult Education Costs		
Adult Education	$4.00 million	
JTPA	$8.86 million	
Category Total	$12.90 million	
Crime and Incarceration Costs		
Incarceration and Post Supervision	$126.19 million	
Judicial Costs	$5.88 million	
Police Protection	$116.10 million	
Property Loss	$119.60 million	
Category Total	$367.77 million	
Unemployment Insurance and Placement Services		
Unemployment Insurance	$15.73 million	
Placement Services	$1.90 million	
Category Total	$17.63 million	
Total Possible Savings in Relation to Social Expenditures in These Areas		**$652.00 million**
II. Possible increase in wages and taxes		
Gross Earnings		
Male Dropouts	$10.955 billion	
Female Dropouts	$5.938 billion	
Total	$16.893 billion	
Minus Tax Revenues	$5.068 billion	
Net Earnings Loss	$11.825 billion	
Total Lost Earnings and Tax Revenues		**$16.893 billion**
Total Benefit Categories I & II		**$17.545 billion**

Cost Categories		
Education and Prevention Costs		
Cost of completing high school	$913.50 million	
Cost of providing dropout prevention programs	$331.90 million	
Cost of college for that group that continues beyond high school	$656.30 million	
Total Education and Prevention Costs		**$1.90 billion**

Current Cost-Benefit Figures

"The aggregate consequences of raising the high school graduation rate for each age cohort are economically large. Each cohort of 20-year-olds includes more than 700,000 high school dropouts. If this number were reduced by half through successful implementation of the median educational intervention, the net present value economic benefit would be $45 billion. This figure is an annual one because each cohort is assumed to include the same number of dropouts in the absence of powerful interventions. And it does not count the private benefits of improved economic well-being that accrue directly to the new graduates themselves. If we were able to obtain these fiscal benefits over a decade, we would approach fiscal savings of about half a trillion dollars."

– Levin, H.M. "The Economic Payoff of Investing In Educational Justice," *Education Researcher* (2009)

"In the nation's 50 largest cities and the 45 metropolitan areas that surround them, an estimated 600,000 students dropped out from the Class of 2008 at great cost not only to themselves but also to their communities. Reducing the number of dropouts by 50 percent for this single high school class would result in tremendous economic benefits to these regions."

- $4.1 billion in combined earnings in the average year
- An additional $2.8 billion in spending and $1.1 billion in investing in the average year
- Increased home sales of $10.5 billion and auto sales of $340 million in the average year
- 30,000 new jobs and economic growth of $5.3 billion
- $536 million in increased tax revenue in the average year
- Increased human capital

– Alliance for Excellent Education. *The Economic Benefits from Halving the Dropout Rate* (January 2010)

Students who drop out of high school will cost Texas up to $9.6 billion in lost revenue and outright expenses over their lifetimes, and that figure escalates as each new crop of dropouts is created… reduction in high school students could save the state up to $1.1 billion in education-related costs each year, but investing in keeping these students in school produces a substantial long-term monetary gain.

– Bush School of Government and Public Service. *The ABCD's of Texas Education: Assessing the Benefits and Costs of Reducing the Dropout Rate* (College Station, Texas: Texas A&M University, May 2009).

(c) implement dropout prevention efforts.

The benefit categories total approximately $17.5 billion. The cost categories total approximately $1.90 billion. In essence, for every dollar expended on prevention and the education of the would-be dropout, nine dollars will be returned.

Note also that the estimated losses in social expenditures related to welfare, crime, incarcerations and unemployment alone amounted to $652 million. This is not far from the amount we estimate it will cost to complete the high school education ($913.5 million) of all of the 86,000 dropouts we estimated in this study. The question then is: Where do Texans wish to spend limited resources? On the basis of the staggering amount being lost in earnings and tax revenues (i.e., $16.89 billion), the choice is obvious. Indeed, it's interesting to consider how long it will take before dropout education and prevention is funded totally by the increased revenues gained by diminishing the dropout problem.

Consider that the 86,000 students lost in graduating class of 1985-86 will result in a potential tax loss of $5.07 billion over the next 45 years. Also, the students that will be lost in the class of 1986-87 will likewise result in a loss in tax revenues of approximately $5.07 billion over the course of their 45 years in the labor force. And the pattern continues. Given the extraordinary amount being lost in taxes for each graduating class ($5.07 billion), it would not be long before the $332 million we estimated might be required for the prevention efforts could be funded totally from the increased tax revenues paid by the averted dropouts.

Resources

Catterall, J. *On the Social Costs of Dropping Out of School* (Stanford, Calif.: Stanford Education Policy Institute, 1985).

Henningson, Durham and Richardson. *Texas Department of Corrections Ten Year Facilities Study, Executive Summary – preliminary* (Henningson, Durham and Richardson, no date).

Levin, H.M. The Costs to the Nation of Inadequate Education (Washington, D.C.: Senate Select Committee on Equal Educational Opportunity, 1972).

U.S. Bureau of Justice. *Examining Recidivism, Special Report* (Washington, D.C.: U.S. Bureau of Justice Statistics, 1985).

U.S. Bureau of Labor Statistics. *Special Labor Force Report, No. 191, Bulletin 2192* (Washington, D.C.: U.S. Bureau of Labor Statistics, no date).

U.S. Bureau of the Census. *Lifetime Earnings Estimates for Men and Women in the United States: 1979* (Washington, D.C.: U.S. Bureau of the Census, 1979).

U.S. Bureau of the Census. 1980 Census of Population, Volume 1 Characteristics of the Population, Chapter D Detailed Population Characteristics, Part 1 United States Summary, Section A: United States Tables 253-310 (PC80-1-D1-A) (Washington, D.C.: U.S. Bureau of the Census, 1984).

U.S. Bureau of the Census. 1980 Census of Population, Volume 1 Characteristics of the Population, Chapter D Detailed Population Characteristics, Part 45 Texas, Section 2: Tables 230-251 (PC80-1-D45) (Washington, D.C.: U.S. Bureau of the Census, 1983).

U.S. Bureau of the Census. 1980 Census of Population, Volume 1 Characteristics of the Population, Chapter C General, Social and Economic Characteristics, Part 45 Texas (PC80-1-C45) (Washington, D.C.: U.S. Bureau of the Census, 1983).

Originally published in the *IDRA Newsletter*, April 1987